LICKING THE SPOON

Licking the Spoon

A MEMOIR OF FOOD,
FAMILY AND IDENTITY

Candace Walsh

SEAL PRESS

Published by Seal Press
A Member of the Perseus Books Group
1700 Fourth Street
Berkeley, California

Library of Congress Cataloging-in-
Publication Data

Walsh, Candace.
  Licking the spoon : a memoir of food,
family, and identity / Candace Walsh.
    p. cm.
  ISBN 978-1-58005-391-4 (pbk.)
1. Walsh, Candace. 2. Food writers—
United States—Biography. 3. Women
authors—United States—Biography.
4. Walsh, Candace—Family. 5.
Food—Social aspects. 6. Gastronomy.
7. Feminist theory. I. Title.
  TX649.W35A1 2012
  641.5092—dc23
  [B]
                              2012012283

9 8 7 6 5 4 3 2 1

Cover and interior design by
Gopa & Ted2, Inc.
Printed in the United States of America
Distributed by Publishers Group West

I am singing the songs of my ancestors,
so they can dance.

To Zoila, Migdalia,

Maria, Marie,

Linda, and Lisa

Contents

PROLOGUE		ix
CHAPTER 1.	How Cuba Married Crete	1
CHAPTER 2.	Mastering the Art	17
CHAPTER 3.	Cradle of Flavor	33
CHAPTER 4.	Water and Wine, Divinity and the Divine	43
CHAPTER 5.	Of Frying Pans and Fire	53
CHAPTER 6.	The Freshman Fifteen	73
CHAPTER 7.	*The Enchanted Broccoli Forest*	83
CHAPTER 8.	Cooking with Pam	95
CHAPTER 9.	*Almost Vegetarian*	103
CHAPTER 10.	The Way to a Man's Heart	117
CHAPTER 11.	Jack and Coke	129
CHAPTER 12.	Powdered Sugar and Spice	139
CHAPTER 13.	Canned and Green	143
CHAPTER 14.	*The Cake Bible*	153
CHAPTER 15.	A Will and a Way	161
CHAPTER 16.	Inside the Gingerbread House	167

CHAPTER 17. Wedding, Bella   177

CHAPTER 18. *Lune de Miel*   187

CHAPTER 19. Bun in the Oven   193

CHAPTER 20. Baby Food   203

CHAPTER 21. Wine and Chile   213

CHAPTER 22. Down the Hatch, Up the Stump   221

CHAPTER 23. Home Cooking   233

CHAPTER 24. Soul Food   243

CHAPTER 25. *The New Basics*   255

CHAPTER 26. First Course   261

CHAPTER 27. A Moveable Feast   269

CHAPTER 28. Raw   279

CHAPTER 29. Carryover Cooking   287

RECIPES   295

Prologue

Come on, girls . . . do you believe in love?

I HAVE MADE risotto in many seasons and climes, but it's a dish best made in the icy nadir of a New York February. Standing over a hot stove, coaxing broth into swelling Arborio rice grains solely with elbow grease, the burner's flame, and a wooden spoon, is cozy when it's cold outside but masochistic in July.

But it was February 1998, and the man I might marry was climbing up the four flights of narrow, spiraling, tenement-smelling stairs to my postage stamp–size kitchen, where I stood, beaming, dewy, and bare legged, in my black Manolo Blahnik knockoff stiletto mules, midcalf A-line charcoal wool skirt, and sleeveless shell.

On the menu: seafood-mushroom risotto and a dessert of crêpes with chocolate sauce.

Like the favorite dress you give away because it's too small (right before ten pounds fall off), I no longer have the mushroom cookbook, and I feel the regret-frizzled ache of its loss. I gave it to Goodwill because I hadn't cooked from it in years. But at the time, it was a reliable friend, one of the first cookbooks my mother gave me. When I was a vegetarian, mushrooms often stood in for meat, given their chewiness and rich, smoky taste.

After work, I hurried to a Chinatown seafood market to buy littleneck clams, shrimp, and rings of stretchy calamari. I plucked oyster, hen-of-the-woods, and chanterelle mushrooms from the mounds of perfect produce at SoHo's Dean & DeLuca. Shallots and leeks and saffron and stock were on hand at home. But I bought a bottle of tart white wine to add when caramelizing the aromatics.

All of these errands took longer than I had anticipated, and I was forced to call Will and postpone the time of his arrival.

"I don't mind arriving before it's ready," he said. "I love to hang out, talk, have a glass of wine, and watch people cook."

"That sounds lovely and I wish I could say yes," I said, "but I wouldn't be able to concentrate."

I needed a certain amount of Zen, solo space to cook unfamiliar dishes. When peppered with comments and questions, I grew distracted and snippy. The food suffered, and so did the interlocutor. It was way too early in the relationship to reveal my flaws.

I wanted to reveal my cooking instead. This night had a backwardness to it; my usual pattern was to invite a suitor up after a few chaste restaurant dates, cook a toothsome dinner, and then allow one thing to lead to another. Cooking for me was many things, but in these moments it was a form of foreplay. And it could be quite telling.

"I *love* chopped salads," Ralph exclaimed. That, along with his too-small feet and the low-fat Entenmann's cookies in his closet-size kitchenette, did not count in his favor.

"This doesn't have any protein," Daniel groused, when I placed stir-fried vegetables over rice in front of him. I burst into shocked, embarrassed tears, as if he had just criticized me personally. That would follow.

Jack told me ahead of time that he couldn't bring himself to eat "red things or round things."

Po didn't really like eggs—in fact, it seemed like his goal was to subsist on a diet of beer, wine, and hard liquor.

But Will and I had already gone to bed—precipitously, after running into each other in the same wine bar twice in the space of a week. I was sure, when I woke up the next morning, that I had spoiled something promising by having sex so soon. But instead, he pulled me close to him and smiled. "Good morning, beautiful."

I found myself asking Will to dinner to heighten the chances that I'd see him again. He could cancel, of course, but a plan was better than the bird-on-a-wire suspension of waiting for the phone to ring. Anyone could fake her way through a congenial morning before dropping off the face of the earth. I'd done it myself.

I didn't want Will to drop off the face of the earth. He was different—an ambitious intellectual overflowing with ideas, philosophical theories, opera librettos, wine varietals, and classical composers. He was tall and thin, but moved with economy and precision. His skin was pale with golden undertones, like milk from the grass-fed cows that grazed where his father was raised in the Jura region of France . . . and his hair was the dark ash brown of a graphite pencil.

And although he spoke with the ironclad confidence of a practiced university lecturer, something in his demeanor exuded a vulnerability that caused me to pleasurably collapse inside. When he put on his paper-thin V-neck cotton undershirt the morning after our first night together, the pale inverted triangle below his sternum was so fragile and bare that I swooped in and kissed it.

And here I was, two nights later, freshly showered and made up, adding the seventh portion of broth to the thrifted, thick-bottomed Dutch oven. The rice grains were plump and glossy; the pot soon to be covered, the heat of the delicious glop poised to delicately steam the seafood, and in return, the shellfish would release its liquor.

The crêpe batter was chilled in a bowl in the refrigerator, and the chocolate was prepped to melt in my makeshift double boiler.

Bleat! went the buzzer. I pressed the small plastic button that released the big, heavy wooden door four floors below. Will bounded up the stairs, wine in one hand and flowers in the other. I opened the door and he crossed into my fragrant kitchen, smelling of wintry city air and promise.

It's February 2007. The place: Santa Fe, New Mexico. You could fit my entire New York apartment into my current kitchen, which is nestled in a sleek adobe house at the top of one of the Sangre de Cristo foothills. I have counter space to burn, and my current knockoff isn't a pair of wannabe Manolos; it's an oversize stainless steel stove with six burners that looks like a Viking from a distance. It was one of the reasons we fell for the house, along with the mega–living room, gorgeous views, long, meandering driveway, clusters of piñon trees, and privacy.

My two children, ages three and five, have their father, Will's, milky skin. Honorée has my features and Will's slim body. Toddler Nathaniel's face is Will's, but he's barrel-chested and doughty, like my brothers.

Tonight, I'm making a multicourse dinner for six. We will start with appetizers and aperitifs.

Lillet on ice, graced with a single round slice of orange, and kir royales. I've got a single long, fresh baguette to accompany the cheese plate: pungent, creamy, melting Époisses de Bourgogne, arid manchego, a knob of chèvre, and a wedge of cambozola. It sits on the kitchen island beside a tray of endive leaves filled with rosettes of smoked whitefish mousse and sprinkled with grassy chive snippets.

The mushroom-chestnut soup is warm on the stove and will be served in red Emile Henry footed lion's-head bowls. I had to order the dusky chestnuts online, and threw in a tall, narrow jar of boozy cherries with a label as beautiful as an art deco poster.

The main course: lamb chops Champvallon, with *soupe à l'oignon gratinée.* According to *Cooking with Daniel Boulud,* the lamb recipe was created by a mistress of King Louis XIV who hoped to gain his favor. If he was taken by lamb chops braised with onions, potatoes, and thyme, she was successful.

The onion soup gratin was a 1907 French recipe reprinted by *The New York Times* in 1974, when I was two, and then re-rescued from obscurity by *New York Times* food writer Amanda Hesser in February 2007. It's the kind of recipe that makes people moo with pleasure.

It involves layering toasted, buttered baguette slices with Emmental cheese, tomato purée, and caramelized onions in a five-and-a-half-quart Dutch oven. I used the red Le Creuset that Will ordered for my birthday from Broadway Panhandler our first December in Santa Fe.

The entire construction is bathed in heated salt water, simmered on the stovetop, and baked for an hour in the oven. Hesser writes (one of my favorite sentences in the English language):

"The soup is ready when the surface looks like a crusty, golden cake and the inside is unctuous and so well blended that it is impossible to discern either cheese or onion."

Dessert was made the day before and chills in the fridge: a bittersweet chocolate tart with a walnut crust. The boozy cherries will be spooned atop each dense, satin-textured wedge.

The children will be fed pizza before the guests arrive, since they never like my complicated dishes.

But this time, despite my married status and the children we've sired and nurtured, the house we bought together, three trips to France, thousands of dinners and breakfast omelets, couplings and records played, trips back and forth to the car to unload grocery bags, nights between the same sheets . . . the last person I am cooking for is Will.

In fact, he won't even be here tonight. He's at a work-related dinner. When I found out about the conflict, I was secretly relieved. I *was* infatuated enough to brazen through a dinner with both my husband and the person I had a crush on, but it would be even better to not have him present.

One moment in the last five months, I lost my moral footing. Will and I had spent enough time in France, enjoying the food and wine and swooning over the scenery. But we'd never for one moment thought that the tacit acceptance of infidelity was worthy of emulation. We thought it was wrong.

But look at me now. I've arranged to have my daughter's friend sleep over so that she and my daughter and son will be busy playing all night, and not underfoot. I'm happy that my husband can't be here. I'm cooking a side dish in the pot he gave me as a gift. Who am I?

I've schemed and plotted to get C. into my house—inviting four other people to camouflage the architecture of my designs.

There was a bridge, and I crossed it. A line in the sand that I stepped over. Or did I just go to sleep one night and wake to find myself on the other side? Either way, I'm intoxicated to be here.

How Cuba Married Crete

ONCE I DECIDED TO WRITE about my lifelong love affair with food, I realized that I needed to talk about my *own* ingredients: my family—my grandmothers and grandfathers, my mother and father, who gave me my genes and made the meals that shaped my tastes—one way or another.

And once I began to do that, I realized that my identity, something I took for granted, was entirely different from what I had been told. I thought that the fairy tales my mother told me were make-believe and the family stories were real. But in fact, most of the things she told me weren't just stranger than fiction; they were fiction. The only things that were really true were the recipes, written down on tattered paper, on index cards, in notebooks.

Even though her stories were embellished and outright fabricated, I lived my life up to the age of thirty-nine believing that they were my stories. Like a person who finds out well into adulthood that he's actually adopted, and the family he thought was his genetic kin is not, and he has a whole other biological family somewhere, I discovered that the ancestors in my mother's stories were colorful, but not quite who I thought they were. And yet did my belief in them mold me anyway?

Was it easy for me to live a kind of lie for so long because I was told so many lies and believed them to be true? Perhaps I didn't notice the signals because I couldn't recognize them.

And although that was discomfiting, uncovering my true kin and their own true, far-from-boring stories restored my identity to me in a way that grounded me powerfully in self-recognition. I always feel a little off when I swallow a lie whole (as if I've eaten something tainted), and so each bit of fantasy I lay to rest is one fewer off-kilter element in my being.

So this story is not only the story of my lifelong love affair with food, but a story of identity: how I found out what (and who) I was truly made of historically; what my own truth was, one meal at a time—and whether to live it.

When I was cooking during this time of my life, I found comfort in the elemental truth of each ingredient, and in the end product. Recipes might not always have turned out the way I expected, but they weren't illusions. Each meal I cooked—and ate—helped me find my way back to the truth: the truth of my body, the truth of my heart, the truth of my mind, and the truth of my origins. And it set me free.

My maternal great-grandmother, Zoila, the legend goes, was from an aristocratic *madrileño* family, but, thanks to a combination of squirrely choosiness and parental indulgence, she remained unmarried, despite a series of earnest proposals. She met her husband, Albert Martin, on the *promenada* in Madrid. He was an Irish sailor, and they eloped to Cuba.

The name Zoila is a Spanish variant of the Greek word for "life." She was petite, with high cheekbones and a wide face. After a glance at her photograph, my daughter and I now know where we come by our bold, batwing eyebrows (which strive to meet in the middle if not waxed into submission), and my brother Jimmy inherited her flat, broad nose.

I grew up thinking that my great-grandmother was a noble-woman who threw off convention and privilege to marry a sexy Irish seafarer. How very adventurous! They bought a sugar plantation with her dowry and lived a gilded life until Albert died. Then Zoila had a nervous breakdown and the kids were forced to beg on the streets.

In fact, Zoila and Alberto met on the *promenada* in Sagua la Grande, Cuba. Zoila was a native Cuban (her photo hints that she's Afro-Cuban), and Alberto was also Cuban, although he did have some Irish blood.

My mother has never been too attached to *what truly happened*. As a child, I had trouble with making sense of sharing an experience with my mother and then listening to her broadcast a much more exciting, suspenseful, and heroic version into the telephone.

Growing up with my mother taught me to be a better-than-average detective and storyteller. I try to make the best and most truthful stories out of my experience of what happened, but straying from the truth makes me nervous, given that I grew up within so many layers of fiction intermingled with truth.

Alberto *did* obtain a job as the accountant at a Cuban sugar plantation, Ulacia Central, in Sagua la Grande. He and Zoila were allowed to live in a modest yet handsome house on the property. They had a bevy of children. In 1921, my grandmother Migdalia was born into this big family. The night she was born, Alberto placed a bundle—the payroll for the whole company—under her pillow before distributing it the next day, an act he believed would give her a lifetime of good luck.

My grandma Migdalia and her siblings played hide-and-seek amid the tall, bamboolike stalks and climbed up to play king of the mountain on mounds of sugarcane. They chewed and sucked the nectar from juicy, fibrous bits of peeled cane and spit out the pulp. When they were thirsty, they drank chilled lemon juice mixed with sugarcane juice fresh-pressed from hand-cranked machines. Even the cows chewed on the thick stalks, which made their milk and butter sweet.

Along with guavas, mangoes, citrus, and pineapple, the children feasted on mameys, which resemble giant toasted almonds. The coral-colored fruit within tasted of pumpkins, chocolate, and vanilla.

They also loved cherimoyas, which are covered in green, reptilian skin but, once sliced open, offer a yielding, white, custardlike flesh that tastes like a mixture of coconut, strawberry, and mango.

Inside, the house was cool and dark, white curtains fluttering in the arched windows, coffee-colored wood floors polished underfoot. In the evenings, under the shelter of a canopy, the family sat outside during the rains and enjoyed the cool air. Zoila did needlepoint and Alberto smoked a cigar, his hand proprietarily on his wife's knee. Migdalia loved to play the piano and was allowed to practice and play during the day at the plantation owner's house. She couldn't read music, but she learned to play songs by ear.

"He was the first man in town to have a car," my uncle Rickey told me. "He had a boat and hunting dogs. He was in charge of the general store. When she was little, Migdalia used to break her shoes just so she could go see her dad. He would give her a new pair. He was the *man*. But then the two sugar plantation owners got in a fight and one killed the other. The remaining owner asked Alberto to get rid of the body, but he refused. He was banished. Persona non grata. Lost everything except his car. They moved to Havana and he became a taxi driver."

In 1931, when Migdalia was ten, Alberto contracted tuberculosis and died, leaving Zoila and her children without a provider. There may have been women in her situation who could have figured out an ingenious plan to stay afloat, but she wasn't one of them. She promptly had a breakdown.

Zoila asked the older children to look after the younger ones, and she lay down on a mattress in one of the two bedrooms. She closed her eyes and felt the natural-cotton, tropical-weight spread below the slight body that had carried ten children, and she felt her ominous grief, which kept circling back whenever sleep blotted out consciousness. It tracked her like prey, waiting for her eyes to open. She blinked.

And then her vision loosened until darkness rushed between the threads, and she fell.

The godmothers arrived to take Migdalia's sisters and brothers into their care. They left Zoila and Migdalia, one staring vacantly, one string-bean thin with flashing eyes fighting back tears.

Did Migdalia want to leave her mother? No. Would Zoila have

been left alone? It's uncertain. Perhaps if all of the children had been claimed, one of the godmothers would have taken Zoila, too. But since Migdalia's godmother was also dead, the other godmothers reasoned that they could get by as a pair.

"Zoila needs to snap out of it," one said. "She always was too soft."

"Migdalia will never starve," said another. "She's more of a *chancletera* than the rest of the children put together."

"*La flaca* needs to learn how to make herself useful," said a third.

"With that *visaje como una payasa . . .*" murmured a fourth, uncharitably referring to Migdalia's prominent eyes, fierce brows, and plump lips.

Migdalia became a ten-year-old caretaker and breadwinner. Each morning, instead of walking to school, she knocked on the doors of nearby houses and offered her services as a housecleaner. She soon had a regular clientele, and often worked for food. But she wished she could cook. That way she could get paid in money, make something thrifty, and save the rest. When she didn't bring food home, they ate corn mush with sweet potatoes.

One fruitless day, she started home. Her mouth watering, she paused in front of the open-air butcher shop. The woman behind the counter waved her in. She remembered Migdalia's family. "How is your mother?" she asked.

"*Se chifló,*" said Migdalia, not in the mood to hide the truth.

Ximena nodded. "You take care of *her* now."

"I'm cleaning houses," said Migdalia with complicated pride.

"How's that going?" Ximena asked.

Migdalia needed no further prompting to unleash her laundry list of complaints. The uncertainty of compensation. The woman who never played her piano and wouldn't let Migdalia do it, either. The time she brought home dinner to her mother, only to find used (used!) toothpicks mingled in the food. The loutish sons who lurked around, pestering her like *moscas*.

With long deft fingers, Ximena packaged up scraps of *bistec de tipa de pierna*. She put the package into a bag with a few vegetables and a sachet of spices and handed it to the girl. She hesitated, then went into the back. A few minutes later, she came out with a small jar. "Here's some *sofrito,*" she said. "With this you can make your mother *ropa vieja.*"

"Thank you, Ximena," Migdalia said, and looked around, noticing with regret how clean it was and how much her services would be superfluous.

"How do I make it, and why is it called *ropa vieja?*" she asked.

The butcher's wife couldn't tell her how to make it before she told the story: A poor man's relatives were coming to his house for dinner. He didn't have enough food for the meal, so he took some old clothes from his closet and held them close to his heart until they glowed with his love. He put them in a pot with vegetables, herbs, and spices. As the ingredients simmered, the mixture transformed into a delicious beef stew.

~~~~~~

ROPA VIEJA
~~~~~~

½ pound flank steak
1½ tablespoons oil
2 cloves garlic, minced
1 small onion, diced
½ green pepper, diced

1 pinch black pepper
1–2 finely chopped or puréed tomatoes
1 cup water
2 ounces *sofrito*

Cut flank steak in strips, and brown in oil in a skillet. Remove from heat to rest in a bowl while you sauté the garlic, onion, and green pepper until they are soft and limp. Reunite the meat with the skillet, and add black pepper, finely chopped tomatoes, water, and *sofrito.* Simmer for about an hour. You'll know it's done when the meat shreds like old rags. Serve on top of rice, if you have any, or just eat it by itself.

Serves 2.

~~~~~~

Migdalia made *ropa vieja* for us when I was little, but because my father had rules about what could be cooked in his kitchen ("no spic food"), she called it beef stew. Although she and my father fought like cats and dogs, as long as he didn't know she was serving him Spanish food, mealtime was a reliably harmonious time of day.

Like a recipe—or a dancer with a thousand veils—an ocean freighter's passenger list contains secrets that don't immediately reveal themselves.

Not oblique: Constantin and Maria Vourakis, my mother's paternal grandparents, arrived with two young sons on March 4, 1914, on the SS *Athinai,* which sailed from Piraeus, Greece. Constantin was thirty-four, Maria twenty-five. Their sons were Stelios, sixteen months, and Stefanos, six months. They were from Chania, Crete— and as soon as the family arrived in the United States, Stelios and Stefanos became Charlie and Steve.

My mother told me that Maria was fourteen when she and Constantin ran away from home—an estate in Chania. Maria was the owners' daughter, and Constantin was a gardener on the property. She was betrothed to an old codger, and she was horrified. Constantin took pity on her and helped her to escape. They eloped.

That was my mother's story.

When I was older, my mother told me that Constantin may have kidnapped and raped Maria, and because she knew her family would feud with Constantin's and that her loved ones would inevitably die, she lied to her family and told them that she had gone willingly. And over time, their love grew.

Another possibility: Although bride theft and rape are crimes, it's also a common practice for two young people in love to run away until parents agree to the match. And they do, to put an end to the scandal.

"Maria didn't have a dowry, and she wasn't the eldest sister," my mother's cousin Stacie told me. "So they did what they had to do to get married." Maria's father or brother shot Constantin in the hip, which left him with a lifelong limp.

In Crete, "making love" is a pillar of any marriage—but not in the way you might think. It means to actually *churn* love out of the ups and downs of daily life. In fact, when a couple is overheard arguing, people say, "Ah, they're making love." Discord is seen as a process toward unity.

Constantin had been in America for a few years on his own, creating a life for himself and his family. One of his close male relatives had gone first—on the lam after killing someone in a Cretan bar brawl. He became a soldier in Chicago's organized-crime scene, and when Constantin came over, his cousin introduced him to associates in Brooklyn. They put him to work running a bordello.

That's something my mother never told me, but as I spoke to the Greek side of the family, the beans were spilled.

"When Yia Yia came over, she found out and told him he had to stop that right now. Papou stopped—but unwillingly. He showed her. He never worked another day in his life. He had savings, and the property—the apartments—and his garden, but Yia Yia had to open up a dress shop and do alterations to make money for the family."

As an older man, Papou was a piece of work. He threw an ax at a grandson who made him angry, and sexually molested a young neighborhood girl. "They had to pay off her family. They were poor, so they took the money and didn't turn him in," relatives told me.

From memory, Maria baked *koulourakia*—hand-formed cookies yellow with yolk, pillowy with butter. With the children's enthusiastic help, she formed the sturdy dough into snails, braids, twists, and cursive uppercase *C*'s and *S*'s.

She dabbed the top of each cookie with egg white and then sprinkled sesame seeds on top. Then she put them in the oven to bake until they were golden, but not browned, on the bottom.

In 1916, Maria gave birth to a little girl, Christina. Now that she had her own daughter, to join her sons, she could teach her how to make *spanakopita, koulourakia, kourambiethes, melamacarona.*

❧ ❧ ❧

"My father made the best rice pudding in the world," recalls my mother. "He was famous for it."

His recipe evolved over time while serving with the Seabees (a cognate of "CBs," "construction battalions") in the Philippines. The Navy's construction force recruited Charlie, né Stelios, because of his construction skills, but his acumen in the mess hall set him apart.

As a boy, Charlie helped his father build their family compound in Sheepshead Bay, Brooklyn, and continued to work on construction crews as he grew into manhood. He married a woman named Ethel, the daughter of a family friend, and moved with her into the apartment across the driveway from his parents.

In January 1942, rear admiral Ben Moreell, chief of the Navy's Bureau of Yards and Docks, was given a mandate to recruit skilled laborers for the Seabees. The Seabees have a tradition of aiming to serve above-average food, but rations were sometimes meager and mean. The quality of life of the men aboard a ship was significantly tied to the quality of the commissary staff, and Charlie was cherished.

Sacks of rice became *pilafi kritis,* cooked in stock gleaned from boiled meat bones and all the odds and ends he could salvage. Instead of serving canned vegetables plain in a puddle of their own brine, he drained them, sautéed them in oil, and made *ryzolata me lahanika,* a mixture of rice, chopped vegetables, and mayonnaise.

He coaxed life into the least amenable staple, dehydrated potato cubes, by grinding them up and making a makeshift *skordalia* out of the potato meal, dehydrated eggs, garlic powder, toasted stale bread, oil, and vinegar.

The ground potato cubes also found new life as potato pancakes, croquettes, hash browns (with the help of waffle irons), and sauce thickener.

Soon, mail deliveries from wives and girlfriends included sachets of dried herbs, which were brought to Charlie like *prasad* to be blessed and transmogrified in the gleaming stainless-steel kitchen.

Charlie never got any mail from Ethel. However, Constantin

rarely missed an opportunity to send his son his own dried *rigani* (oregano), *dyosmos* (mint), *vasilikos* (basil), *daphni* (bay leaf), and *glis-tritha* (purslane). After the packets were emptied, Charlie rubbed the wax paper between his hands and then raised his palms to his face and inhaled reverently, remembering the plot of land, which grew bushels of cucumbers, onions, tomatoes, pears, arugula, fennel, squash, string beans, and grapes.

Once he was back on dry land, Charlie was more than ready to take his talent for feeding hungry crowds with bare basics and turn it into a profitable livelihood.

Things with Ethel did not improve upon his return. Although Constantin and Maria had gotten married in opposition to Maria's arranged marriage, they had cajoled Charlie's relationship with Ethel along, and when Charlie shipped out, Ethel, according to my mother's story, was unfaithful. When Charlie returned home, his sister, Christina, told him what she'd observed in his absence.

"Find another place to live," he said to Ethel, and removed all traces of her from the apartment.

Although Charlie's ultimate goal was to open a diner in Sheepshead Bay, there was a promising opportunity in Bay Ridge—a beautiful chrome diner at the right price, not much competition—and so he took a leap of faith. He named it the Mermaid Diner, and his mother and father called it the *Gorgoulaki* (Dear Little Mermaid).

The first few days, when business was sparse, Charlie stood outside, swept the three half-moon steps, straightened his sign, polished chrome, taking every opportunity to smile and make eye contact with passersby.

Pictures of Charlie are arrestingly similar to those of young Al Pacino. In fact, after his death, my mother could not watch an Al Pacino movie for decades without sobbing uncontrollably.

"Hey, this is my grand-opening weekend," he said to teenagers, fishermen, grandmothers, young marrieds, and mothers pushing baby carriages. "We're celebrating. Come on in and have a free cookie. My own mother made them this morning." He passed out the sesame-encrusted *koulourakis,* which begged to be consumed with the fragrant, dark coffee waiting to be poured from pot to heavy, cream-colored mugs.

The mug's pleasing weight seemed to anchor people, sink them into the cushions of the spinning diner stools and booths. A bud vase of Constantin's flowers decorated each speckled Formica table.

Charlie talked shop with construction workers and fishermen, talked military with soldiers and their family members, and found something kind to say to each mother about her baby or child.

"Are you a good boy for your mama?" Charlie asked while winking at elfin-faced five-year-old Albert Karlson, who spun around on a diner stool once before his mother's finely manicured hand stopped him gently.

Charlie was getting ready to launch into his usual banter, but then he looked at Migdalia and lost his train of thought.

Young Migdalia had Salma Hayek's high forehead, strong chin, and sooty lashes. Her eyebrows arched like gulls. Beneath them, her heavy-lidded eyes drooped slightly at the outer corners, and her smile did the same. Those qualities, paired with her creamy skin, led people to compare her to Dorothy Lamour.

Charlie saw the resemblance but decided not to mention it. Flirtatious yokels must blurt that out to her every day. He wanted to compliment her more memorably, even if he had to let his admiration steep for a while. And maybe it would be better not to, given that she was wearing a wedding ring and had a child.

Her masses of glossy black hair were artfully pinned back with barrettes. As silly as it was, her hairline reminded him of black coffee against the side of a pale diner mug. That wouldn't be a good compliment, either, though. Instead, he smiled and held her gaze.

The features that had made her seem *como una payasa* as a child— the full lips, strong straight nose, and large eyes—had settled on her adult face in a manner that was distractingly, fearsomely beautiful.

Migdalia looked at him haughtily, as she did with strangers (and loved ones, too), but a smile played around the corners of her mouth. She was twenty-eight years old, lonely and hungry for social contact. Over the past eighteen years, much had changed.

She'd nursed her mother back to health, and then, when she was sixteen, met a Danish merchant seaman, Gustav, who married her and brought her to America.

Gustav took Migdalia and little Albert to the apartment he had selected for them in Bay Ridge, Brooklyn. It was the second floor of a two-family house, with a front patio to enjoy on summer evenings. She smoked and felt the bay breezes cool the hot residential streets. In one photo she sits sideways, dressed in a Katharine Hepburn–like camel silk pantsuit, on a canvas and wooden-framed folding chair, a stuffed lion under her arm inches away from the lit cigarette between her fingers. Solemn.

She still looks young enough to have a favorite stuffed animal, and also old enough to be smoking in an urbane tailored suit.

When Migdalia saw the plainly furnished apartment for the first time, she began to imagine ways to make the space warmer, less tame, more like home. She was an accomplished seamstress, like all of the women in her family. Perhaps she could glue seashells to the coffee table in a spiral pattern. She could swap the stuffy lampshades for large, droopy straw hats, adding a beaded fringe. The pale blue panel curtains—the same color of a dying woman's transparent eyelids!—could be replaced with palm-printed tropical barkcloth she'd seen for sale in the window of a fabric shop.

Before Gustav left, he bought Migdalia a sewing machine, handed her a bank account booklet and showed her how to withdraw money, and even took mother and son to see the sights in Manhattan.

For the first time in Migdalia's life, she was completely cut off from her family, except by mail. She and young Albert took walks, went to the beach and to the playground, but she had no friends and felt shy about extending herself. She was comfortable practicing her English on shopkeepers but didn't feel ready to function socially in a second language.

As Migdalia sewed, cleaned, mothered, and stitched, aromas wafted into her apartment from the floor below. Heavenly, mouthwatering smells, of garlicky tomatoes stewing, rich meat browning, soft cheese melting, bubbling, and becoming crispy in places.

The downstairs tenants were a middle-aged Italian couple. They and Migdalia smiled at each other, and Mrs. Sticcho always let loose a torrent of child-adoring Italian whenever she laid eyes on Albert, but they weren't at the food-sharing point. Migdalia could only savor the morsels of Romance language that trembled in Mrs. Sticcho's sentences, different yet familiar.

The daily caravan of good smells was so different from the vinegary, spiced, sweetish smells of Migdalia's own Cuban cooking, which is perhaps why she decided to take Albert out one day in search of Italian food. If Mrs. Sticcho had come up the stairs with a welcome basket of lasagna and garlic bread, the course of Migdalia's life would have turned out very differently.

She passed one Italian restaurant that was closed until dinnertime, and a second that looked too formal, and a third that was filled with men, and a fourth that looked dingy.

She noticed that the shiny silver diner was open. Nothing inside would slake her craving, but at least she could bring Albert in for a milkshake and hamburger. He was already pulling on her hand, leading her to the half-moon steps that glimmered in the sunlight.

As they crossed the threshold, Migdalia smiled. She smelled the same aromas that had taunted her for weeks: tomato sauce, garlic, browning cheese.

"Where would you like to sit, Albert?" she asked in English. He pointed to a stool at the counter, attracted to the dessert case, which sheltered crumb cake, fruit and custard pies, and cherry Danishes. They settled themselves on the round red vinyl seats.

"Are you a good boy for your mama?" the counterman asked.

For a second, Migdalia translated it as, "Are you a good mama for your boy?" *Qué cosa!* But then the words rearranged in her head and she saw that he addressed the question to Albert, and noticed his teasing smile and kind brown eyes.

Charlie rattled off the specials, and Migdalia ordered the ziti for herself and a burger and fries for Albert.

"How do you make the ziti?" she asked.

"Well, I get the pasta, ricotta, and mozzarella from Mario around the corner, and then I blend up some diced tomatoes with basil, garlic, salt, and pepper. Cook the pasta, put it in the tray, then pour over the sauce, mix in ricotta, and cover everything with enough mozzarella to choke a horse. You can't go wrong—pasta, sauce, two kinds of cheese—how could anyone mess that up?"

She smiled. He was funny and cute, like the boys she had grown up with, but he was also humble, with an air of needing to be cared for.

He placed stemmed glasses of vanilla pudding in front of Migdalia and Albert, and then pulled a metal bowl out of a low fridge and dolloped each serving with whipped cream. "On the house," he said. "Although you're probably sweet enough," winking at Albert.

Migdalia thought of the sugarcane she and her sisters and brothers used to suck on, the lemonade sweetened with cane juice. Her favorite meal as an adult was the following trio: a cup of strong instant Yuban coffee with four sugars and evaporated milk, a piece of cake, and an unfiltered cigarette.

"I'm like black coffee," she said. "I need cream and sugar."

His gaze jumped to hers from where it lingered in the middle distance, feigning a restaurant manager's distracted air. Her reply seemed suggestive, but her English language skills were too rudimentary to flirt quite so deftly . . . yet who knows? Who hasn't said something accidentally suggestive to a future lover? Sometimes the tongue has its own wisdom.

She looked at him innocently and then lifted the spoon to her mouth. She tasted the pudding and put down the spoon. "Not bad," she said, "and thank you so much, but I prefer my mother's *natilla.*"

"What's *natilla?*" he asked. "Can she bring some in for me to try?"

"My mother is in Cuba," she said shortly. "But she taught me how to make it, and the next time I do, I will bring you some."

NATILLA

1 stick cinnamon	1 teaspoon vanilla
¼ teaspoon salt	4 heaping tablespoons sugar
¼ cup water	2 cups milk
4 egg yolks	2 tablespoons cornstarch

Add water, cinnamon stick, and salt to a saucepan and bring it to a gentle boil. Separate eggs. Beat *(baté!)* yolks with a whisk. Add vanilla and sugar to the yolks and *baté*. Add milk and *baté* once more. Hear the word *baté* in your mother's voice; remember when you were small enough to hang on to her skirt as she cooked at the stove, the cinnamon, yolks, vanilla, milk, and sugar combining into one velvety mix that scented the space you shared with her. Now you are the one cooking the *natilla,* far away. Your son loves it. You and he will eat it all tonight, because otherwise you'll go back to the Mermaid Diner far too quickly. You are alone, but you are not lonely. You are lonely, but you're not *medio descarada,* half-shameless.

Pour the mixture into the saucepan and add cornstarch. *Baté* to distribute it well. Cook the golden liquid over medium heat, stirring continuously until it thickens. Then take the pot off the heat and let it cool a bit, sidling over to lift up a small spoonful every now and then. Blow on it and dip your upper lip into the bowl of the spoon, coating it. Lick it off and repeat, until you step away to the patio, to have a cigarette and stare down the darkening street, children being called in, husbands hurrying up the steps and into the arms of their wives.

Pour into custard cups, sprinkle with cinnamon, cover, and chill until set.

2

Mastering the Art

WHEN MY MOTHER married my father, two families were linked: the hard-drinking, garrulous, one-pot-dinner Irish Walshes and my mother's clannish Greeks and Cubans, who stuck to their mother tongues and kept to themselves. They mixed about as well as corned beef and cabbage goes with *spanakopita,* which gave me another understanding of the term "distant relatives."

The phone rang in a small cottage in Mastic Beach, New York, in 1973. My mother, Linda, picked up the phone with one hand and slid it between her ear and shoulder, then put her hand back on the baby in her arms.

"Hello?"

"Hey, Linda, it's Dad. What are you thinking about making tonight?"

"Well," she said, flipping through Julia Child's cookbook, "I'd like to try *boeuf bourguignon.*"

"I heard a couple of commuters talking about that on the train the other day. What should I pick up from the store?"

"Hang on," she said, doing the intrinsic hip sway that she hoped would soothe me while she finished the phone call. "Six ounces of bacon, three pounds of stewing beef in two-inch cubes, and a bottle of 'a full-bodied, young red wine'—Julia Child says you can use Chianti—two dozen small white onions, a pound of mushrooms, and a bag of egg noodles."

"Okay, Mom and I will be over at about five. That work for you?"
"Sure, sure! Looking forward to it."
"Kiss that baby for me."
"I will."

Charlie and Migdalia's meeting in the Mermaid Diner was fateful. It's impossible to know when their friendship turned into something more, because the accounts vary, but it did.

Migdalia moved into one of the Vourakis compound apartments with Albert, and lived with Charlie when Gustav was away. When he came back to visit, Charlie retreated. At that time, he had a diner in Sheepshead Bay called the Tip Top, and Migdalia and Albert ate most of their meals there.

"Charlie was always very good to me," Albert said. "He never treated me as less than his son."

When Migdalia became pregnant with Linda, it may have initially been unclear who the father was, until Linda was a child. As she grew older, you couldn't help but notice that she had the knife-blade features and olive skin of the Vourakis clan.

But Migdalia assured Gustav that Linda was his, and he went along with it, although he also noticed her resemblance to Migdalia's landlords, the Vourakises. He may have gone along with it because he had his own setup in Japan (and perhaps other countries—we know only about his Japanese wife).

"It never came up as a conversation for me," Albert said. "It was the fifties. We didn't talk about things like that with our parents."

Linda felt different than other children, because her father was always away, but Charlie was happy to play a paternal role.

Migdalia's pregnancy with Linda's younger brother, Rickey, so out of sync with Gustav's last visit, triggered their divorce. Gustav retired to Japan.

Once liberated, Migdalia and Charlie got married in a discreet city hall ceremony. No party, no pictures, no gifts. It was gift enough to be legitimate in the eyes of the law, to stop sneaking around, posing as married, or as less than what they were, depending on the context.

In 1966, when Linda was sixteen, Migdalia and Charlie decided to move their family to Center Moriches. They traded the denser population and urban texture of Brooklyn for the spread-out, gentle community on the south shore of Long Island, buffered from the full brunt of the ocean's swells by the long, thin shinbone of Fire Island's barrier beach.

It was beautiful, but Linda was miserable. She loved the city, never would have left if she hadn't been forced. That's where her friends were—in her two thousand–strong Sheepshead Bay high school class. Here, she was one of one hundred, and she was keenly peeved that everyone was so country.

And the food! No longer could she stop at the pizza place under the elevated subway station, or at the Hebrew National deli for a hot dog or knish, or at Goody's, which had the best chocolate and vanilla egg creams in the world, and ice cream cones, sundaes, malts, nickel and penny candy.

Nor could she stop in at the Tip Top Diner and order anything she wanted, on or off the menu. She even missed Lundy's. Once a month, Migdalia and Charlie took Linda out for a family luncheon there. It was famous for its capaciousness, and for its clam chowder and pillowy biscuits.

In Center Moriches, she also missed being across the driveway from Maria and Constantin, whom she called Yia Yia and Papou. "None of the other kids were allowed in Papou's garden, but I was. And every afternoon, Papou and I took a nap on the couch. I leaned against his shoulder."

My mother's cousin said, "When I was little, the relatives told my mother about what Papou did to the neighborhood girl, and that she should keep me away from him."

Apparently, nobody told Migdalia (or sought to guard Linda)—because she was very overprotective of Linda in every other way. She used to spy on Linda at junior-high dances, peering in the windows of school gymnasiums and rushing in to physically pull a too-snug dance partner away from her daughter.

In Center Moriches, Linda missed Yia Yia's kitchen, its ceramic cookie jar filled with fresh *koulourakia,* and the spinach pies Yia Yia always had on hand to warm up if Linda was hungry.

Every day, Maria and her sisters went outside and received the daily haul of tough, wrinkly savoy spinach leaves from Constantin and his garden. They rinsed them in big tubs of water. Then they removed the stems, dried the leaves, and began to add them into a mixture of three cheeses, kneading them until they broke down and released liquid. "Kind of like what sautéing would do, but without heat," my cousin Stacie said.

Linda could also help herself to fresh bread with cold butter, or the yogurt Papou made each day—thick, silken, tart, and as unctuous as sour cream.

"So-called Greek yogurt from the store would not hold a candle to Papou's," my mother sniffs.

Each night, he poured milk into a large glass rectangular baking dish and added a little bit of yogurt from the day before. He warmed the milk ever so gently, testing it periodically with his finger, nudging the temperature up bit by bit until it reached the exact right level of warmth. Then he placed it in the oven on the lowest setting and let it transform overnight.

In the morning, he poured the yogurt into a cheesecloth-lined bowl and lifted up the cloth like a sack, so that the liquid whey drained from the yogurt. Papou kept the whey in a jar in the refrigerator—Yia Yia used it in place of water when baking bread, and Papou liked to drink it. Papou returned the yogurt to the glass dish, covered it with a white cloth napkin, and refrigerated it.

"Why don't you like anyone at Center Moriches High?" Linda's friend Colleen asked.

"They're hicks," my then-teenage mom dismissed, flipping her long, dark, ironed hair over her shoulder. "I don't see you dating any of them."

"Well, that's because I'm going out with Joe," Colleen said. "Hey, Joe was wondering if you wanted to come out with us on a double date."

"That depends," Linda said. "Who's his friend?"

"That's the thing—his family moved out here from Brooklyn, too. So you have that in common."

"Really?"

"*Really.*"

"What does he look like?"

"I don't know, but he's probably halfway-decent-looking," Colleen said. "He and Joe are good friends. They go to school together in Mastic, and they also work at the same restaurant."

"What's his name?" Linda asked.

"Peter."

"Well, I guess there's no harm in going. Especially since we'll be in it together."

At some point, Linda had gone from a scrappy, skinny tomboy who hid her braids in a baseball hat to pass as a boy and play baseball (girls weren't allowed to play) to a petite young woman with head-turning curves.

The night of the double date, Linda and Colleen got ready together at Linda's house. Linda wore a form-fitting T-shirt and hip-hugger bell-bottoms.

Peter was fifteen, tall and lanky, with Irish-pale skin, the kind that never tans, only burns. He had faded-jeans blue eyes, fluffy sideburns, and a mustache above slightly gappy teeth, and combed out his curly hair so that it rested on his head like a shallow layer of pale gold cotton candy.

"He wore sandals with *socks,*" my mother always repeated, years later, shaking her head, first fondly and then less so.

Bonnie and Clyde was playing at the Rocky Point drive-in, about thirty minutes away. After the movie, they went to the Carvel soft-serve ice cream parlor and Peter bought Linda a hot-fudge sundae with marshmallow sauce.

Colleen and Joe got married, but it was doubtful that either of them could have predicted that five years later, Linda and Peter would do the same.

When Linda was eighteen, the September of her senior year at Center Moriches High, Charlie died of a heart attack. Like Zoila before her, Migdalia was devastated.

"Yia Yia and Papou were away, on vacation in Crete, when he died. This was something they had saved for and looked forward to for over fifty years," Albert recalled. "They said, 'Don't bury him until we get back. Wait.' So for nine days, we waited."

It took days to find and notify Charlie's parents, and then money had to be wired to them to buy tickets for the earlier passage. They boarded the series of flights back to their home.

"But did you know that he was your dad then?" I asked my mother.

"Yes, damn it, that's when they all told me! After he died, when we were waiting for my grandparents to get back, my aunt Christina and uncles sat me down and told me the truth. I thought I was going to go out of my mind. First I lost Charlie. Then I realized I had lost out on acknowledging him as my dad, all those years that he was alive. And I was so angry that he never told me, 'You're my daughter.'"

When Yia Yia and Papou arrived, the grief reached a fever pitch. Papou sat in the corner and howled, crying torrents of tears. Yia Yia screamed and repeated a chant over and over as she rocked back and forth: "*Kyrie eleison.* Have mercy, Lord, have mercy on me."

Aunt Christina did her part. She cooked and fed everyone for nine days straight, tears falling into the mixture of spinach, onions, feta, parsley, and eggs and on the phyllo sheets as she brushed them. Maybe it helped her to cook, to tend, to feed the assembled. People sent over casseroles, odds and ends, but she was responsible.

After taking trains and subways to get to Linda, Peter ran up the subway exit steps, wild-haired, in an ill-fitting suit he had borrowed from his brother. They'd been dating for three years, going steady after two, and he'd been coming in to spend time with her as much as he could. She wasn't at the funeral, and she wasn't in any of her family's apartments, so he started looking in places he knew she loved. He found her at the ice cream parlor, washing down Valiums with an egg cream.

"When he came and comforted me, he encouraged me that I could make it through this. No one else had said that—I had been surrounded by people who felt like they couldn't go on, either. It was a turning point."

Peter, who had been a casual boyfriend, who liked her more than she liked him, transformed into her rock.

As she stared into his pale blue eyes and felt his large, cool, dry hand take her damp, sticky one, she imprinted on him, eyes and nose red and swollen from crying. Supported by him and the round red vinyl diner stool, the same one that she used to spin around in circles on when she was a little girl—a lucky girl with two dads. And now she had none.

After Charlie's death, Peter's family, who had loved Linda before, took her under their wing in earnest. It was a nice place to hide.

There were his parents, Jimmy and Marie. Jimmy was strikingly handsome—a fair, blue-eyed Gregory Peck type, talkative, quick to laugh, fond. Jimmy was a union organizer and train conductor on the brink of retirement, and he loved people, but his family especially.

Marie Reichert Walsh was pleasingly plump, flame red–haired, with hazel eyes and a pealing laugh. She'd had a tough life, which maybe honed her razor-keen bullshit detector. She could lay you flat without raising her voice. You knew not to push Marie.

Pictures of young Marie show her small mouth, penciled to show off its petite cupid's bow, a bit pursed. Her eyes look out from under her brow, wary and alluring. Her face is a perfect oval, perhaps the slightest bit long.

Jimmy doted on his grandchildren, embraced the presence of all of his children's spouses, and made sure everyone had a drink, something to eat, and a place to sit down.

Marie turned out deeply satisfying, thrifty one-pot meals for a crowd most nights of the week: pot roast, meat loaf, lamb stew, Salisbury steak, Manhattan clam chowder made from the daily haul of local clammers. When something went on sale, she stocked up on it—down in the cellar, she had a second refrigerator and lots of extra pantry space.

She stood in front of the stove, periodically stirring, tasting, salting, a cigarette in one hand and a tumbler of whiskey on the rocks in the other.

Marie also cooked dishes passed down from her father's German-born mother: *Frikadellen,* savory meat patties enrobed in subtle, creamy gravy; and toothsomely lumpy potato pancakes with sauerbraten and red cabbage.

Thanksgiving was Grandpa Jimmy's favorite holiday. Everyone went to Grandma and Grandpa's for Thanksgiving. Grandpa made Grandpa Jimmy's Stuffing, a mix of bread crumbs, onions, crumbled loose breakfast sausage, and celery, and Grandma took care of the rest.

Their small Cape Cod–style retirement house seemed to expand at the seams to fit the thirty or forty people who arrived to eat on that holy day of gratitude and benevolent gluttony.

It was there that I learned that it's much better to cram people in like sardines on a joyful gathering day than to underinvite. You're forced to talk to people, everyone's face takes on a beautiful postcoital rosiness, perfume mingles with cooking aromas, and the idea that you are an individual, a lonely and unique individual, is squeezed out of the room entirely.

Beer, wine, and liquor flowed freely. Grandpa couldn't drink because of his ulcers, but Grandma could put it away, and she did, along with all of the adult children. Nobody really stayed on top of whether the teenagers were stealing nips—and they were.

Getting "in her cups" might have helped Marie to do it all—be a matriarch who maintained an ever-flowing font of hospitality, given the tragedies that gouged sizable divots out of her capacity for joy.

Marie and Jimmy were no strangers to loss. Their second-oldest son, Gregory, drowned at age seven in an upstate lake under the care of his aunt and uncle.

My father, Peter, was born after his death. His parents kept bags of Gregory's old clothes and favorite toys in Peter's closet, and his first memory was that he had a dream that Gregory opened the door and came out, and Peter was so glad, because he knew that it would make his parents happy again.

Their eldest son, James Junior, was the black sheep. Although he was a drinker in a family of drinkers used to exercising latitude around the behavior that went along with it, Jimmy Jr. pushed the envelope.

He drove drunk and crashed his cars, went AWOL on his first wife and children, moved out of state to avoid paying child support, and then had to sneak in and out of New York to visit family because there was a warrant out for his arrest. He, too, had ulcers but figured out a way to minimize the agony of drinking by packing his stomach with ice cream and milk.

There may have been more forgiveness ladled out for Jimmy Jr. because he was acting out the grief and fury that his parents kept quietly stored inside them. All of that grief, however stoically held in, displaced other things. For at least seven years, the grief of Gregory's death blotted out Marie's consciousness. She had no memories of her daughter Carole's early childhood. It was all a blur.

Jimmy lost his son, but for many years, he also lost his wife. She went through the motions, drinking heavily, numb. He couldn't drink, so he threw himself into the railroad and labor organizing.

But they loved and enjoyed the children they were able to keep close at hand: Carole, their only girl, Frank, and Peter.

My father was their youngest child—an accidental child conceived when Marie was forty-two. Jimmy and Marie were Catholics, and although they did their best not to get pregnant via the rudimentary options available to them, Marie noted the absence of her period at the end of May 1950. She thought, as one would, that she was menopausal. But about halfway through the pregnancy, she realized, when my father moved in her belly, that her vaguely bemoaned midlife weight gain was in fact a baby.

There really aren't any photographs of Marie with young Peter, not one, where she is even pretending to be happy. She looks at the camera with heavy-lidded, glowering eyes, almost lizardlike, with a cigarette dangling from the corner of her mouth.

Just as Peter's birth year was a source of ire for his mother, his birth date became a source of panic. In 1969, the draft lottery gave all men with my father's birthday, March 2, the draft number 29. Low numbers meant a higher chance of being sent over to Vietnam.

Jimmy wanted Peter to get a job on the railroad, like his brothers before him. Given that Jimmy Jr. was now in Pennsylvania and Frank was regularly getting disciplined for drunkenness, tardiness, and absenteeism, perhaps Jimmy thought Peter was his last chance at having a strong filial successor.

Or maybe Jimmy didn't want Peter involved in all of the campus protesting, drugging, and radicalism, or he didn't want Peter to surpass him.

In 1963, President Kennedy signed an executive order exempting married men from the draft. But in 1965, married men without children were once again eligible. The only thing that kept men out was having a dependent.

"Your parents had you to keep your dad out of Vietnam," my cousin once said. "But then, once he knew you were on the way, your dad dropped out of college and started working on the railroad. And that was a big sacrifice for him. He wanted to do something different with his life."

Grandpa Jimmy kept the family together. He invited his children over for big family dinners once, twice a week. They ate and drank together, and if it was true that there was an unspoken watchfulness and caretaking around who was drinking the most, there was also an osmotic, common bombed-ness that rendered going sober and staying in the group's good graces unthinkable. Marie drank to forget about Gregory. Her children drank, in part, to forget the nurture they missed from Marie, who spent their formative years in a numb lockstep of grief. And nobody was about to rip the scab off of that one.

Grandpa Jimmy also kept my parents together by assiduously looking after my mother and keeping her company. He knew she loved Julia Child's recipes but couldn't really afford to buy the recipe ingredients for more than a few meals a week. So he called her up and asked which ingredients she needed, then he and Marie shopped for them and came over and helped her cook.

Right on time, Jimmy and Marie turn up with paper sacks in hand. Linda lets them into the beach cottage, which is decorated with Beatles posters, Indian shawl throws, and paintings they made in college art classes.

"Hi, Mom and Dad!" Linda calls out. "Come on in."

"I got some formula ingredients, too," Grandpa Jimmy said.

After I was born, my mother had huge, melon-swollen breasts just aching to feed me, but because her doctor told her that breast-feeding would interfere with her C-section recovery, she did not. She'd also been paying attention to news exposés that revealed that baby formula contained lead, monosodium glutamate, and "all manner of horror."

She was used to making things from scratch. Why not formula? And so she turned to her well-worn Adelle Davis book, *Let's Have Healthy Children* (she'd been studying it since she got married), and read the baby formula recipe. It called for raw milk, brewer's yeast, rice syrup, and eggshells. Where could she find raw milk? She called the one health foods store on Long Island, in Rocky Point, and asked the rawboned, yellow-haired hippie owner for advice.

"I can order that for you," he said. Stuck with me, screaming bloody murder because I could smell the perfect breast milk just millimeters away from my mouth, and recovering from surgery, my mother asked my grandfather if he could go get it.

"What for?" he asked.

"I'm going to make Candace's formula from scratch. You know how much she's refusing to drink the store-bought formula. She turns her head away and *screams.* Even when I finally get her to take it, she projectile-vomits it across the room. I don't blame her. It tastes terrible."

He wondered if she was having dangerous postpartum delusions. "Is it safe?" he asked.

"Please, Dad, I wouldn't give it to her unless I was 100 percent, totally and completely, sure that it was safe. I trust Adelle Davis with every fiber of my being. Please?"

"Linda, you know I'd do anything for you. I just want to make sure it's the best thing for the baby."

"It is," she said, starting to cry.

"Okay, I'll go get it."

Jimmy made his way to Rocky Point and into the fervently healthy, modest little storefront, and sniffed its almost pleasant odor: a mix of curry, armpit, pot, and lemongrass.

"I'm here to pick up . . . to pick up the raw milk for Linda Walsh," he said.

"Linda told me you'd be coming. It's right here."

"How much do I owe you?"

"This first order's on the house. Our gift to the baby."

"That's my granddaughter," Jimmy said, smiling, thawing.

"Congratulations."

"Thank you, and thank you for the gift. Have a good day, now."

Back in Mastic Beach, Mom got up gingerly and began to make my elixir while Grandpa Jimmy gently bobbed with me in his arms, and then sat down softly to hold me as I slept. Linda heated the goat milk and added the eggshells, brewer's yeast, and vitamin powder. It bubbled on the stove, filling the room with a rich, pleasant odor.

"Now I have to let it cool a bit," said Mom, "and hopefully she'll wake up when it's at the right temperature. I hope she likes it. She can't go on like this, not eating."

"Well," Grandpa said, "why don't you give me a cup of it? I might as well test it out. If it could make her sick, I'd rather find out by getting sick myself."

After one sip, his eyebrows shot up. "This is delicious!" he declared. "It's so good! Like a vanilla milkshake! This . . . this is wonderful. I still want to wait and see if it agrees with me, but it *tastes* great. Much better than regular baby formula."

"You've tasted formula?"

"Well, not like this. But just a drop on the wrist to make sure the bottle wasn't too hot. And then I figured, why not taste it? I only did *that* once."

Linda sipped it. "You're right, it *is* good."

"Let's let her sleep, and when she wakes up we can give her some, provided I don't keel over between now and then," Grandpa said.

When I woke up, Grandma, Grandpa, my mother, and my father were staring at me with solemn faces. My mother picked me up, then placed the bottle's nipple at my lips, tapping it to allow a drop of liquid to enter my mouth. I took the nipple and sucked it until it was empty. Then I let out a loud burp and fell back to sleep. Mom put me in my bassinet.

"Eureka," said Jimmy.

With Jimmy and Marie over, Linda's hands were freed up to cook. She cut the bacon into *lardons* and placed them in a saucepan of hot water to simmer. She made Marie a cocktail and Jimmy a club soda, then perched on the edge of the chair and watched the news with them for a few minutes before going back into the kitchen to brown the bacon and then the cubes of beef in a Dutch oven.

Jimmy left me dozing against Marie's cozy bosom and wandered into the kitchen. "Need any help?"

"Sure, could you cut these mushrooms in quarters? We need to sauté them separately and add them in at the end. I'll slice the onion and the carrot."

"Is this good?" Jimmy asked, handing her the bowl of quartered mushrooms.

"Yes, thanks." She added the meat and bacon back to the pan where the vegetables were browning, salted and peppered the mixture, then dusted it with flour and gave everything a good stir. She poured the wine over the hot browned meat and vegetables, added the tomato paste, garlic, thyme, and bay leaf and brought it to a simmer on the stovetop.

"Okay, we're almost done here," she said. "We can start the water for the noodles."

"Good, because this stuff smells amazing. I'm famished."

"Oh, nuts."

"What?"

"It says I have to cook it for three to four hours! We can't wait that long."

Jimmy and Linda looked at each other, crestfallen.

"Hey, no problem. Put it in the oven, we'll go out to eat at the diner, and then we can have this tomorrow night."

"O . . . kay," Linda said. "You know, I could definitely drown my disappointment in a malted milkshake and a cheeseburger right now."

"At least Peter will enjoy it, because it will be ready right about the time he gets home."

Mom brightened at the thought. After dinner at the diner, Jimmy and Marie dropped us off. The house smelled divine. She checked on the stew, blew on a spoonful, and tasted it. Rich and darkly savory, with a hint of winey sweetness. It was definitely cooked through, but Julia Child advised letting the flavors marry for a few more hours.

She decided to set aside a portion for Peter and put the rest in the fridge, so that she could finish cooking it the following evening. Linda put a small saucepan filled with a hearty portion of the stew in the refrigerator, and left a note on the counter: "Pete, leftovers in the fridge. Heat up! French beef stew, we loved it."

My mother fed me a bottle of homemade formula, put me in my crib, and read to me from the *Anthology of Children's Literature* until I fell asleep. Then she went to bed.

Dawn broke, and Linda stretched out her hand to touch Peter. He wasn't there. She bolted upright, with panic clamping down on her chest.

She walked into the kitchen and looked out the window to see if maybe he had passed out in the car. No car. With a trembling fingertip, she dialed Jimmy and Marie's number on the avocado-green rotary wall phone.

"Dad, Dad! Peter never came home!" she gasped.

"Okay, I'll call the police and then go out looking for him. Try to stay calm for the baby. I'll drop Marie off on my way."

Jimmy called his friend the police chief, and patrol cars from three towns combed the streets looking for Peter's blue hatchback. One policeman who drove down to the beach noticed a flash of blue against the paler blue water.

It was the roof of a car with part of the windows showing. The cop waded out to the car, opened the door, and pulled Peter out. He was passed out, dead weight, and so the policeman slapped him on the face a few times and yelled in his face. "Wake up, you drunk motherfucker! I don't care whose son you are—this is bullshit."

Peter came to, flailing around and mumbling, "What the hell? Why'd you hit me? I just wanted to take a nap."

"You almost drowned, asshole."

Peter looked at the car, the ocean swirling around his waist, into the cop's eyes, half-hostile, half-pitying. He waded and lurched with the policeman back to the cop car. "You're not getting in this car all wet. Bad enough that I am. You can wait here until I get your family to pick you up. You're their problem, not mine. But here—take this card. It has information about meetings."

"What, AA? I don't need to go to AA. I'm not an alcoholic," Peter laughed. "I was just having a few beers after work. Don't tell me you don't do the same thing."

The policeman looked at Peter, wet and disheveled, and past him at his car, almost covered by seawater.

"No, pal, I don't do the same thing."

Jimmy arrived in his sedan. "Get in, son."

Peter's shoulders slumped as he got into the car.

"Linda's sick with worry. Let's get you home."

"Can we stop and get something to eat?"

"No, Linda cooked beef stew."

Serve in its casserole, or arrange the stew on a platter surrounded with potatoes, noodles, or rice, and decorated with parsley.

—Mastering the Art of French Cooking

Cradle of Flavor

Bitter

MY MOTHER HATED COFFEE so much that my father drank his only outside the house, black, no sugar, in Styrofoam cups from silver concession trucks that perched at each railroad stop.

But whenever my grandma Migdalia came to visit, my mother's distaste ceased to be an issue. The stainless-steel percolator with its fabric-covered cord came out; the Yuban coffee, tins of evaporated milk, and white sugar were bought, and a center of gravity took hold in the house. It wasn't like sweetness and light descended.

My earliest memories of Migdalia are of a strikingly handsome woman in a housedress, cleaning. Her hair was a careless barbershop shag, her face lined with deep grooves—a mixture of laugh lines and frown lines.

Because she had so deeply embodied the young beauty, the sultry woman, I think she took a certain satisfaction in casting off all of the trappings of femininity, like a drag performer on his day off. Her middle and old age were the day off she never allowed herself while she was a maiden, lover, wife. She lived as if all men died the day Charlie died, as militantly unadorned as women's land separatists can be—except for one thing.

Her hands, scored by work, stroked my hair or my arm absently, and I admired her pretty oval nails, painted in tropical Cuban hues of pink and orange, because that was the one bit of grooming she did not give up.

"Grandma, will you do my nails?" I asked, knowing the answer.

"Oh, Candooch, you're too young," she said, pronouncing it *joe-ng.* "When you're older, after your sweet sixteen, then I'll paint your nails."

My mother spent days cleaning before Migdalia's arrival, but it didn't matter. Grandma still picked up the broom, the rag, the duster, the mop and pail, and went to work.

She was the roughest kind of tender. Her voice, deepened by years of smoking cigarettes, reminded me of a crow's caw. Her laugh came out as a cackle—and she loved to shock me and my cousins by taking out her false teeth and smiling, bare gummed.

She still sewed, commandeering my mother's machine to make me fanciful dresses and nightgowns. She and my mother collaborated on sewing projects as they had when Linda was a teen.

On summer evenings, when I came in after playing barefoot in the backyard, she sat me down on the couch and washed my feet with a cool, wet washcloth drizzled with rubbing alcohol.

The sharp hit of cold caused by the evaporating alcohol tickled and zinged along the surface of my soles. I knew this act was one of tenderness, but it also teetered on the edge of discomfort. Because she was so brusque, I endured it, in my hunger for her to be more like a Mrs. Claus kind of grandmother and my fascination at her difference.

"Teach me how to speak Spanish," I begged, but she did not. My father forbade her or my mother to do so. He didn't want me to grow up acting or appearing to be Hispanic.

"You're 100 percent Irish," he told me. "If anyone asks you, you tell them that you're 100 percent Irish."

"Okay," I said, accepting what he said at face value. I was a blond, fair toddler, but as I got older, I began to look more and more . . . something.

As I grew too old to be left on the church steps, and even more so when I hit puberty, the sleeper cells of my Mediterranean genes woke up. People guessed Sephardic, Italian, Spanish. As an adult visiting the Middle East on a layover in Dubai, I felt women's eyes flashing on mine with recognition and curiosity. They were mostly in burqas, but the ones who weren't looked like me.

It was an issue that my father had married someone Hispanic, although his family loved Linda so much that they welcomed her into the family without a fuss. But Peter and Linda both felt uncomfortable. He felt uncomfortable with her Hispanic blood, and she did, too. She was always trying to minimize it, as if it were a genetic predisposition for something unsavory. They both had a very old-Brooklyn, queasy resistance to dating outside of their community. Linda was too spliced to have a community, but she knew she was on shaky ground, almost there on a trial basis.

But there was no minimizing Migdalia. She got on the phone with her sisters and held forth at the top of her lungs in florid Spanish. She talked smack about my dad in front of him, in Spanish, glorying in the spite-spiked relief of being able to vent freely without his knowing what she was saying.

He felt it, though. When she felt sufficiently fed up, she would haul off and read him the riot act in her cawing English, which triggered my father to no end. They'd brawl like two alpha dogs in a pen; my mother recalls having to get between them once because they were about to come to blows.

Grandma Migdalia did not, however, push the topic of talking to me in Spanish. I didn't even know the Spanish word for "grandmother" until I took Spanish in high school. *Abuela.*

And Migdalia made no Cuban food, nor did my mother—at least none that I could suss out at the time. She flew from Miami with sleeves of rosy-colored Ancel guava paste and bags of puffy Rika crackers in her luggage, but she and my mother ate them furtively, when my dad was at work.

She made *ropa vieja,* but she called it beef stew. She made *arroz con pollo,* but pulled the chicken out at the end and served it beside the rice. *Natilla,* however, was a different story. The wafting scent of that dulcet custard turned my oft-surly father into a wide-eyed, compliant lamb. And we didn't call it anything but what it was.

Sweet

Dad loved sweets. He ate so much candy when he was a child that it rotted his teeth, and his frequent, painful 1950s visits to the dentist gave him a phobia about dental care.

One evening, he shot me a conspiratorial look. "Hey, Candy," he said, "go sneak into the kitchen, climb up on the counter, and get the bag of chocolate chips. Bring it over here and we can share some."

"But Mommy says we shouldn't have any, they're for baking," I said.

"I *know*," he said, grinning mischievously. "But aren't they delicious? Don't you want to have some with me? I won't tell. It'll be our secret."

I walked to the kitchen, pulled a chair over to the counter, climbed up, and grabbed the bag of chocolate chips. Sharing a secret with my father was almost as intoxicating as the chocolate chips that melted between my tongue and the roof of my mouth.

Just as Jimmy and Marie took pains to be so good to my mother that she almost didn't notice how absent my father was, they did the same for me. And given that my mother was attentive when she was present, my grandma Marie's affection was the icing on the cake. But my grandpa gave me something I wasn't getting from my father: steady, benevolent fathering. I am sure that my grandpa Charlie would have been just as nurturing a presence, but he died before I was born. I can look back and feel the loss in an abstract way, but I can feel the loss of Grandpa Jimmy physically.

His cashmere-soft, oft-washed white cotton crew-neck T-shirt against my cheek, his large, strong hands wrapped around my waist. I loved the way he smelled—like Ivory soap and French toast—and I loved the warmth of his attention. He engaged with me with the assumption that I was good, and smart, and interesting.

❧ ❧ ❧

Sour

Grandpa liked to open Martini & Rossi Asti Spumante before dinner. Although he didn't drink it, he liked to serve it to mark festive occasions. One time, I picked it up and drained the last drop or two from the bottle. Everyone laughed and pointed, and someone snapped a few pictures. The drops were sour, but fizzy and sweet at the tail end of the taste.

Although Jimmy was still involved in his union duties, he had just retired and was enjoying his time with Marie. They went out to dinner almost every night. After decades of her thrifty-one-pot-meal duty, he whisked her out of the kitchen. They were blithe, hale gadabouts.

When I was four, Grandpa went to sleep and didn't wake up in the morning. I didn't know what the word "death" meant, but I was sure he was hiding in the attic. I could not understand the concept of death, and I missed him so much that for months, I went up there and poked around in mothballed closets, looked under the guest bed, and just sat, feeling him. I was so sure that he was there that I didn't cry tears of loss, although I may have cried tears of frustration. It was time to come back, come out of hiding, and spend time together.

I don't remember anyone crying. I wasn't brought to the funeral, which might have helped it to click for me, although not in a way that would have been decorous, neat, and tidy. My neighbor, who had a daughter my age, took care of me until my parents were finished burying my grandfather.

Irish wakes blunt the edges of grief. They're humane in some ways, and in other ways, they skim the surface of healing like a stone.

"I was so angry at the wake," recalls my mother, "because people were laughing, telling jokes, drinking. They all had flasks. It was a party atmosphere. I didn't understand it because I was so used to Greek funerals, with people screaming and crying and throwing themselves on the casket. That, to me, was mourning."

Grandma Marie was stoic. She didn't say a word and didn't shed a tear. She slid back into the place she lived when Gregory died, as if into a long, form-fitting coat.

Screaming and crying is cathartic, and getting drunk and having heartfelt conversations with your otherwise distant family is also cathartic. Weddings and funerals are the times, at the bare minimum, when Irish families get together, and they have a similar conviviality.

I do think my grandfather was up in the attic. He couldn't bear to leave. And although Jimmy was in his sixties and his babies were all grown up, they still needed him desperately in order to stay on course.

Salty

When I was four, we moved from one Long Island town to another, from our condominium in Babylon to a worn-around-the-edges house beside the railroad tracks in Patchogue. After Grandpa Jimmy died, my parents declared bankruptcy and defaulted on the condo's mortgage. We became renters.

There were no more vacations to visit my grandma and uncles in Miami. The one time we went to Disney World became the only time. Now my parents drove us to the Poconos, to visit my father's brother and his wife at their lakefront house, for weekends here and there. I waded in the water, scampered amid the tall pines, and accompanied my uncle on drives to get ice cream or just ramble around. Sometimes he scooped me onto his lap and let me steer his truck.

At home in Patchogue, my parents and I spent a lot of time in the living room. There, they played records—my mother played Anne Murray and Judy Collins, and my dad favored Gordon Lightfoot and Livingston Taylor. My dad liked to play with me and a puppet called Newton. He made the brown felt dog say all sorts of silly things in a voice all his own. He also got a kick out of tickling me. I screamed and begged for him to stop through my treacherous laughter. He tickled my stomach, my underarms, under my chin, under my knees, and the bottoms of my feet. I hated it; it made me panicky and crazed. But he took my laughter as encouragement.

Sometimes we all danced. My father loved to dance. His body coiled and snapped, his large hands clapped, together and separately, his head bobbed, his torso dipped and shimmied. There was a beauty in his uninhibited flails and spirals, not so much connected to grace as to lack of artfulness. It was a little bit scary, and yet he was happy, so I felt happy, too. I loved to dance with him. But when we tried to dance together, he stopped, irritated, and said, "Stop trying to lead." And he'd pick me up and dance with me, or we'd break off from each other and dance alone.

The living room was also where I got punished. If I did something spanking-worthy—anything from chewing gum loudly during prayer time at church to lying or being mulish—Dad took off his belt, snapped it at me, and then beckoned. If I came, I only got three straps. If he had to come get me, it was four. Sometimes I ran and hid under the bed, but I knew as I was under there, with the dangly dusty fibers and lost bouncy balls from vending machines, that eventually I'd have to come out, and when I did, he'd be waiting. He never, ever forgot.

Around and around I ran, his hand clasping my hand, and he was the axis, landing a black leather belt so true on my bottom that the sound was clean and sharp, like the sounds of horses springing into motion on *Little House on the Prairie*. He had a knack for it.

But because I ran so fast, he sometimes missed, and it landed on the bony base of my spine or on my free hand, which reflexively covered my father's target. Either way, it blew my mind apart. *White-hot pain!* Mother holding her hand to her mouth, frozen. I was screaming and he was bellowing.

That was our other dance.

I cried so hard that it felt like a bumpy boat ride. I couldn't talk. I could spurt syllables in between heaves. *I'm so sorry. I didn't do it. Please never hit me again. Don't be mad at me anymore. Mommy!*

Right about the time that I started to feel the soft edges of exhaustion, the same kind of exhaustion that maybe makes it easy to drown, he would pick me up, place me on his lap, wrap his arms around me, and let me cry my last few tears onto his broad throat. I was smarting with pain and panic, but I was not unloved. The embrace was tender, shot through with rescue, and wordless.

I tried hard to be good, and all he had to do, most of the time, was give me The Look, and I'd stop doing whatever he forbade.

Eating was another matter.

I was five, and it was time to eat what was placed in front of me. At the time, my mother was making a lot of brothy stews with big chunks of potatoes and carrots, hunks of stringy browned stew meat the size of ice cubes. Her current go-to cookbook was Betty Crocker's red primer, much easier to face down than the Julia Child tome that she used to dig into with Grandpa Jimmy. That phase of her life seemed so distant now, so plangently hopeful that it hurt.

The carrots softened and caramelized as they simmered, and the glaze of sweetness over savory flavors repelled me. I liked broccoli tops; my best friend, Stacey, a redhead with lots of freckles and an earnest expression, liked the trunks—between the two of us, we polished off the little trees, pretending to be hungry giants.

"I love that you finish the broccoli all up together!" my mom exclaimed. "It makes me wish that you were both my daughters."

"Oh, we don't want to be sisters," I said. "Stacey and I are going to get married when we grow up."

My mother's smile froze and then faded. Then she put it back on again. "That's so silly! Girls can't marry girls and boys can't marry boys. Boys can only marry girls."

"*Icky!*" we both screamed and ran away, laughing.

Dad had rules about mealtime. I had to chew everything thirty times, and I couldn't drink anything until I had cleaned my plate. I was taught not to follow my own sensations of fullness, but to restore the plate to its empty state. If I was thirsty, I couldn't drink. I had to eat to drink, even though eating made me thirstier, and I couldn't imagine chewing and swallowing any more food.

He placed my glass in the center of the table, filled to the top. I looked at my mother. She looked back at me with a dip of her chin, saying without words, *Obey your father.* She made a big, big pot of stew, and we'd eat the leftovers tomorrow and maybe even the next day. I took a bite of the stuff and choked it down, chewingchewingchewing while thinking desperately of other things. But there were at least twenty more bites remaining. He stared at me with the look of a firebrand preacher in his eyes.

I took another spoonful, of a shred of meat and some broth.

"Your next bite should have carrot and potato in it."

I dug grimly for that combination, and then closed my mouth around the spoon, pulled it into my mouth, and began to chew. Suddenly the sheer, towering wave of flavor threw grappling hooks into my gag reflex, and I upchucked into the bowl.

"Oh, you think you're so smart," he said, with his angry smile. "You're going to eat that bowl of soup anyway. We do not waste food in this house."

I shook my head, eyes wet with throwing-up tears and disbelief.

He grabbed the spoon with one hand, clamped his arm around me, and fed me. I gagged a few more times, but I ate it.

Water and Wine, Divinity and the Divine

My mother's *Betty Crocker Cookbook* pages were Braille-speckled with floury drizzles and droplets. She faithfully referred to the cookbook for roasts, soups, and casseroles, but my interest lay solely in the sweets. Those recipes had enchanting, beckoning names that evoked heaven, astronomy, and theology. No-Cook Divinity. Galaxy Cakes photographed against a starry sky. Cherry Berries on a Cloud. Stained Glass Cookies. A frosting rose on the head of a nail. Our home life was rocky and chaotic, but when we strapped on our aprons and gathered in the kitchen, peace and harmony reigned and the end product was reliable.

The Cold War, inflation, and assassination attempts colored the outside world in drab tones, and my mother was sure the end times were nigh. Any day now, the Rapture would happen and we'd be whisked off to heaven, leaving the multitudes behind to suffer a miserable fate. My aunt, uncle, and cousins, a few of the recipients of our cookie bounty, hadn't accepted Jesus into their hearts, so they'd be among those left behind. But at least in the meantime, they could enjoy our sweets.

At Christmastime, my mother and I spent days making hundreds of cookies and gave them out as gifts in tins lined with wax paper. The whole house smelled of warm vanilla and caramelizing sugar, and the bounty covered all available counter space. Everyone was so much happier with a heavy tin loaded with cookies than with a generic sweater or mug. Even my father came in with his face alight, hugged my mom, and swung her around in a circle before grabbing a handful of cookies. My sister and I had matching homemade aprons, but my brother was still an infant.

Before we began our marathon, my mother and I put our heads together to decide which cookies to make. We had to include perennial favorites, like the cunning spritz cookies that looked labored over but were popped out assembly line–style with the cookie press. When it came to flavors, she was despotic. She didn't like gingerbread, so that was out, as well as peanut butter. We chose Russian tea cakes because they looked snowy, coated in powdered sugar. Stained glass cookies were time-consuming but beautiful.

Mom was also a blue ribbon–winning pie baker. She made pies so pneumatically voluptuous they looked like fantasy cartoon constructions come to life. She learned at Yia Yia's elbow.

With her firm belief in using the freshest, most basic ingredients (no margarine crossed our threshold, nor did Sweet'N Low) and precision when following recipes, she turned out perfect baked goods.

She lit up when her creations were praised. "If you can read a recipe, you can cook" was her motto. There was no magic or mysticism about it, which was perhaps why she disapproved so much of mothers who relied on store-bought baked goods.

It was a testament to my mother's patience that she didn't throw me out of the kitchen, as I was an unrepentant batter and dough hound. The second her back was turned, I nabbed a glob of sweet, gritty goodness, and then, when she turned back to me, I had to freeze the workings of my mouth. This made my salivary glands ache, but it was a good kind of pain. As long as she didn't ask me any questions, I was home free. Otherwise I nodded or said a noncommittal "hmm," which reverberated through the glob and got me busted. No matter how many times she scolded me, no matter how much discomfort I suffered in the form of stomachaches, I persisted.

One of my mother's favorite cookies was the *koulourakia* her Greek grandmother taught her to make when she was a little girl.

Like her Yia Yia before her, she made them regularly enough that there were always several in the very same cookie jar that used to adorn her grandmother's counter.

When I was a child, the cookies seemed dull to me. As I grew older, I realized that *koulourakia* were best appreciated as a breakfast biscuit—not too flavorful, the perfect accompaniment to a cup of tea or coffee.

When my mother wasn't baking, she was embarking on other, short-lived projects: the Cambridge diet (shakes), Weight Watchers, Grey Sheet, "fasting," the grapefruit diet, the Scarsdale diet, Overeaters Anonymous, the Pritikin diet, the Ayds candy diet, and the cabbage soup diet. She always felt fat, in a super-dolorous, self-disgusted way, and couldn't pass a reflective surface without making a moue of disappointment.

I didn't know what she was talking about. She was my mommy and she was beautiful. She had given birth to three kids, ate cake and cookies all the time, and was still only a size 10. But as a teen, she'd won the genetic lottery of being a skinny girl with big boobs who could eat burgers, shakes, and cake without gaining a pound, and she wanted that back.

Outside of the kitchen, there were too many reasons we needed to move again, too many arguments, and (I thought) too many siblings. If my father hit me up to borrow my honor roll reward money but then claimed he couldn't pay it back, was it really wise for them to have more babies?

My mother leaned heavily on me to help her change diapers, change clothes, and bathe, tend to, and feed my sister and two brothers. I wasn't able to focus on what I loved most: reading and spending time up in the tree in our side yard, thinking.

My father seemed to be happy to start fresh with them, children who knew him only as a sober man walking the straight and narrow. When he looked at me, he saw the child who had witnessed him at his worst (he stopped drinking when I was six). Instead of making peace with that, I thought he held it against me.

There were moments, though, startling ones, like the sun breaking through an overcast sky, when my father looked at me with love. He gave me nicknames and told me that my name meant "Shining Bright." He was the only person on this good earth I let call me Candy after the age of six. Me, a Candy? Only in his gaze.

When I achieved, starred in plays, signed up for track, was praised by teachers, won awards, I came into focus for him. After he stopped drinking, I was suspended between wanting to please and distract him and the fear that I'd find myself at the charring end of an accusing stare—because what I thought would please him could so easily backfire.

He abruptly cut ties with all of the relatives on his side of the family because they drank. We no longer spent time with cousins, aunts, uncles who had loved and played with me since I was born. My mother still mailed them cookies at Christmastime, though.

He did maintain a relationship with Grandma Marie, and even stopped in at a liquor store on his way over to her house, to pick up large bottles of gin. Whenever we parked in front of such a store, I held my breath as he walked in. How could he go in there, into a temple of booze of all stripes, and not snap? But sure enough, he'd come out with the value-size jug, and to Grandmother's house we'd go.

The one time Dad was reliably cheery was after dinner. Dessert made him so happy that he forgot any grudges.

"I stopped at Friendly's and got *ice cream,*" he said, eyes googly with camped-up excitement. "Who wants *ice cream?*"

"Me!" we all chorused, hands raised.

When we finished, he asked, eyes agleam, "Want another bowl of *ice cream?*" Sure. That bought me another five minutes of being on Dad's good side. And it was delicious.

My parents fought about lots of things, the way you do when you're so over someone that the slightest thing makes you see red. And they fought about his decision to stop going to church.

A few years earlier, Dad had "gotten saved" by another trainman, Bob, and then he turned my mom onto it.

That night, she asked Jesus into her heart, too. And for a while, our family "grew in the Lord" together, studying the Bible and praying, going to church, and reading me Bible stories before bed. We were soon regulars at the hippie church Bob attended.

Shortly after my parents were saved, my mother sat me down and told me that if I wanted to invite Jesus into my heart, that was all I needed to do to become a Christian, and when the Rapture came, I'd go with my parents to heaven. But if I didn't ask Jesus into my heart, I'd have to go to hell, which was a place of burning, fiery misery inhabited by Satan, his army of torturing demons, and all of the evil people in the world. My eyes as wide as saucers, I went with option A.

After a while, though, Dad quit going to church. And the one thing they enjoyed together faded. Not only that, but my mother's fervent, passionate faith—of a tenor that led her to witness to strangers in parking lots—blossomed, pushing them ever further apart.

The Bible guided her in ways that pleased my father: It told her to be submissive, that he was the head of the house and she was the weaker vessel. She waited and prayed for him to change, and sent me upstairs each Sunday morning to ask him if he wanted to come to church with us (and each time, he groaned a sleep-furred "no").

Christianity gave my half-orphaned mother a source of strength. Her new wine was prayer, her new Valium, reading the Bible. And I was her fine Christian girl, snuggling with her in the big marital bed when my father worked late, I with my small white leather kiddie Bible illustrated with snow-white lambs, she with her King James version. We no longer read from the *Anthology of Children's Literature,* because it contained mythology with false gods. That also meant no TV or even Disney movies. Only Christian radio. My mother aimed to be in a spiritual bubble now.

I switched schools in fourth grade, and public school was so different from the church school I'd attended that it made me sick. It didn't show up in my body temperature or something measurable—but I felt depressed, anxious, and dry-mouthed. I felt queasy.

I missed my favorite teacher, Mrs. Anderson. She was strict and tough. She had a soft, old-Brooklyn accent, milky skin, and root beer–colored eyes under heavy lids. She said, "I coont" for "I couldn't." She wore half-moon glasses on a chain around her neck and unleashed a sharp look (paired with a pursed mouth) on any student who was out of line. The few times I drew that look, I felt gored through the heart.

"You have Mrs. Anderson? She's strict, she's hard," other kids said.

She *was* strict, but she gave me the gift of knowing at a very early age that I could do strict, I could do hard.

My mother left my father for the first time when I was eight. Although my father was just as unhappy with my mother as she was with him, he saw no reason to get a divorce. Their discord was familiar and grounding to him. And his affairs with women he met at AA meetings provided some release. Mrs. Anderson, after listening to my mom's sad story, offered to let us stay in her family's cabin in upstate New York.

My Mom loaded me, my infant brother, and my toddler sister up in her red Volkswagen bug and drove us to the small, bare-bones cabin, its water pump and outhouse all it had to offer in the way of plumbing.

Before we left, my mother packed the freezer with a month's worth of meals for my father, along with instructions on how to prepare them, written out in her loopy handwriting. My father eschewed this option and ate fast food for the mere two weeks it took for him to send her a letter and woo her back.

My mother was excited about my starting at Rocky Point Middle School because she had sweet-talked the principal into putting me in fifth grade. She thought I should skip a grade.

I landed in toadlike, jaundiced Mrs. Moran's class when I was eight years old, in my sweet little calico dress and tight ponytails.

The air was metallic with hormones. As was par for the course at Rocky Point, half of the kids had repeated a grade somewhere along the line, and so I was sitting beside ten-, eleven-, and even a few twelve-year-olds.

My mother was very angsty about the new curriculum. "Just pray when they teach you about evolution," she said. "Memorize it for the test, but tell Jesus that you don't believe those lies. And I think I'll go to the principal about it, but for now, just do that."

The fifth graders were nice to me. They treated me kind of like a little sister. Even when I began to cry. I began to wake up each morning so nervous and filled with dread that my stomach roiled with queasiness.

"Eat your breakfast," my mother urged, but I had a nervous stomach, apparently. Nothing had made me this nervous before. I picked at the oatmeal. Pushed around the cereal. Could not take even one bite of slimy eggs. Felt like gagging when she lovingly presented Eggs in a Basket, dough pressed into muffin tins, then topped with eggs, ham, and cheese, and baked.

I used to happily eat soft-boiled eggs each morning. One school later, the very thought made me heave.

The first time the teacher caught me crying, she asked me if I didn't feel well. I didn't, so she sent me to the nurse's office. Soon I was going every day.

It was quiet and calm, and I got to lie on a seafoam-green cot and stare at the pinpricked dropped ceiling. The two nurses were so very nice. One was slight and gray-haired, and the other was large and brunette. Both were gentle and concerned.

I threw up a few times, just from nerves, and when I did, I got to go home early. I had never realized how great home was before. It was safe, and it was familiar. My mother gave me tea or broth and crackers.

My parents and the principal decided that I should try out fourth grade, since I wasn't handling fifth very well. It was less overwhelming, but the kids did not think of me as a younger sister. They thought of me as an idiotic peer.

They teased me the way you tease a new kid who cries a lot, has Amish-odd hair and clothing, believes in Jesus, admits to liking *Sesame Street,* and reads freakishly fast, especially all through lunch period, so as to avoid noticing that she's eating all by herself. My classmates thought it was especially hilarious when they asked me, "Are you gay?" and I said yes, because I did feel happy at that moment.

I had to learn to come up with answers to "Why is your purse so ugly?" and "Do you have a staring problem?" and "Are you retarded?" In the moment, I had nothing to say, and the questions weren't repeated when I had good retorts freshly filed away in my mind.

Gym class was in the afternoon, and I had anxiety about getting dressed in time and playing field hockey. So I told the teacher that I had a stomachache, went to the nurse, walked into the nurse's office lavatory, stuck my finger down my throat, and puked. I had read about it in a book, and what do you know, it worked.

The less nice nurse walked in when I called out and examined the bowl. She also saw me wipe my pointer finger with toilet paper. She looked in my eyes.

"Did you make yourself throw up?"

"*No!* I would never do that!"

She paused. "Okay. I'll call your mother and see if she can come get you."

My mother called up Mrs. Anderson, told her what was going on with me, and invited her over for lunch.

I was giddy with anticipation. I helped my mother clean, put on a pretty dress that would not be wrong in her eyes for being handmade, set the table, helped prepare the roast chicken and biscuits. Mrs. Anderson was coming to *my* house. Yes, because I was imploding, vomiting, crying, and otherwise losing it, but still. She was coming over to my house!

I picked through the drawer of mismatched silverware, found the setting with the most curlicues, and gave it to her. We must have talked about what was going on, but the one thing I remember from that day was the thing she clearly wanted me to remember most.

"When my father died," she said, "I was a little girl. And my mother was so upset that she couldn't comfort me. My aunt told me, 'This is going to either make you or break you.' And she was right."

"What do you mean?"

"It can either make you stronger or break you, make you weaker. For the rest of your life. So, Candace, you have to decide: Is this going to make you or break you?"

It *could* make me? I wasn't just in an unending hell that set me free each Friday afternoon but delivered me into Monday morning as if into a nightmare?

Fifth grade was miraculously better, but in sixth grade, I ended up with another group of kids who shunned me. After I went down into the school's cavernous dungeon of a basement after gym class to get a forgotten sweater, my classmates turned off the light at the top of the stairs, closed the door, and ran off laughing. After I inched my way across the squishy gym-mat floor (rather directly, I am proud to say) to the cold, dark, cement stairwell and slowly climbed each step, blood pounding in my ears, made it to the top, opened the door to a shocking wash of light, and strode the hallways to my classroom, filled with tittering, giggling, smirking sadists, I went home that day, burning with impotent fury, and stopped eating. What my mother got me to eat, I vomited up. On purpose. Anything was better than going back to school.

"She can't keep anything down," my mother told the doctor.

After a few days of that, I was hospitalized. I spent two weeks on an IV, in the very hospital where I was born plump and uncomplicated. My father visited me in between work shifts; my mother came every day during visiting hours.

My roommate was a girl my age who was truly physically ill. She had some kind of horrible blood disease.

Her mother stared at me one day when her daughter was sleeping, and she said, "I think I understand your situation. But it's time to start eating again and go home." She alone (not my parents, not the doctor) had my number. I was shamed into it, but righteously so.

I could say that I now ask myself if something is going to make me or break me, but I've been very lucky so far, because my conditioned reflex, when confronted with a setback, is to shift into survivor mode.

When I was in ninth grade, I somehow stumbled up against my own moxie, and when someone called me a name, I called him a worse name. When I got shoved, I shoved back harder. I finally got that nobody was going to magically decide to be my friend because I was unfailingly nice all the time. It got me nowhere. And the tide began to shift.

Of Frying Pans and Fire

MY MOM LEFT MY DAD for good on Christmas Day 1984 when I was 12. She packed us up and spirited us off to a wan, shabby two-bedroom bungalow, hours after my dad went on his merry way to work. The torn wrapping paper was still strewn across the floor, and the tree's lights twinkled impertinently, as helpful church friends carried the last overflowing box and kiddie chest of drawers out the front door.

I had been in on the plot for months; I knew we were going. She swore me to secrecy, and I, weary of noting my parents' utter lack of love for each other, and of breathing the air of their mingled malaise, colluded.

After my parents split up, I had access to two houses, two kitchens instead of one. But neither of them resembled the kitchen my parents used to share.

Before family court sorted out child support, my mother signed up for welfare and food stamps to keep food on the table. I had been used to my parents' arguments about money and to an atmosphere of frugality, but we had never been poor.

Whenever it came time to pay—with food stamps—the register was inevitably staffed by an older classmate of mine. I told my mother I'd meet her by the car. I just couldn't face the humiliation. It was already embarrassing to be twelve and at the store with a parent. (Later I would realize that everyone I was afraid of running into was also there with at least one parent.)

My mother's kitchen now contained government cheese: a long, solid brick of uncut processed American cheese—think generic Kraft, but less yielding. To engage with it was to be reminded that you were financially disadvantaged. Presliced, cellophane-wrapped cheese slices suddenly seemed like the height of bourgeois splendor.

We hacked away perilously at the cheese brick, because of course we didn't have a sharp knife, a knife sharpener, or a cheese slicer. Poverty consciousness put those items in the "nonessential" category—way too high up on Maslow's hierarchy of needs. Our lumpy grilled cheese sandwiches melted unevenly, but they got the job done.

My mother's cooking ceased to be a presence. For the last eleven years, she'd been in charge of dinner—back when going out to eat was saved for very special occasions. Suddenly, those galley chains were cut. On the nights when she got dolled up and went to Christian singles mixers at area churches, I was the one in charge of dinner. It made me feel grown-up, even though I was inept. One night, I heated up frozen fish sticks and served them with chocolate-covered Entenmann's doughnuts to my three younger siblings.

We spent the weekends with Dad, and before we arrived, he stocked the pantry with brownie mix, chocolate chip cookie mix, and cans of frosting. I was encouraged to bake cookies and brownies, but breakfast, lunch, and dinner were his department. It was a wonder that we didn't get food poisoning and die from all the chicken he served medium-rare. New to anything but osmotic parenting, my dad rented piles of videos each weekend and popped them in, one after the other, which pacified us, as did the bags of chips and frosted brownies.

Dad began using the slow cooker, probably after the legal fees started rolling in. Frozen sandwiches were replaced with pea soup that cost mere cents per bowl. Luckily, soon after that he began dating women who jumped on domestic duties with all the verve of women auditioning for a Stove Top commercial.

My mother's husband hunting also paid off in record time, and we soon bid welfare and its trappings adieu. She was back in the kitchen. I was free to spend more time doing homework, talking on the phone with my friends, and daydreaming myself into a narcoticed, sensual torpor over whatever boy I had a crush on that day.

Mom's new husband was named Bill. He was very tall, and very inarticulate, and not the most handsome man you'd ever meet.

"He's smart!" my mom insisted. "He may not sound that way, but that's because his parents immigrated from the Ukraine and he grew up in a very anti-intellectual household."

The week my mother met him at a Christian singles get-together, she came home with a weird expression on her face. "I gave a man my number," she said. "But I don't know why. I don't like him that way. He's funny looking. He looks like the monster in that library book *There's a Monster in My Closet.*"

She got the book off the shelf and showed me the illustration. It was of a hulking, snaggle-toothed, craggy monster. He was a monster, and he was in the child's closet, but he also happened to be a nice monster who had so much love to give. Monsters got such a bad rap. That was the book's message.

Bill worked nights, as a postal employee out at JFK airport, supervising the mail's delivery onto planes. He had an ex-wife and two children, but his daughter refused to see him. He could see his son twice a month.

As my mother's first date with Bill made way for many more, she told me about his life. "His mom was vicious—used to hit him on the head with a frying pan if he wouldn't get out of bed in the morning. And his ex-wife is a witch. Poor Bill."

I didn't know why his first wife was so terrible. I glimpsed her only once, as she opened the door to take little Billy back into their condo. She was bottle blond and a little heavy, with a neck brace and a cane.

"I know that guy," my dad told me. "I used to see him at AA meetings. He's an alcoholic. I don't know why she would leave me just to get together with another drunk."

"Your father's a crazy liar," my mom said. "Bill's not a drinker. He never has been."

Mom and Bill got engaged after just a few months, and by the time the divorce was final, they got married at Sound Beach Community Church. Bill stood there, in a *Miami Vice*–inspired liverish mauve (pronounced in this context as *mawve*) sport coat, and my mother wore a white satin dress with lace leg-of-mutton sleeves. And I wore a candy-pink polka-dotted dress with a four-tier skirt, a hand-me-down from my dad's new girlfriend Lita.

Wham, divorce, bam, remarriage. The first wedding was not quite for love; the second one seemed like a move calculated toward stability and security. Would my mother ever partner with someone for love? Or was she acting out some old genetic pattern of arranged marriage—except that in this case, she was doing both the arranging and the marrying?

On my mother's wedding night, Bill turned on the TV, surfed channels until he came to a porn channel, and settled in to watch.

"What are you thinking?" she asked.

"What's your problem?" he shot back, grinning.

"This isn't of God," she said.

"You actually believed I was a Christian? I just pretended because I knew you wouldn't marry me otherwise."

Welcome to the real Bill. Lest you think he was 100 percent evil, he did buy a bag of Egg McMuffins for breakfast the morning after my fourteenth-birthday sleepover party. And when my father bailed on paying for my contact lens bill midstream, which led the doctor to hold the lenses hostage, Bill paid off the balance of it and told me not to worry about paying him back. Nobody is 100 percent evil.

But the very first time Bill yelled at me, it went on for fifteen minutes. He yelled so loudly and for so long that his voice cracked and grew more and more hoarse, as if he were a dog straining against a choke chain, barking until he gagged. What was the cause of this outburst? I had left the outside light on all night.

I cried. But that was the last time Bill hurt my feelings. I didn't love him and he wasn't my dad. I guess we weren't all going to live happily ever after. At that point, I was pretty familiar with "unhappily ever after," so familiar that it was almost a relief when mom's Cinderella story went sour.

"He feels like you disapprove of him," my mother said. "He feels like you don't appreciate him. He's spent his whole life feeling inferior and 'less than.' Can't you please try harder?"

"What do you want me to do?"

"Just try to let God's love shine through you. It will heal him and all of his emotional wounds."

I couldn't fix Bill, and neither could my mother. I could only hunker down, do my homework, and count the days until I could go away to college. But then an opportunity for an early escape presented itself.

At the end of sixth grade, we were asked to pick a language: French, Spanish, or German. My junior high school was odd for including German; French and Spanish were usually the only options in area schools. It is an indicator of how disenfranchised I was from my Cuban heritage that I never seriously considered taking Spanish. Of course, there were other factors. It seemed like all of the popular, snobby girls were taking French, and the burnouts and nonscholars took Spanish, because it had a reputation for being the easiest language. The nerds were taking German, and I was closest to being a nerd.

The only German I'd been exposed to had been via Nazi movies and *Hogan's Heroes*. My sense was that it was guttural and comical. But if there was one class that was near guaranteed to be free of mean girls and smartness haters, sign me up.

When my teacher spoke English, she did so dourly, rather like someone who feels that enthusiasm is the province of idiots. But in German, Frau Fischer trilled and singsonged, her *r*'s and *ch*'s were held back in her throat like caged birds, and her lips made kissy-face shapes as she unleashed *ö*'s and *ü*'s.

Her passion for the language didn't prevent my classmates from mangling German. It didn't matter that Erich had a throated *ch* in his name; every *ch* came out like the hard *k* of a tap shoe's heel, or like chewy chowder in others' mouths. The language's sounding rules snapped to fit my tongue and teeth, their precision and clarity pleasing in contrast with Long Island's beleaguered English, where all manner of dipthong ruled with shameless brio.

My diligent attention to the task of pronouncing German, along with my "good ear," was not lost on Frau Fischer. When it was my turn to read aloud, her face fell into an expression of relaxed pleasure, as opposed to the pinched, long-suffering mien she exhibited for others.

And so, two years later, when I saw a flyer posted in the German classroom for the Nacel short-term foreign exchange program, I became obsessed with the idea of traveling to Germany and staying with a *Gastfamilie* (host family). It didn't matter that students usually waited until they were juniors or seniors to go. I wanted to go that summer. It didn't matter that my mother and Bill said no because they thought my plane would be blown up by terrorists, or that my dad said no because he didn't want to pay for it. Back in 1986, the cost, including airfare, was $640.

My parents' nays fell on deaf ears. I began saving my babysitting money and papering the refrigerator with my German tests. It paid off: My mother and stepfather decided to give me their consent, and also the rest of the money needed to pay for the trip (which was most of it).

"You're going to be eating lots of sauerbraten!" my parents promised me.

In fact, I ate none.

My guest family and I had already begun corresponding. The teen girl, Nicole's, letters were written on A4-size graph paper in what I would come to learn was the orderly yet undulating and near universally identical German-schoolgirl handwriting. Hans-Joachim, or HaJo *(Ha-Yo)*, was in the German army, and Mute *(Moo-teh)* was a housewife. Nicole went to a scholarly gymnasium, which was a type of German high school you went to if you weren't shuttled off to a trade school at the tender age of ten or eleven.

They lived in a charming-looking thatched-roof cottage on the windswept island of Sylt, which was north of the German mainland and just east of the Danish island of Romo. The Nacel matchmakers might have thought that I, from Long Island, should be on an island that in some ways very much resembled the north shore of Long Island. I may have regretted not being in a bustling, urbane city, but being with the duRoi family was pure heaven.

First off, it was clear that HaJo and Mute loved each other very much, in a way that was unquestioned and deep. Although Nicole sometimes got impatient with her little brother, Frederic, and he sometimes fussed, overall, nobody ever raised their voice. Ever. And it wasn't fake or smacking of repression. They just didn't see the need, and given that the grownups were very grown-up and the household was very orderly, there wasn't a lot to get upset about.

Nicole had her own room on the second floor, but for the duration of my stay, we two were given the run of the furnished basement, which had a queen-size bed, a stereo, a bathroom, and a dresser for all my things.

It was like a monthlong sleepover with a cousin who was smart, funny, and thoughtful. We tickled each other's backs every night before we fell asleep, at Nicole's suggestion. It was cozy and harmonious, and I fell in love both with them as a family and with being a part of it. The thousand little withered-up and traumatized cilia that my heart had all but discarded came alive and began to palpate.

Frau Fischer hadn't warned me that German breakfasts, lunches, and dinners were different. Every morning, out came the cured meats and cheeses and crackers and bread, the unfamiliar jams *(Konfitüre),* cloudy, creamy-looking Langnese honey, and *Quark* (cream cheese–like, pronounced *kvark)* and yogurt. I watched Nicole take a slice of bread, spread it with butter, add a slice of cheese, and then layer that with a few pieces of sliced, rosy, white-speckled cured meat.

Every day, HaJo and Nicole and I went back home for lunch. There, Mute had prepared a hot, hearty spread—sometimes goulash, sometimes a recipe that I remembered from my grandma Marie's kitchen: *Frikadellen.* They looked like small burgers to me but were flavored more intensely—a mixture of ground meats, bread crumbs, spices, and minced onions, sautéed and then drizzled with a delicious creamy gravy. Mute served them with boiled potatoes, which went perfectly with the extra gravy.

When the duRois had tea, they sweetened it with beautiful chunks of sugar that looked just like bits of amber.

"Das ist Kandis Zucker," HaJo said with a smile. *"Es Hört wie deine Name." Kandis* in German did sound exactly like my name.

My time in Germany was divided into three phases: my adjustment to Sylt, the duRois, and their house; the middle period, in which I loved the family and the peacefulness of each day with them; and the third and last phase, in which my departure was imminent and I felt like I would die of grief and dread. It was kind of like birth, middle age, and death, squeezed into a single month.

I'd already been through a few heartbreaks, thanks to my tendency to have outsize, moony crushes on boys and then take their lack of interest as confirmation that I was completely unlovable. So I recognized the sensation of heartbreak, but it was multiplied times four. I also knew that I really couldn't explain it to the duRois. They liked me, maybe even loved me, and I knew they'd miss me (though they'd also enjoy having their normal family structure back), but they weren't losing the only safe family experience they'd ever experienced. I was.

But my introduction to *Schneewittchen Kuchen* occurred in the middle period, and to this day, each bite of it reminds me of the sensation of my soul's blossoming.

Mute took out what looked like a large jelly roll pan, although with slightly higher walls. She mixed up a delicious, slightly dense vanilla cake batter and poured it into the greased pan. Then she dropped in beautiful dark, sour morello cherries, individually and at intervals, plucked from a jar topped off with cherry juice. The cherries sank into the batter, sometimes submerging and sometimes peeking out a bit.

After it was baked and cooled, Mute spread a buttercream layer over the cake and then drizzled a bittersweet chocolate syrup over the top, gently spreading it out, covering the buttercream, careful not to disturb it. The dark chocolate hardened to a luscious shell, and Mute put the entire dreamy thing in the refrigerator to chill. Later, she cut it into squares. Then the source of the name, Snow White cake, became apparent. Like the Brothers Grimm fairy tale character, the cake was pale like *Schneewittchen*'s skin, the cherries were red like her lips, and the chocolate was dark like her hair.

The night before my departure, tears spilled out of my eyes, and I probably didn't stop crying for the rest of the time I spent with the duRois.

They were likely a little bit confused by the floridity of my grief. I hadn't told them anything about my interesting family life. I was just beginning to understand how interesting it was, and that awakening was creating a lot of inner turbulence.

I would be catching a ride to the Hamburg airport with another Nacel family. Nicole traveled south with me to their house and held my hand. We hugged goodbye tightly, and her answering tears made me feel like less of a freak.

After meeting the other exchange student and seeing her German guest family's house, I realized that I was even luckier to have been matched with the duRois than I had thought.

The American girl, Kerry, was two years older than I was, but she was about a foot shorter and she smoked incessantly, even in the house. Apparently, she had noted on her application that she was a smoker and had been matched with a smoking family. "I've been smoking since I was eight," she said. "They say it stunts your growth, but . . . "

But you're freakishly short, I thought, *and not too easy on the eyes, regardless.*

I arrived just in time for lunch, and the food was white bread and chipped beef, with sauce ladled on top. Kerry piped up, "My dad's in the service, and at home we call this Shit on a Shingle."

I couldn't believe she had just said that. "*Was ist* 'Shit on Shingle'?" the dad asked.

Kerry got the dictionary. *"Scheiss auf Dachschindel,"* she proclaimed. Hearty laughs were had by all.

The next morning, we got up early to get to the airport on time. Kerry's guest parents and guest grandmother were along for the ride, and it poured down rain. They and Kerry chain-smoked in the sedan, all of the windows closed the entire hour and a half to the airport. I thought I would vomit if I didn't pass out first. But the foulness of that ride, apart from infusing my hair, skin, and clothing with nasty smoke, distracted me from my sadness over leaving the duRois.

When I arrived at JFK, my mother ran up to me at the airport gate and hugged me as if I were the most precious thing in the world to her.

"So, how was it?" she asked.

"It was really peaceful," I said. "Really calm. Nobody yelled."

"You know, you've got some nerve," she said. "You're cruel. What's that supposed to mean, 'nobody yelled'? I missed you like my heart was being ripped out of my rib cage from morning till night, and all you can say is that nobody yelled?"

"It's true," I said.

"You're ungrateful."

"I'm not."

And so life resumed.

So far, my adolescence had been one long awkward stage. My eyebrows were coming in thick and heavy, like Zoila's. Each new dusky hair taunted me with its not-goodness. My mom applied Jolén Creme Bleach to my upper lip a few times each month. The strong chemical paste stung my skin like a thousand little wasps.

After my return from Germany, the crushes I had, back-to-back, sometimes overlapping, became my escape. I fantasized about being loved, adored, and desired. I had taken stock and already knew that my parents loved me, but my friends clearly were loved more

actively and thoroughly. The solution was to get older and find better love outside of my family. I was so hungry for it that daydreams
made me dizzy with poignant warmth. I stared at high school
couples, awash in each other, mouths wide open like baby birds',
sucking each other's tongues like ripe fruits, hands kneading each
other's flesh, whole bodies burrowing into each other's before their
next classes, or on the school bus, or at a school dance. Their heed-
less passion gave me goose bumps and dry mouth.

As much as I fantasized about making out with the boys I liked,
or even just being adored from afar, those sensations never led to
erotic release. Trying to combine them was like mixing oil and water.

For that, I had to recall the lesbian scenes I'd glimpsed in
stumbled-upon porn magazines. They set me off as easily as flying
down a water slide and splashing into the pool below. There it was.
That was the divide. But I didn't fret about it explicitly. I wasn't
gay. That wasn't possible. If I were, I'd ignore it, deny, it, keep it in
that tiny box inside me that only opened, glowingly, late at night
and then snapped shut again.

In Rocky Point, after so many years on the fringes of happy
groups of friends, I made one friend, Emily, who made up for her
singleton state by being the friend of my dreams. She was a new kid,
who hadn't witnessed my loserdom for the last three years. She loved
reading as much as I did, and her parents were witty intellectuals.

Em and I were inseparable; we both wished to be popular and
have a roaring social life, but that was a pipe dream. Instead, we
were companionable, making the most of what we had.

But then my mom and Bill decided that Shoreham was a better
school district, and we moved.

Shoreham was a few miles down Route 25-A, but it felt like
another world to me. It had the imprimatur of Mrs. Anderson's
presence. She lived in Shoreham with her husband and had raised
their two sons in a white house on a quiet, shady country lane.

The high school, dubbed the Country Club by other districts,
was indeed far more slick than any other public high school in the
area. Our community received this gorgeous, modern, architecturally

clever high school on acres of nicely landscaped grounds because it agreed to host the local nuclear power plant. (And yet there was so much public outcry around the plant that it never did open.)

Shoreham was much more of a good fit for me, nukes politics aside. I dove into the extracurricular activities and was able to reinvent myself in many ways. I made friends with a klatch of brainy, creative, open-minded girls who welcomed me into their crowd.

But on Saturday mornings, I entered the "Weekend at Dad's" reality. Our pattern was that he was supposed to come at 9:00, but then we'd call at 9:20 and he'd promise to be there in a few minutes, and we'd call again and eventually get picked up at around 11:00. I don't know why we didn't just do our thing and make him wait when he finally showed up. Probably because my mother and Bill were ready to have their time off and were pushing us out the door just as my father and his new wife were reluctant to start their two-day shift. We spent the interstitial time sitting on the curb, in a cruddy-feeling purgatory of not being all that wanted.

Once I got to my dad's, though, there was tons of food, and I ate it, justifying it in the following way: I was "good" all week, and I exercised every day after school on the track team. So if I wanted to pig out on the weekends, that was okay. Also, how could I say no to my father when he was brandishing a serving spoon?

Like his father, Jimmy, Dad welcomed his children with stocked cabinets of sweet treats. His second wife was only seven years older than I was, and just as food-obsessed as my dad. She was an enthusiastic cook who loved to feed my father as much as my father loved to be fed. She didn't try to sneak Cuban dishes past him or put him on the Pritikin diet, as my mother had. She was Irish like him. She also hadn't learned how to make dinner at my grandmother Marie's elbow, either, but did a fair job of approximating the meals my father had grown up on.

My stepmother's meals tasted good going down, but my siblings and I always suffered stomachaches after eating them. She didn't drain the fat from the ground beef she browned for sauces, or remove the skin from chicken. She poured oil with a heavy hand and didn't skimp on the butter.

More often than not, I went to the bathroom and brought the increasingly bilious load up with a tickle of my pointer finger upon my tonsils. As my sister crossed the line from childhood to adolescence, she also began coming out of the bathroom with watery pink rabbit eyes, although we never discussed it. She had her own sources of information: After-school specials, school talks, and young-adult books all covered eating disorders. And we were both steeped in our mother's criticism of all but the leanest women's bodies. Including our own. My sister didn't need me to give her a primer on how to eat enough to avoid guff from Dad *and* not so much that we got the diet talk from Mom *and* also avoid feeling uncomfortably full.

And that way, we had room for dessert. Because there was *always* dessert.

College brochures began to arrive in the mail.

"Why don't you live in the basement and go to Suffolk Community College or Stony Brook?" my dad asked.

Yeah, right. Like that would ever happen. I wanted to go to Sarah Lawrence, or Colgate, or Carnegie Mellon. I didn't have the grades to make it into an Ivy League, but I had a B-plus average, a long list of extracurricular activities, and a pile of writing awards.

"I'm not filling out financial aid forms for private schools, because I'm not paying for them. I'm in school, and so is my wife. I can send you to a SUNY," my father told me. "And I think you should live in my basement and go to SUNY Stony Brook."

He'd picked a great time to go back to college and then on to law school, and my stepmother was going to college now, too. I, of college age, was third in line. Even though my father wasn't forbidding me to go to college like his father had forbidden him, he tried to clamp down on what kind of college experience I could access.

"Dad, filling it out doesn't make you liable. I need this to turn in my application. I can take out loans."

"Pick out the SUNYs you want to go to, and I'll fill out those forms."

I sent in the private college applications anyway, with a letter explaining why the financial aid forms weren't complete. I had to pencil in boxes stating my parents' occupations. Father: train conductor. Mother: school bus driver. Stepfather: mail man. Stepmother: secretary.

I lived in a middle-class neighborhood and went to school with students who had maids and boats and BMWs, but it was then that I realized how baldly working-class I was. My father checked tickets for the fathers who worked in the city as investment bankers, attorneys, and upper management. He helped them get to work. My mother helped their children get to school. My stepfather helped mail to arrive. My stepmother helped her boss be successful. Who knows what my father would have been able to achieve if his dad had supported his educational goals? And who would my mother be today? She'd been accepted to Pratt and Parsons, but had decided to go to Stony Brook so that she could help to put a roof over my father's head as he went to college in spite of his father's wishes. Fat lot of good that did her.

I wanted more.

My gang's college acceptances rolled in. I was wait-listed at Binghamton and got into state universities in Albany and Buffalo, cities I'd never even visited. My parents had neither the time nor money nor interest to take me around to visit colleges.

I was accepted at Colgate, Sarah Lawrence, and Carnegie Mellon. I hoped that I could wrangle the financial aid package to attend one of them. In only six months, I'd be on my own.

And then, just like my mother's before me, my high school senior year packed a debilitating surprise.

One day in late February, I woke up and took a shower before heading to my job at Pizza Hut. The house was quiet. I walked from the bathroom to my bedroom in a bathrobe and closed the door, then turned on the radio. I always took great pains to be covered up in front of Bill. We were never one of those half-naked families, especially since there was a stepfather in the mix.

I took off my robe, dried myself off more thoroughly, and put on a bra and panties. Just then the door flew open and Bill walked in and turned off my radio. I grabbed a towel and pulled it up to cover myself. "Asshole!" I sputtered, mortified, as he exited and closed the door.

The door swung back open, and in less than a second he had me by the neck, on the bed, knees on either side of my hips, his huge, empurpled face screaming at me, "Oh yeah, who's the asshole now?"

I could not breathe. He shook my neck and screamed, and I began to fade out. He grinned. Would the last thing I saw before I died be his gray front tooth, the Cro-Magnon fold of his brow? That gave me a spurt of adrenaline. I jerked my head around and sank my teeth into the soft inside of his wrist.

"Ahh! Bitch! You bit me!" He let go and looked at his wrist.

As soon as his hands released my neck, the screams flew out.

My mother came flying through the door and saw me on the bed, in my underwear and bra, and him standing over me.

"What the hell is going on here?"

"She bit me!"

"He choked me!"

"Okay, everybody calm down."

"I'm not gonna calm down, I'm getting out of here!" I said.

Bill opened the second-story bedroom window and started throwing my folded laundry out of it. "You're not running away, I'm kicking you out. Get the fuck out!"

I grabbed my jeans and shirt and ran out of my bedroom and down the stairs, then dialed my father's number as my mother and stepfather argued upstairs. I pulled on my clothes as the phone rang and rang and clicked over to their answering machine. I left a crazed, incoherent message and then, "Oh my God, he's coming!" I hung up the phone and ran around the staircase and out the front door.

"Who do you think you're calling? You're not calling anyone. That's right, get the hell out of here, you little bitch." He laughed. My mother came out of the house with the keys and a pair of my shoes.

"Come on, we're leaving." My sister and brothers, wide-eyed, scurried toward the car.

"Here, you forgot something," Bill said, throwing my clothes at me from where they had landed on our lawn.

"Fuck you!" I yelled.

"Oh yeah, you want more?"

He lunged toward me, and my little brothers, nine and seven years old, each grabbed one of his legs and screamed, "No!"

"Get in the car, Candace. Come on, kids. Bill, go in the house, now."

My mother told me that if I reported Bill or told my dad the truth, Social Services would take the kids away and she would commit suicide. It was all up to me.

"Why don't you leave him? He just tried to kill me."

"I don't think he was serious. I think he was just trying to scare you."

"Scare me about what? He barged in on me when I was getting dressed. He didn't even knock."

"You called him an asshole."

"Because he barged in on me!"

"He thought you weren't in there."

"Then why would the radio be on? Mom, he choked me and cut off my oxygen. I almost died. Look at my neck."

There was a ring of red fingerprints around it that shortly there-after turned to angry purple bruises. His brand.

"I can't deal with this. I can't get another divorce. I'm taking you to your father's, but do not tell him what happened, or you know the consequences."

My father was more than happy to take me in. He didn't waste any time making a child support agreement change to reflect that I was living at his house. My stepmother was also welcoming. She went out of her way to buy food I liked and to make sure I felt at home, and I began to eat weekend-heavily all week long. What was the point of caring so much about my appearance, away from my mother's watchful eye, when I could gain pleasure and comfort, and ensure harmony, with every mouthful? It was also harder to work out, since I lived two towns away from my high school gym and had to get rides home based on my dad's and stepmom's schedule. I gained ten pounds between February and August.

I overheard my stepmother arguing with my father late at night.

"We're *newlyweds,*" she cried. "I didn't sign up for this."

My mother didn't understand why I didn't want to come back and live with them.

"We can work it out," she cried. "You live with me."

"No, I don't. I cannot live in the same house as someone who almost broke my neck."

"He wasn't serious. He was just trying to scare you."

"I have to go now. But I'll see you on Sunday. We can go to church together."

I was so sad that my mother refused to accept what he had done to me; that she brought me into this world but didn't even seem to have a problem living with a man who almost took me out of it. And that she couldn't believe he was a threat to my sister and two brothers. No. I was the problem. Now that I was out of the house, everything would settle down. I felt leaden, collapsed inside. I missed my sister and my brothers, our dog, and the house that was now unbreachable. In one bizarre, random moment, everything had changed.

The following Sunday morning, I called my mother and told her I couldn't make it to church. Performing at work and school—pretending that everything was normal, though everything had changed, in ways that weren't addressed—took every bit of energy I had.

After I got off the phone, I heard a noise. It sounded like cats in heat, weird and yowly. My stepmother stormed past my bedroom and into the bathroom, where she slammed the door.

Hmm.

Finally, she came out.

"What's the matter?"

"I've been waiting all week for you to go to church so I could have sex with your father, and now you went and canceled! Don't you realize how hard this is for me? We never have any privacy! We're *newlyweds!*"

"Okay, I'll go to church," I said, flustered. "I'm just tired, and I thought it would be better to rest."

"That's right," she spat as she stormed into their bedroom/the living room. "As usual, you were only thinking about *yourself.*"

Those six months were exhausting. My stepmother took me to school every morning, but just late enough for my first-period Spanish teacher to shoot me dirty looks. My homeroom teacher had been apprised of the situation (the edited version—I had moved to my dad's house, full stop), and she was very kind. I told my friends the real truth. They were sympathetic, and my feistier friends were angry, but it also isolated me a little bit. They couldn't quite process what happened to me, even though I pulled down my turtleneck to show them the oval finger marks.

Strangely, that spring, another Long Island teen girl's boyfriend killed her abusive father or stepfather. I was jealous of that girl. No one cared about me enough to punish Bill. It was for the best that I didn't have an overly protective boyfriend, because I had never felt so murderous. A switch was flipped inside me when he took so much away from me—almost took it all away—and was free to go on with his life, a life more convenient thanks to my removal. And it solved the mystery of his ex-wife and her permanent neck brace.

When I received a phone message from the nice Sarah Lawrence financial aid counselor, who wanted to work with me to come up with a way for me to attend their beautiful school, I didn't call her back. I lived with my father, he wanted me to go to a SUNY, and I felt frozen at the thought of rocking the boat.

I chose Buffalo, because it was the farthest away.

6

The Freshman Fifteen

MY DAD DROPPED ME OFF at the college dorms in August 1990 with a meal plan card, a hot pot and a mini-fridge, bags of clothes, a pile of journals, a box of my favorite books, and my yearbook.

Ellicott, a futuristic-looking complex, was a magnet for kids from Long Island who were *psyched* to be from Long Island, and tame, bland upstaters. Over time, I realized that I was in the wrong "neighborhood."

The eight-hour trip from Long Island to Buffalo had been tense; Dad was focused on getting there and back in time to make it to one of his law school classes, and his inability to study or write papers while he drove weighed on him.

By the time I left Long Island, I'd lived in twelve different houses. My mother had left my father at least three times; the third time had stuck. My childhood was one long anxiety attack, relieved only by reading or baking, when my mother and I would take the butter out to soften, wash our hands, tie on our aprons. We'd assemble the mixing bowls, measuring cups and spoons, the handheld mixer, the liquid measure, the vanilla and baking soda and powder. Preheat the oven. Begin again.

I couldn't imagine cooking myself dinner every night. I was on the meal plan. I had a little laminated card with a terrible, sweaty picture of me.

I could drive a car and be left at home without parental supervision, take out student loans, and have sex (not that I had, yet), but pick up a no-nonsense Jane Brody–style cookbook and whip up a meal? Inconceivable.

It also wasn't high on my list of priorities. It was much easier to go to the dining hall, or to any of the on- or off-campus spots that catered to students. Perkins was a lot like Friendly's, the grill and ice cream spot my dad took us to on the weekends. I also occasionally walked to the student deli to buy a pint of Ben & Jerry's Chunky Monkey: banana ice cream studded with dark-chocolate slabs and walnut chunks. When my roommates were out for the night and I felt like the only college student on the whole campus without a life, it soothed.

But could I afford to eat in the dining halls? No, although I hadn't figured that out yet. My father had told me, a few short months after I began school, that I had to make a choice. Although he'd set me up at UB, he couldn't sustain the expense. Either I could come back home, live in the basement, and go to the local community college or I could pay my own way.

Live in the basement and go to community college with all the burnouts from my high school? After busting my ass to get good grades in high school, all the extracurriculars, Mentathlon, school plays, college-essay writing, peer tutoring, and even fasting to raise funds for Global Club's Oxfam benefit?

The only way I'd live in the basement would be if I drank a tumbler of hemlock and expired in a plushly lined casket the very first night.

"I'll pay my own way," I said.

"Good for you, kiddo," he said. "Let's go to Marshalls. I'll buy you some clothes."

And he did, to the tune of $300. If he was deeply disturbed that I bought nearly everything from the men's section, he didn't say so, although he did ask, "Don't you want to . . . look in the women's section?"

"No," I said. "I wear men's jeans because they fit me better."

And they did. The early-nineties women's jeans were the kind that came up to my belly button, squeezing me into an hourglass shape that I wasn't born with. I also hated tight clothes, preferring men's button-down shirts and V-neck sweaters. The clothes felt like a hug from some comforting masculine figure—"boyfriend jeans" a few decades early.

And with a few bags of new-smelling clothes as my cushion, I became independent. Except not in the eyes of the IRS, since my father refused to stop claiming me on his taxes.

At first, I felt lost in a sea of engineering students, people in flannel shirts, college sweatshirts, and uniformly stonewashed jeans from the Gap—people who were trying their damnedest to look exactly like as many other people as possible. But at an off-campus party, I caught glimpses of people who were different. Although I had landed in the huge maw of a public state university, I'd had cherished hopes of going to a tony private college with an artistic, literary bent. These people looked like they'd ended up at UB by accident, too.

They wore purposely clunky glasses and quirky, natty outfits made up of thrift store finds. The girls had sleek bobs, which looked especially chic in contrast to the ruling style for college girls: big, poofy eighties hair still going strong in 1990. The boys, on the other hand, had shaggy mops that contrasted with the mainstream guy hair, which was close-cropped, conservative.

I told my dorm friends I'd be right back and got in the bathroom line behind one of the guys from that crowd. He wore a charcoal J.Crew rollneck sweater, an ironic bowl haircut, and a huge, incandescent grin.

He spun around and trained it on me. "Hi!" he said.

"Hi!" I replied.

Apparently, here at college, people actually talked to each other instead of staring at each other torturously for three years without making a move, like in high school. The beers in our hands didn't hurt, though at the time I hated the taste of beer and just used the cup as a prop.

"I'm Po," he said.

"Po? Like, as in Edgar Allan?"

"Yeah, but spelled *P-o*," he said, his smile acknowledging the pretentiousness of it. We were both English majors. He was a sophomore.

While the bathroom line inched forward, we talked about our favorite writers (mine, Wilde, his, Beckett) and our lodgings (I in suburban-lame Ellicott, he on South Campus in Goodyear, shabby but cool).

We continued talking as the night went on, and moved out to the front porch, where he kissed me. His mouth was beery, and I'd never kissed a smoker before, but soon I was lost in making-out land, each enervating second blotting out a lifetime's weight of feeling locked out of love.

"Come on," he said, and I walked with him the few blocks to South Campus and then to his dorm.

I, seventeen, was walking with Po, nineteen, to his dorm room, just a few weeks after going away to school. Nobody would fret or miss me; I didn't think much more beyond that as we stepped into the hospital-size elevator and it whooshed us up to his floor. Then the hallway, starting to feel a little tawdry, but this is what happens in college.

He opened the door to a dark room. "Shh, my roommate is sleeping."

It was a small room with cinder block walls and a brown linoleum floor. I sat down on his bed as he shuffled to the record player and put on the Smiths' "Reel Around the Fountain."

Then he came back, sat beside me, and planted his mouth on mine. And as we kissed, he wriggled out of his clothes and began to peel off mine.

So the kissing led to this room, and opening the door led to his bed, my bra showing, his hand sliding down the back of my tights, bases flashing by. He thought we were going to have sex. He was wrong. I had just met him. If for some unlikely reason I decided to go ahead and have sex before marriage, I'd not do it like this! In a dank-smelling room with his roommate just a few feet away!

His skinny hips bracketed a big, engorged penis with a dark thatch of hair. It seemed to be poking me everywhere at once. In a few minutes I'd gone from being a girl who had never gone past breast groping to being a mostly naked girl in bed with a totally naked guy, on his not recently laundered, ripe-smelling sheets.

I would have happily gotten him off with a hand job or even a blow job, but I was so damned inept and he was so drunk that nobody got release. My release wasn't even on the agenda.

Our bodies debated wordlessly.

Let's fuck.

No, I'm not doing that.

Okay, I'll kiss you and palpate your body partially to acquiesce to what you're saying and partially because I think it will lead you to saying yes.

Hey, don't try to put that there.

Okay. I'll try to do this with it instead.

"Watch your teeth!"

"Sorry." Mortified. Whatever mystique I'd built up with him at the party was now blown, since I was such a spaz in bed.

We spent another tussle-y hour *not* getting off, and then he fell asleep beside me, his body clamping me down as he snored so loudly that my own sleep was absolutely out of the question.

But despite the loutishness, the snoring and the beery saliva and nicotine-scented fingers, the manky boxers and his foxy odors, my guilt and ebbing sense of adventure, as dawn grayed the darkness and then the low western New York sunrise yellowed the grayness, I fell oddly in love. When wasn't love this way? It was a water cracker in place of a feast that only bred more hunger, but still, it took the edge off.

Po showed me a new way of being drunk. Like my father, he was truculent and terse when sober, his happy moods tweaked sideways, his laughter sardonic. But when he was drunk, he was lit up from the inside, aglow with good times. He was like a questing philosopher prince, awash in ideas, hugs, approval. He was fond of me. And I was completely in love with him. He told me that he was in love with someone else—Pam. She went to a different school, was older. She'd been his first.

"She was my prom date senior year. After the prom we went back to my parents' house and slept over. Her sister was there with us, asleep on the floor. And she and I did it right next to her." His expression was hard to read. He seemed to feel sheepish, but not sheepish enough to keep it from me.

It was a very hungry love. He didn't love me back, not in the way that would have turned him into my boyfriend: someone who'd study with me, take me out to dinner, hold my hand, and adore me.

I was at a college with thirty thousand people and I chose to focus on just one. If I could make him love me, my horrible childhood would be a random piece of bad luck, not a predictor.

I hadn't let a drop of alcohol pass my lips in high school, afraid that I'd instantly morph into a Skid Row dipsomaniac, but one night soon after I got to college, I went to a dorm party that featured a White Russian punch bowl and I became someone who drank cautiously. With Po's friends, who were (I hoped) becoming my friends, I became someone who drank copiously. They called it "getting fucked up." After we got fucked up, people usually "hooked up." There were a few couples in the group who hooked up only with each other, but the rest of the people tended to grab whomever was cute and closest of the opposite sex and wander to someone's room or apartment. Getting fucked up was nothing to hide—it was more something to brag about. Hooking up was also nothing to hide, although there was a point—some chalkboard calculation —at which too many hookups turned girls from fun-loving into too slutty.

Thursday nights, we all headed to Anacone's, an old-man bar on the dodgier side of University Heights that didn't check IDs.

Pitchers of cheap beer were $5, and we sat around table hopping and relishing the feeling of being grown-up—sitting in a dark bar, talking, laughing, flirting, hundreds of miles away from our parents.

After the closing night of *No Exit,* I got high for the first time. I played Estelle, a matricidal narcissist, in the Jean-Paul Sartre play about three unsympathetic people trapped in a room together.

My friends J. and Kathleen came to see me perform on the last night and then took me out to celebrate. They spirited me off in J.'s two-tone Honda CR-X. J. pulled into the Tops supermarket parking lot. "Come on, Kathleen," he said. "I have a great idea. Candace, stay in the car."

"Okay," I said.

I sat in the darkened parking lot. It took a bit longer than I had anticipated, but they returned, grinning.

"We got you a cake!" J. exclaimed as he opened the car door. He placed it in my hands: a large purple sheet cake festooned with frosting roses, the words "Congratulations, Candace!" written boldly in skillful script across the top.

"Wow, thank you!" I said. J. wanted to be a chef. Of course his "bouquet" to me would take the form of something edible.

He drove us to a slightly ghostly park and pulled out a joint. There was no question that I would smoke it. We were celebrating. A lot of my friends smoked pot. I had even taken a few puffs, which had done nothing because it was my first time. I doubted anything would happen this time, either. We stood in a circle and passed it around in the dark.

I realized I was high when I got lost in the middle of my sentence. I could vaguely sense the words that were meant to be the end, but they no longer made sense without the beginning.

"Wait a second," I said. "What happened to the end of my sentence?"

They burst into laughter. "You're high, Candace!" J. said.

"Let's have cake," Kathleen said.

J. popped the top off of the container and handed us forks. After a few decorous bites, we put the forks down and dug in with our fingers.

"This is so good!" I exclaimed. "I've never tasted supermarket cake this good."

"The pot makes it taste better than it actually is," Kathleen said. "Isn't that great?"

The crumb of the devil's food cake was slightly gummy, and the frosting shone with some deplorable industrial oil, but it was still so *good*. It also felt good to be so uninhibited in my enjoyment—like a baby turning one, given a cake to mangle, wade through with my fingers and face, experience without worry of seeming gluttonous or punishable.

J. had to finish a paper, so he dropped Kathleen and me off at the Ellicott dorms and vanished into the night. We hugged good-bye and then I went up to my room, but not before stopping in the bathroom to wash the frosting out from underneath my nails. I'd been initiated.

High, I would happily eat the vanilla ice cream leftover after my friend Anna ate all of the chocolate chip cookie dough chunks out of the Ben & Jerry's pint, J.'s fluffy broccoli omelets, greasy taco salads served in tortilla bowls at Amy's Place, ruddy, glossy Buffalo wings that left reddish streaks in cups of blue cheese dressing, tabbouleh salads at hippie potlucks (the pot helped make the last one appealing).

Sometimes when I was high, I'd imagine a time warp wherein my college-age toker dad and I hung out at a party. We'd laugh until we cried, and share a box of Cheez-Its. My father hadn't smoked pot for years, and got incensed if my older cousins joked about how they used to try to find his stash when they babysat me.

I couldn't bond with my dad sober, couldn't game the system by smoking pot with him, so I smoked pot in remembrance of the skinny, long-haired guy who stared out from the black-and-white photo my mom took at the beach before I was born. He and I would have gotten along, I thought, and there was no way to prove that theory wrong.

At the end of freshman year, I planned to stay in Buffalo over the summer. My friends were renting a house, and Anna, one of the housemates, needed a subletter for the summer months. I could stay in Buffalo and get a job, romp with my friends, and enjoy the one beautiful season the city had to offer, or I could go home and get a job and coexist tensely with my father and stepmother, with the surety that we'd have epic brawling fights that were ostensibly about my leaving a wet washcloth on the shower stall floor or whether I drank the last Fresca but were really more about how much they'd rather not put up with me. I could see this, but my father fought with me for weeks, sending long, irate letters in single-spaced nine-point Times New Roman, printed on both sides, and called me to insist that I was coming home, because if I didn't, he knew that I'd sabotage my chances of success for my entire life.

Go home? It was time to make myself a new home.

The Enchanted Broccoli Forest

MY VERY FIRST off-campus room was beautiful, thanks to Anna's clout. If I'd been moving into this four-bedroom house share with Bridget, Zack, and Sean, and not just holding Anna's spot for the summer, I would have happily accepted the worst room. But Anna was a tall, buxom, alpha Swede, and she took what she wanted without much resistance from any corner. Because of her chutzpah, my very first nondorm, nonfamilial room was in fact a large room with another room off the back—a small study with a slanted ceiling, with a desk and chair that overlooked the backyard, and flowering trees with blowsy petals waving beyond the windows.

I had *A Room of One's Own* on my bookshelf, in a room of my own. The next very good thing that happened that summer was meeting Steve, a cute, funny friend of my housemate Bridget. He asked me out on a date—a picnic in the park.

"This is soooo good," I said, biting into a vegetable-and-cheese sub. I was too embarrassed to tell him exactly how good it was to me; in the two weeks between the end of the spring semester and the beginning of my work-study payments, I had survived on perhaps a tenth of the calories I needed per day. Staying in Buffalo for the summer against my father's will meant that when my meal card became null and void, so did my access to food. One day I ate a cadged hot dog from a biology department grad student picnic. Another day I boiled up a 22-cent box of generic macaroni and cheese, adding only water. My roommates were happy to share coffee in the morning and cheap beer at night, but I hated to jeopardize our friendship with any further grubbing.

Between that and my need to walk everywhere, those two weeks saw me go from a cafeteria-and-keg-beer-plumped girl to a (light-headed, weak, frequently salivating, food-fantasizing) lithe young woman. If everyone got high, the munchies took over on a communal level and food came out of cupboards and fridges, so I could tank up without feeling quite so conspicuous.

I did check in with my dad once and mentioned that I had no money or food and was hungry. "There's plenty of food here at home," he said tersely, and sent me a $5 bill and a stack of irrelevant coupons (cat food?) he and my stepmother had clipped. As long as I did what he wanted, I could be loved and fed. But if it came down to that, starving was more appealing.

There were plenty of pliable, daddy-devoted daughters out there. I just wasn't one of them. There were lots of laid-back, accepting, doting dads out there. For whatever reason, he and I had ended up together, and I wasn't yet ready for us, with a sigh of relief, to have hardly anything to do with each other. I walked around dogged by sadness that I couldn't make my own decisions, be my own person, *and* have the love and support of my father.

With Steve, I had my first casual, fun relationship. We got high, drank beer, watched movies, laughed with friends, and fooled around. Po was in Buffalo, too, and now that I had another romantic focal point, he seemed eager to have an actual friendship. He turned up at my house and took me on walks.

One buttery summer afternoon, we took the subway downtown —to the gentrified stretch of Elmwood near Buffalo State College. I'd been there a few times; it was always a shock to note that a neighborhood so overridden with charming bakeries, used-book stores, and bistros was only a few miles down the road from the faded student ghetto I lived in.

"Let's go in here," Po said, as we approached Rebels, the one hip, and correspondingly expensive, clothing boutique in that city. "Maybe Aaron's working."

"Okay." I wasn't surprised that he was working there—he was a guy on the fringes of our crowd who everyone agreed was stunningly beautiful, so beautiful that he seemed like a supernatural being.

As we entered the store, Aaron erupted from behind the counter, a dark, handsome vision in distressed jeans, scarves, and other world-music chic. "Po! What a great surprise!"

I saw that when he smiled, his whole face smiled—his cheekbones, his nostrils, his ears, his forehead, his honey-brown eyes, and his wide, full mouth, which revealed white teeth just crooked enough to put the final off-kilter flourish on his looks.

We sat around the store, as Aaron played DJ, and we talked literature, sociology (Aaron's major), and, of course, philosophy, the ideas tumbling over each other like puppies. Although I usually felt like a student around Po, with Aaron there we all engaged with each other like equals, and our voiced thoughts added up to things far beyond what we would have come up with on our own.

And then it was time to move on, to have more perfect moments in an already perfect day. The sun shined, Po and I were having a blast, without all of the negativity and disappointment that had haunted us before I met Steve, and although we were still in Buffalo, it felt like a different city.

As we left, I walked a few steps down the street before I realized Po wasn't beside me. Then he exited Rebels, a funny smile on his face. We walked past a few storefronts and he said, "Aaron thinks you're beautiful."

"What?" I may have washed my face that day, but I wasn't sure. I felt entirely unremarkable.

"Yeah, and he really likes you. He just told me. Isn't that awesome?"

"*Aaron* likes *me?*"

"Why not?"

"Well, I'm not an Italian supermodel, for one."

"Aaron's really down-to-earth," he said. "And you *are* beautiful, Candace."

Dang.

I visited him at the store a few days later, and that was all it took. We went to dinner that night, and then he took me to his mother's apartment, where he was staying to save money before he left for his semester abroad in London. London! But we had the summer. I needed to jettison Steve, but there was an overlap. I told him that I thought we should clarify that we were both okay with our seeing other people.

He said, "Yes, of course" and hugged me as if I were the absolute coolest woman on the planet.

Aaron and Candace. Candace and Aaron. I felt like I had been discovered. And his love for me made up for every boy who called me ugly, every girl who called me retarded, every time my mother hinted that I needed to lose weight or my father told me I was a disappointment. Every ding in my soul felt healed by his love, and I was grateful that any relationship that came before did not work out, because it would have kept me from this. To Aaron, I was amazing, extraordinary, fascinating, and precious, and for the first time, in his ardent eyes, I felt so.

Another park, another picnic. This time Delaware Park, on a blanket, a few hours after we dropped acid. A sociology professor he adored, a pal of Timothy Leary's, had given Aaron the tabs.

Now the blades of grass were extraordinary and fascinating, as were the ladybug on my arm and a butterfly's fluttery levitations. As we embraced, we were one pulsing, sweaty being within the whole world's pulsing, sweaty clasp.

I remember when the acid hit: We were on my bed, and I wasn't sure if I'd actually feel anything or if the tabs might end up being too old. Then the Georgia O'Keeffe painting, reproduced in a magazine spread that I had painstakingly removed and taped up, began to melt. It was an odd image—not a big flower, but Ranchos Church One, slabs of thick sand-colored adobe with soft edges, like flesh as it shifts around the joints of the body. I had many of her flower posters, initially innocent of and then enthusiastic about their labial connotations, but the adobe structure seduced me in a different way.

And . . . I was ready to have sex. My friends had lost their virginity in bedrooms at parties, in cars, in summer houses, tree houses, and dorm rooms. I had held out, but this was a perfect opportunity. Beautiful Aaron, who loved me, wrote poems about me, gave me uncut, semiprecious-stone jewelry. We'd even named our daughter, because I knew, when we got married after grad school, that I'd have a girl first and we'd name her Violet Daisy. We'd do it in my bedroom, with Enya playing and candles burning.

And we did. All of our passion, which had ended before in orgasms not tempered by pain or tentativeness, was now going to relieve me of my maidenhead. Despite my mother's imprecations, her many, many very special talks with me about how I'd be basically losing an emotional limb, so to speak, if I had sex before marriage, and the cow and the milk for free, and how a woman's body was like a sleeping tiger that should not be awakened, I was ready. In spite of my father's belief that I was abnormal if I wasn't having sex by the age of sixteen, I had not, until that moment, been ready.

And so, lights out, candles lit, incense burning, Enya singing "On Your Shore," we began. Something gave, and it *hurt,* but he was definitely making headway, and then by the time "Storms in Africa" launched into the second verse, we both heard an audible *pop* and he edged further into me, until there was no doubt that I'd been deflowered. We held each other, feeling velvety and blessed, kissing and awestruck. At that moment, we definitely felt like we'd invented sex.

And then, my nervousness gone, my body mine in a new way, my love consummated, I felt a new sensation. "I'm so hungry," I said. "Let's go make something to eat."

Aaron grinned. "Okay!"

I threw on a wrap, he pulled on his jeans, and we went out to the kitchen, which was happily empty, along with the rest of the apartment. In the one lightbulb's glow, I made a big, fluffy omelet, studded with cheddar cheese, diced tomatoes, onions, and green peppers, and we ate it, my first meal as a nonvirgin. It tasted exquisite.

My stepmother and I were chummy at that point, and she'd always been more like a big sister to me when it came to matters of sexual experience. So the next morning, I called her to tell her. I didn't want my father knowing such personal details, though, so I always swore her to secrecy, and she promised.

"Oh, that's so exciting!" she enthused. "Tell me all about it."

That night, my father called. His voice sounded tender.

"Hi, honey," he said.

"Hi," I said, realizing how awkward it was to talk to him while my entire vulva throbbed with postcoital pain.

"So, how are you doing?" he asked.

"Fine."

"You sure?"

"Yeah . . ." *What the hell!*

"You're doing okay?"

"Yes. The weather's beautiful, I'm enjoying my classes, things are good. How are you?"

"I'm good. Busy with the law school summer session, the railroad . . ."

"Well, I was just about to go to bed." (*Shit!* "*To* sleep," *I meant.*) "So let's talk soon, maybe Thursday?"

"Okay, Candace. Take good care of yourself, okay?"

"Okay."

"I love you."

"I love you, too."

"Be good."

"Okay."

"Bye."

Of course my stepmother told him. But it would take me years to figure out that anything I said to her in confidence might as well have been whispered directly into his ear.

Sail away, sail away, sail away. Four months. Like a magical prince, Aaron unlocked my sexuality, opened my mind, and, most notably, steeped my stray, bedraggled heart in his fervent love—and then he took off for England. I only had to get through the next four months, though, so I found a tiny room for rent for a mere $120. It was perhaps a few feet bigger than the writing room off Anna's bedroom, and my three housemates were guys.

In my summer sublet, the kitchen was a toxic-waste dump of days of dirty dishes and empties. My new house was much better, but dishes in the sink were still an issue.

My housemate Keith's girlfriend Helena also lived off-campus, but differently—in an orderly and tasteful apartment with two other girls who were also orderly and tasteful. They were all vegetarians who relied on *The Enchanted Broccoli Forest* for recipes.

Helena's apartment seemed like a Zen sanctuary in comparison with other student dwellings: earth tones, pretty curtains, area rugs. The furniture may have been quasi-Goodwill-sourced, but it didn't look like it. Glass canisters held lentils and grains, and the earthenware bowl on the kitchen table cradled actual fruit that the girls ate, not faux, velveteen, and gemstone-encrusted fruit in a wicker bowl, like one friend's ironic nod at domesticity. Helena came back from visits to her mother's house, which was a stately townhouse off Elmwood, with Kona coffee, imported chocolate, and handmade pasta from artisanal-food shops.

Helena invited me over for dinner one night, and as she serenely cooked dal and rice, I paged through her cookbook. I was intrigued. I'd never seen handwritten recipes inside a published volume. I marveled at the regularity of Mollie Katzen's letters. What a dependable human being! Never a *t* crossed askew or even a scribble.

The cheerful, plucky pages reminded me of the handwritten recipe cards my mother exchanged with her friends and stored in squat boxes. This cookbook intimated that *I* could cook. I could be a serene vegetarian woman with an orderly yet creative life. I could wake up, do a series of yoga poses in my tidy, spacious bedroom, drink herbal tea in my kitchen, eat homemade yogurt and granola for breakfast, and ride my bicycle to campus, where my assignments would be complete in a satchel and my classmates would wonder about me, a mysterious human being who was winsomely beautiful and smelled faintly of lemon verbena and lavender. I couldn't have been further from that persona.

I was chaos, frayed hems, lost pens. Maybe that's why I was so enchanted.

Mollie Katzen would not have cheated on Aaron with not one, but two, men. She wouldn't have told him about it in a letter, weeks before she was set to arrive in London. She would have known that it's a really destructive thing to do to even a perfect and other-worldly love. That even though I'd waited until I was eighteen and a half to begin having sex and then had only a few weeks to enjoy it before Aaron left, even though that was hard and I felt entirely different in the world, looking at people as potential sexual conquests for the first time, and even though his leaving felt so much like all of the other brutal abandonings, rejections, and slights in my life that it triggered the seven dwarves of corresponding reactions (Angry, Sad, Frustrated, Distrustful, Resentful, Brooding, and Needy), it was an unbelievably stupid thing to do. Twice.

As soon as someone offered me very exquisite love, I found myself acting out, becoming an agent of hurt, instead of the victimized kid I'd been before, with only shreds of love to tide me over. A heaping portion of love activated parts of me that I never wanted to own (and still don't). It made me into a hurtful person.

It didn't matter that Aaron was doing the same thing in his world, because I didn't know it at the time, not in a concrete way. When I did find out, I was already there, in London.

He went out to buy milk and I fell asleep. When I woke up hours later, he still wasn't back and I worried that he'd been in a tube bombing, as they were happening that December. Finally, he returned, wild-eyed and teary and trembling. Beautiful Aaron had just been crying in the arms of his other girlfriend.

And he would tell me, on my birthday in Edinburgh, Scotland, that he was in love with her but would try not to be, so we decided to continue on to Paris, because it might work magic on our broken love, but it didn't. On Christmas Day 1991, he broke up with me and left.

So, yeah. Paris, Christmas, *truly* abandoned, with about $40 to last me a week. It was damply cold, and I remained in our dirt-cheap hotel in the Latin Quarter, moving from our already miserable third-story couple's berth with en suite bathroom to a tiny room with only a sink off the ground-level courtyard, next to a shared bathroom with very scratchy squares of brown toilet paper.

I woke up at four o'clock most mornings, because I never did get adjusted to the time change, and my consciousness of what had happened settled on my chest like a wet wool blanket. I journaled obsessively, trying to write the poisonous grief out of my body as if it came through my pen. As soon as the closest *boulangerie* opened its doors, I crept outside in the damp, windy cold and bought a *pain au chocolat* and a hot *café au lait,* which I rushed back to my room, which was at least warm. I had those things, and my writing, and a journal, with lots of blank pages, and I was in Paris—and damn it, I was going to see Paris.

I wasn't heartbroken in Buffalo (yet) or Long Island. I was heartbroken in Paris, that's how it happened, and I vowed to also *be* in Paris. When I had to, I took the metro, but mostly I walked all over, to save money. I walked to the Cimetière du Père Lachaise and wandered among the graves, looking for Oscar Wilde's, passing Jim Morrison's. Although I was hardly at my best, two young college students, Sylvain and Sophie, came out of the woodwork and befriended me. After we finished our exploration, they took me back to my neighborhood and then to dinner.

Although I usually subsisted on street cart *croques madames,* crêpes, or a baguette and cheese, one afternoon, after walking for miles, I saw a small restaurant in an unglamorous neighborhood. The surrounding storefronts were gray and dusty, but this restaurant's windows were polished, with yellow dotted Swiss curtains.

On the small chalkboard easel outside, the prix fixe special featured a *fricassée de poulet* and a glass of wine, for hardly any money. Chicken fricassee. I was homesick, in the especially stricken way one is when the feeling descends for the first time in adulthood, but seeing the name of my grandma Marie's most comforting meal felt like someone wrapping a warm blanket around my heart. I walked a few steps, then turned and darted toward the restaurant.

If this were a romance novel, I'd have met a dashing Frenchman or a violet-eyed, mysterious Frenchwoman who helped me to forget all about Aaron and my own idiocy. But instead, I was a real person who had just spat in the eye of true love, and so the restaurant afforded me only the realistic, though not insignificant, comforts of warmth and a meal that would arrive magically from the kitchen. I would be served as if I were a princess, but only for that hour.

I opened the door cautiously and walked inside. The tables and chairs were mahogany-stained, and white plates sat on each polished tabletop, along with sturdy silverware, wine glasses, and white cloth napkins. A soot-smudged worker sat at one table, a prim, elegant old woman at another. The bored waiter inclined his head, and I chose a table beside the window.

As the waiter approached, I ordered, any anxiety I might have felt about using high school French blunted by other emotions. Sipping water, I watched people walk by outside. A mother with her small child. Innocent child! Lovers arm in arm. What a newly precious status—it hurt to see them. An old man. Did he have someone to take care of him? Or did he err tragically when he was young, like me, and regret it for the rest of his life?

Soon the meal was in front of me: browned pieces of bone-in chicken in a creamy white sauce with mushrooms and onions, a glass of white wine to complement the delicate flavors.

My grandmother Marie filled a stockpot with water, a whole chicken, carrots, celery, and an onion and boil it all until the meat was falling off the bone. Then she strained the broth from the chicken and vegetables, reserving the broth. Painstakingly, she picked every scrap of chicken off the carcass, put it aside, then brought the broth to a rolling boil, whisked in a cup of floury water until the broth became a sauce, then added the chicken and vegetables back into the mixture, seasoned it with salt and pepper, and served it over rice. It was so good. Delicate, flavorful, filling, though far from rich. For the cost of a chicken and a few vegetables, the crowd-pleasing meal fed at least six, with leftovers.

The traditional French method of making *fricassée* is to brown chicken pieces in butter, then dust them with flour, brown again, and add wine, stock, and aromatics. The flour thickens the sauce, saving cooks the trouble of a separate step.

My *fricassée de poulet* was a distant relative. The chicken seemed small to my American eyes, and was not shreds but pieces, with bones, ligaments, and skin. But the meat was flavorful, as were the buttery, wine-deepened sauce and silky mushrooms. There was no rice, but instead bread with which to swab up each bit of remaining liquid.

I savored each bite, because when I finished the meal, my idyll in the sleepy restaurant would reach its end.

I knew that if I were back in my grandmother Marie's little kitchen in Mastic, she'd be at the table with a tumbler of whiskey and ice on one side of her and an ashtray on the other, her gold watch necklace marking an axis line between the two. Her fluffy red hair would frame her face: her tortoiseshell green-brown eyes behind glasses, her delicate nose and coral-lipsticked mouth. If I told her, "Grandma, he broke up with me on Christmas Day! He had a girlfriend in London! I was all alone in a foreign country!" she would shrug and smile a little half smile, and I'd get it. "You'll live."

I counted out my francs, got up, put my coat, scarf, and gloves on, and headed back out into the cold December afternoon, the light of which was already starting to dim.

8

Cooking with Pam

PAM STOOD in front of our stove in the dinky galley kitchen of our Elmwood Avenue apartment. With precise economical movements, she added a plastic bag of dried green peas, a chopped onion, and a dash of salt to a large pot of water. The peas were pebble-hard, their shape reminiscent of candy buttons, the hard, sugary dots I peeled from paper with my teeth as a kid.

Left alone for hours to simmer, the peas lost their outlines and became a medium-thick liquid. The onions' sharpness became a sweet, rounding-out flavor, the one discrete textural element to detect. No smoked pork bones or stock making it into something more robust—just peas, onions, and water, satisfying because it was warming and reliably there.

Pea soup was the staple of our small, makeshift household. Pam survived on that, lots of skim milk, iceberg lettuce heads cut into chunks and dipped into ketchup, and a pot of coffee every morning. She used to eat lots of carrots, until she ate so many that they turned her skin orange.

The last thing I wanted to do was like Pam, but not only did I like her, we were roommates. Pam was Po's unrequited love from high school, the reason he gave me that we couldn't be together. But she never wanted anything more from him than friendship. Back then, before moving to Buffalo for grad school, she went to college in Boston and had glamorously geeky MIT boyfriends. Before we moved in together, I knew of her for three years but spent only about twelve hours with her total—all in one night.

One weekend during my junior year, Pam came up to visit for a party. She and I ended up drinking forty-ouncers beside each other in the circle that wound around a campfire in the dark backyard. I was no longer the freshman girl Po had met in the bathroom line. My preppy wardrobe had gone bye-bye, replaced with raggedy Seattle grunge jeans and flannel shirts over camisoles. I had chopped off my long, thick hair and dyed it crayon-red—an external symbol of my confused penitence and grief over losing Aaron. I had gone from being discovered and restored to discarded and rueful.

Talking to Pam felt like a giant dose of soul medicine. This vaunted obstacle wasn't scary at all! She had cute, slightly gappy teeth, burbling unguarded laughter, and bright blue eyes under quizzical eyebrows. She was funny, clever, and a great listener. She threw back beer and smoked cigarettes like the beautiful no-nonsense German girls I remembered from my time in Sylt, Germany—without any posturing or vestigial sheepishness. She had paint on her fingers (not her fingernails), and her rolled-up jean hems revealed muscular cyclist's calves.

As the night went on, Pam and I tacitly talked more and more exclusively to each other, mirthful grins revealing what we didn't come out and say: Out of the corners of our eyes, we saw that our connection to each other was slowly driving Po bonkers. Pacing around our periphery, he veered in sideways to lob carefully casual words our way. They bounced, gnatlike, off our bubble, and so did he.

When nature called, we went to the bathroom together. We took turns peeing, then decided to ditch the party. She opened the bathroom window and climbed out, and I followed her. We ran off laughing into the night.

"What do you want to do now?" I asked.

"Let's go to your apartment," she said, with a winning jack-o'-lantern grin.

My apartment, then, was the one we now lived in together, but at the time I shared it with a devastatingly cool gay man who was down in New York City that weekend, partying with Madonna's entourage. We had no idea, as we walked through the wedding cake–like building's heavy entryway doors and up the staircase surrounded by glitter-stucco walls left over from the seventies, that we'd do that hundreds more times in the coming year.

Upstairs in my high-ceilinged living room, we sat in the candlelit dark, cross-legged on my settee, facing each other, like Jake Ryan and Samantha at the end of *Sixteen Candles*. The phone began to ring off the hook.

"It's Po," she said with a grin.

"I know," I said, and disconnected it with a flourish.

I was intoxicated, only as the until-recently impotent are, by the power of it all. I had run away with Pam. Now what?

Well. We both knew what would make for a really good story. It was just a question of how we were going to get there. I took her foot in my hands and began to rub it. She grabbed my hands, leaned over, and kissed me. Her lips were delightfully full, although she'd later confess that she thought they were ugly, thanks to middle-school boys who told her so.

I wish I could say that we kissed in that way where we forgot to breathe, everything fell away, and we melted inside. It wasn't like that. We were kissing because we had run away from Po. We ran away from Po to break whatever spell we thought he had on us (or more accurately, me), and to rub his face in it.

Hooking up with someone to get back at someone else is complicated because that person is still at the center of it, even if he's not there. It wasn't a soul connection, it was an act of defiance. In the defiance was burgeoning power: action in place of feminine passivity. That was hot. As was Pam—whether the chemistry was there or not. And as I leaned in and our hands moved to each other's waists, I was very aware that I was kissing a girl.

A magnificent surprise: her ample breasts, minimized under two running bras, because she was so not a big-boob person. They came tumbling loose like Uma Thurman's in *Dangerous Liaisons*.

Although Po probably gnashed his teeth and pulled out chunks of his lustrous hair thinking of us having full-on sex—and without him(!)—Pam kept her jeans on. "I have my period," she said, and that was that.

She woke up the next morning all smiles. Unruffled, she made coffee and hung out with me for a little while before she ran off to do Pam things like paint, make soup, and read Teilhard de Chardin.

The following fall, she decided to go to grad school at my university, and after my housemate pulled out at the eleventh hour and Pam needed an apartment, we sheepishly agreed to move in together, I with trepidation and excitement, she with pragmatism and boundaries already in place.

"I'm not gay," she said to me matter-of-factly. "I hooked up with you because it was an excellent prank on Po."

So now we were roommates. But not in the way that would have continued to make a really good story. I was hurt in an entirely new way: as if I had found that I had another limb, and that limb had just gotten slammed in a door. The pain was profound and very different. But as time went by, my nascent crush turned into something even more intractable.

In a way, Po got the last laugh, because I had an entire year to realize just how cool and besotting Pam truly was. She was indeed very smart, and in fact a very good artist. Thoughtful, funny, quick-witted, and insightful, but also someone who jumped out of bed every morning happy to see what the day would bring. She took walks *just to take walks.* She responded when a street person called out to her, and was able to hold her boundaries and end the conversation on her own terms, without either party feeling bad—in fact, they both usually took something good away from it. She made beautiful mobiles out of purposely broken wine bottles reassembled with golden wire, called Phoenix Bottles. She was impulsively generous and sent people the kinds of letters that were hard to throw away, or even put away.

So, on top of her being all of those things, I fell for her because she demonstrated so many qualities that I didn't have and wanted, or might have had had they not been occluded not by nature but by my not very comme il faut nurture. If she was sort of mine, then I could feel all of the goodness of being less crabbed and pin-tucked than I currently was. Exercise that was claimed as avidly as one drinks a draft of cold water from a tin cup, instead of a self-flagellating chore. Not making time for art, but creation as a default mode, and making time for everything else. The simplest, cheapest food, made well and without agitation.

I clung to our little microculture: our pea soup, cheap jug wine, cigarettes, and artwork made on our bellies, stretched out on the hardwood floor, our soundtrack songs by Belly, the Story, and Shawn Colvin, with ambient sounds provided by the wino hooker who strutted back and forth in front of the Bakermans donut shop across the street, the Shabba Ranks music vibrating up from the apartment below.

We called the apartment the Haven and decorated it simply, cheaply, and well. We wound up white Christmas lights in a spherical tangle and hung them from the ceiling as a light fix-ture. We bought a piece of sunflower-printed fabric and placed it, unhemmed, on our kitchen table—a $2 tablecloth that everyone admired. We hung our artwork on the walls: hers sure and skilled, mine fledgling and proud.

She had boyfriends and I didn't. I put up with them gamely, although seeing her with a boyfriend felt like my heart was being rapped with the business end of a cat hairbrush. One tried to lounge around on our living room couch in his blue underwear and nothing else, but I sent him back to Pam's room to get dressed posthaste.

My plan was to move to New York after graduation; Helena had graduated the previous spring and had made a place for herself on the Lower East Side. She said she'd help me find an apartment, and I'd been accepted into Brooklyn College's MFA program for poetry. I planned to get a summer job and then find something part-time once school started.

"Can I come?" Pam said one night over beers at the Old Pink, the dank, black-walled local dive frequented by us, our friends, locals, and sundry lowlifes.

"Sure!"

Pam wanted to come! Our year would not end with the end of college, and in a way, college wouldn't end as long as Pam was by my side. And maybe she'd have a change of heart and decide she loved me back, that way.

Pam sent red tulips to a guy named Matt the Valentine's Day before we left. He was in a band, cute in what I thought was a somewhat doofy way. Other boyfriends Pam had were friendly and liked to hang out at the apartment. But with Matt, Pam seemed to want to secret herself away—at his apartment or in her room. The energy was huddled. I didn't like that Pam had boyfriends, but we were friendly and they got a kick out of the way she and I had first ended up in the apartment. But for the first time, it seemed like Matt didn't like that Pam had a pining, Sapphic roommate, and I didn't go out of my way to be conciliatory, either.

And yet it was a complete surprise when Pam sat me down one spring evening and said, "Candace, I've decided not to go to New York with you. I'm going to stay in Buffalo with Matt."

The words floated in the air and then sank into me like nineteen little swords. I got up and walked aimlessly somewhere in the living room. I laughed.

"So you're cool with it. That's so great!"

"No, I am *not* cool with it."

She knew a Candace who cried when she was sad, or got all quiet and mopey. But this was different to both of us.

She rushed up to me and put her arms around me. "Candace Bear."

"Don't touch me." I backed out of her embrace, grabbed my purse and keys, and left the apartment. I automatically turned toward my friend Frank's place, a few avenues away, on stately Delaware. He and his boyfriend were like doting big brothers to me, and lived within a bubble of tasteful sensibility that soothed me with its beauty, order, and proportion—in less fraught moments. After walking the six blocks in high dudgeon, I rang the buzzer.

"Yes?"

"It's Candace."

"Oh!"

I took the elevator up to the fourth floor and knocked on his door. He opened it, a little abashed. "Hi, Candace! What a nice surprise. My friend Christopher is here. From my internship."

Somewhere in my consciousness, I sensed that this thirtysomething *real* adult was over at Frank's to talk about grown-up things, not to listen to his hot mess of a younger friend in thrift store clothes and statement shoes drink palliative beers and rant about Pam's betrayal for an hour.

Frank and Christopher did soothe me, bless them, and I left to go to the Old Pink and sit at the bar nursing a drink, too sad to even tie one on. Close to midnight, I quietly entered the apartment and went to sleep. In the morning, Pam was not up when I got up, for which I was grateful. I saw a wine bottle on the table, from a dinner we had shared a few nights back. She was keeping it to make a Phoenix Bottle. Noting that there were no cars driving by, I threw it out the third-story window and it landed on the street with a high-pitched, satisfying crash. Then I went to class.

Over the next few days, we had a rapprochement of sorts. I was used to having my feelings without having satisfaction, and this was just another level of that particular, precious hell. And it was also a lightening of my burden. Deep down I knew that Pam and I would never be that other thing. To go on living with her and it, constantly just slipping out of my grasp, as she brought me coffee, hugged me goodnight, wrote me cute notes, and mussed my hair, was to live in a state of acceptance of the almost, to look inside the windows of a party where everyone was eating sumptuous food at a beautifully laid table but taste only the rush of saliva in my mouth.

I brought with me to New York the sunflower tablecloth, the knowledge of how to eat for days on a dollar pot of pea soup, and a new standard—a model of living together with someone. When I lived with Pam, there was unspoken understanding, an alignment and a harmonious hum, despite the fact that I wished it to be more.

For the first time since Germany, my living space had cradled my spirit so I could thrive.

Almost Vegetarian

I came to New York City with a tiny amount of cooking experience, and so my first and last kitchen there was right-size. Standing smack dab in the middle of the narrow rectangle, I could reach out and *just* touch both of the longer walls with my fingertips.

Across the street, a pungent-smelling, chicken-overrun community garden thrived beside a school's concrete play yard, which emitted the aggregate screamy clamor of hundreds of children Monday through Friday, from 11:15 to 2:45. Their pent-up energy erupted from them, like toothpaste squeezed from a tube by a toddler's gleeful fist.

My kitchen sink was so shallow that the making of an egg caused it to overflow with dirty dishes. All it took was the pan, the plate, the fork, and the knife. The stove was meager but had four burners, and the oven worked. It was a far cry from the hot plate and "do your dishes in the bathtub" arrangement that some of my friends endured.

Two narrow, speckled Formica shelves ran along the wall, and a sunken cabinet housed my thrifted dishes, emblazoned with the motifs of the sixties and seventies. City scunge settled on everything, and I periodically washed it all down: the walls, the plates, the cups and mugs, the soup cans, and the shelves.

But it still took me a while to grow into the kitchen. I could spring into action to cook for company. I seldom cooked for myself, though, reasoning that in the city, it was cheaper and so much easier to order delivery and it was at least easier, if not cheaper, to eat out.

Elegant Japanese, cheap, veggie-studded Vietnamese, gratifyingly greasy Chinese, with never one mouthful exactly the same. The dense, rich Southern soul food I ordered to soften hangovers: crustacean-crispy macaroni and cheese, fried chicken, collard greens, finished off with chocolate bread pudding or banana cream pie, mashed unceremoniously into plastic pint containers.

I have no idea why I was not seven hundred pounds. If there were ever a time to enjoy my youthful metabolism's largesse, I couldn't have been in a better place to abuse its generosity.

But that was later. Initially, I was broke, unemployed, and job hunting. Barely getting by. Too poor to afford takeout, delivery, or even good, sturdy groceries for make-at-home dishes. Remembering Pam's econo-meals, I bought bags of dried beans, peas, and rice for cents, plus an onion, and got by. Salad days—ha! I couldn't afford salad. The mesclun and arugula, the tony goods on offer at the Union Square Greenmarket, were far beyond my grasp. Mine were soup days.

My first job, after weeks of panicky pavement pounding, entailed working as a foot messenger in Manhattan. Not even a bike messenger. That would have been truly badass. I was just a hoofer. And I was happy to be so.

Between the walking and chugging up and down subway steps, hauling mysterious envelopes and briefcases, and surviving on pennies a day, as well as the occasional dollar hot dog (with pickles, ketchup, mustard, onions, everything, including roach parts—extra protein), the chubbiness that seemed to sneak up on me whenever I wasn't starving melted off for a while. I was almost—mostly— vegetarian. Too poor to be picky when meat was the cheapest thing, too poor to buy meat otherwise.

Slim, with pixie-short hair and glasses, in thrifted calico cotton tank dresses, I stood out. Most foot messengers were wiry young guys from the boroughs or plodding, middle-aged male under- achievers with paunches and dolorous expressions.

"*You're* the messenger?" I heard a lot. "You don't *look* like a messenger."

They were often the only words I heard all day, besides the thoughts inside my head. Pressed in by crowds but parched for social contact, I was eager to parlay that opening into a few more sentences of chat, but they weren't interested. They were at work, doing their important jobs, and I was a pack animal. A young, hungry, impoverished pack animal, nonetheless feasting on the city's energy and its billows of glittering, taunting promise.

At the end of the day, I walked home in the gathering dusk, past basement-level restaurants that let out gusts of tantalizing aromas and tinkling bon vivant chatter.

On toward my neighborhood, through rings like a tree trunk's—the West Vill's avenues plushly encrusted with NYU's Left Bank–ish prosperity, the East Village's down-at-heels yet steadily gentrifying dazzle of cafés, bistros, bars, and boutiques—and on to my new home base: pre-Giuliani Alphabet City, its sidewalks dappled with kids on the nod, the low refrain of hooded drug dealers on every stoop humming out at me like beseeching old flames. The storefronts were bodegas and botanicas, Dominican bakeries with dusty plaster of paris wedding cakes in their windows, selling guava *pastelitos* and hot, creamy, sweet *café con leche*. And dry cleaners, dusty hardware stores, shoe repair places that offered for sale the mended shoes people never came back to reclaim.

I climbed up the four flights of tenement stairs, smelling a different dinner at each landing, unlocked my door, and ate cold beans and rice out of the pot in the refrigerator. I ate to satisfy hunger, alone, standing, no bells and whistles of flavor, no company, no pretty linens or seductive seasonings making it into an *experience*. It was just maintenance.

Sometimes I bought a pint of Ben & Jerry's Chunky Monkey ice cream, and if the night stretched on without a call from Helena and I didn't feel quite scrappy enough to brave the hipster blocks to write self-consciously in my journal in a café or bar, I'd eat the whole pint and then bring it back up.

But if I were too poor to even work the next day—because working entailed fronting money on subway tokens when I couldn't save by walking—I took the train to Long Island, using an old tattered family pass, and walked from the Lawrence train station to my mother's neighborhood in Inwood.

Lawrence was a posh, predominantly Jewish hamlet, all the more opulent in contrast with its shabby cheek-by-jowl neighbor, Inwood. On Long Island, class lines were drawn by a turnpike, a waterway, a shopping center. Here they were etched by the train's groove, a double scoring, aligned with the cliché: wrong side of the tracks.

My mother's dream life lay across the tracks. She would have loved nothing more than to be the pampered Lawrence wife of an attorney or stockbroker, accountant or surgeon. Instead, her latest valiant effort to escape from loathsome Bill landed her in Inwood, a Black Neighborhood.

Fresh from my totally liberal-politics college experience and years spent as a downtown Buffalo resident, I wasn't fazed. My mother, however, was vastly ashamed. It was what she could afford, as a school bus driver. And it was, at the very least, free from Bill. It was also in the Lawrence school district, which was very well appointed, despite the fact that my siblings felt like low-life trash in the sea of designer-clad girls and boys whose parents rented out Windows on the World and the Rainbow Room for their bar and bat mitzvahs.

I walked to my mother's house and let myself in. I rifled through the cabinets and ate whatever wasn't nailed down or clearly earmarked for dinner. I asked my mother for money, and she gave me what she had: $40 here, $40 there.

I could tell from her drawn expression that she had other plans for that money, but it didn't stop her. She knew I was struggling to survive and hopefully find a toehold in New York, to take my four years of college and parlay it into a viable livelihood. I just needed a little time and a few more sustaining handouts. It was classic postcollege mooching, done on a micro level.

Did I think about asking my father and stepmom for money? I knew better. It felt awful to be broke, but it would feel worse to be broke *and* shamed, accused of trying to sponge off them.

Mom didn't last in Inwood. She was soon accepting Bill's offers to take her to lunch, accepting, once more, his remorse as valid— that he was sorry and he would change, that he loved her. She flowed back into the plenty of reliable grocery money, dinners out, bills paid, a roof over her head. That she couldn't rely on the safety of her children or the peace of her household was the price.

I didn't last as a foot messenger, either. While waiting for my beeper to go off to alert me to my next pickup, I circled ads in *The New York Times'* Help Wanted section. An employment agency was looking for a secretary. Great! Working there, I'd scan the jobs and position myself for something good.

I walked to a pay phone and dialed the number. A garrulous woman picked up and asked me to come in that afternoon. I walked home, showered, changed into my best approximation of acceptable office wear, and took the subway all the way downtown to the small, shrunken streets in the shadow of the Woolworth Building. Ann Street, historic. The building's ceilings were low and the offices were mean. The woman, also named Ann, was thrilled to meet me.

For real? I mean, I knew I was smart and hardworking, and ablaze with *potential,* but I'd spent weeks being ground down by the profound knowledge that I didn't have experience. I needed to be given a chance, because I didn't have a history. My references were thin, my experience limited to internships and work-study jobs. But I knew German. Ann didn't see me as the secretary at this employment agency. She saw me at Commerzbank, in the German company's American HQ occupying three gleaming, marble-rich floors of the César Pelli–designed World Financial Center. This was her account, and if they hired me, she'd get a commission. They could find a secretary another day. After weeks of fretting, I had a real job. I was the new technical writer. My immediate supervisor was a perky woman named Philippa Roberts.

With my first paycheck came access. Suddenly, the doors of the city's more affordable restaurants and more expensive markets were open to me. Balducci's, Zabar's, Fairway, Gourmet Garage, Dean & DeLuca.

Work lunch choices abounded. The building's atrium, the Winter Garden, was decorated with stories-tall palm trees (which had understudies in the sub-basement, should one suddenly die or become infected with an unsightly bark disease).

Once I ventured out of the marble-and-glass carapace, the surface of the city held scads of options. There were cheap sushi and noodle joints, French fare, greasy diners, souvlaki carts, delivery Chinese, and pizza by the slice. Leaving one way meant taking a vast footbridge over West Street to the World Trade Center, dress shoes squeaking on the rubbery floor as people scurried along.

I spent many a lunch hour browsing and buying in the Rizzoli bookstore, which seemed like a gateway school of lifestyle to my callow young self. I paged through books while luxuriating in the sounds of plush opera arias and Spanish guitar noodlings that played over the top-notch sound system.

The cookbook section called to me, too. I wanted nothing more to do with pots of poverty soup, but eating out and ordering in was draining my bank account. I wanted to be inspired.

It was there that I found a book that seemed made for me. Its cover featured no gleaming-faced chefs, nor was it a tome or the be-all, end-all of anything. It was a soft-cover book with charming pastel lettuce leaves, mushrooms, and crucifers milling around on its cover.

Almost Vegetarian, "a primer for cooks who are eating vegetarian most of the time, chicken and fish some of the time, and altogether well all of the time." I was very "almost" at the time, and in these pages, "almost" was not just tolerated, it was celebrated.

Almost adult. Almost vegetarian (there were those hot dogs, and I'd recently become enamored of sashimi, and lamb korma and prosciutto and Kung Pao chicken and . . .) Almost straight, but aching to fall for a girl who'd reciprocate. Almost a poet, but I wrote fewer and fewer poems in the "real world" and had deferred the MFA program indefinitely. Was I anything? Was I everything? I was soft-boiled, not fully fired. It never occurred to me that I was well within my rights, at twenty-one, to be a mishmash, an exploratory opportunist. Almost a hipster, but I worked in the financial district. Almost corporate, but I lived in the barrio.

On Fridays, "professionals" gathered at the upscale bars on the World Financial Center's ground floor. I, in my growing-out pixie haircut and barely corporate attire, was terrified at the thought of entering the fray and possibly engaging with these brash bucks in their sharp suits.

But even if maybe, possibly, I had electrified some trader's libido, given that I was a dewy twenty-one and messenger-svelte, it would have entailed throwing around confidence that I was years away from cultivating (from the scorched earth up). Not to mention, I was more interested in women and trying to seek that one out. And it was a lot harder.

Trying hard meant staring at the ads for Let's Have Lunch!, a dating service promising to set me up with other women on my lunch hour. I was intimidated about finding out how much it was to join. And it seemed pathetic and terrifying. I imagined sitting down across from hard-boiled corporate lesbians with pointy hairdos, smelling of Liz Claiborne perfume, and my insides quailed.

Trying also meant mentioning my interest in women to Helena's friend Yetta, as we sat in Tompkins Square Park drinking iced coffee. Unfortunately, she was a snapcase.

"You bisexuals fucking ruin it for everybody! You want the best of both worlds, but you ditch out on lesbians and break their hearts because you always go to a man. You always go to what's easier. Who wouldn't? Fuck you bisexuals."

Yetta had had some issues with her last girlfriend, a woman from a traditional Korean family, who'd shacked up with her for a while and then left her for a man.

I was pierced, wounded, humiliated, furious, defensive, indignant, intimidated, terrified, green. I argued with her for quite some time, until her fury unleashed my tears. I felt humiliated. She was a bully with an ax to grind. But it did make the whole thing a lot scarier to deal with.

Trying hard also meant that I was still holding a big fat scented candle for Pam, who was upstate, living with Matt and working in his family restaurant. She came to visit every few months, which was wonderful. We made soup, smoked a profligate amount of cigarettes, made art, read poetry aloud, listened to our favorite tapes, and passed out in the wee hours of the morning on my futon, chastely spooning like twins in a wine-soaked womb.

My friends knew better than to expect me to do anything social when Pam came to visit. Outside of those sparse, ambrosial weekends, I went to bars with my friend Helena. And I did sometimes make my way to a gay bar with Emily, my best friend from seventh grade.

It felt just as awkward—nay, more awkward—to be in this lesbian bar, with its fair share of women who looked very truck driver–ish as well as cute, though extremely remote, women our age who had probably been playing musical girlfriends since the first day of freshman orientation at Smith. I wondered: *How do women ever pick each other up?* Emily and I had struck out heterosexually in junior high. But in a way, we had expected to. Would we fail in this arena as well? Did everyone think we were a couple? Or just invisible?

Going to lesbian bars was like finding myself in a dysphoric dream: hungry, smelling delicious food, but encountering fun house mirrors, dead ends, and mirages at every turn. Was it because I wanted it so badly, or because I was so afraid of how success here would destabilize my life everywhere else?

As I began to think about my exit strategy, I looked unexpectedly into the eyes of a lithe brunette with paper-pale skin and blue eyes. She looked like an accidentally pretty camp counselor. She held a beer in her hand, but unlike my drink, it was more like a prop than a lifeline.

"Hi," she said, with a faint Southern lilt. "I'm Deb."

So women introduced themselves to each other, casually, as if at a dorm mixer.

"Hi," I said. "I'm Candace."

I was at a college friend's Halloween party a few weeks later. In the way that I choose most Halloween costumes, I stood in front of my closet for about fifteen minutes before leaving for the party and figured out what I would be. I had a sword, a pair of loose white karate pants, a blousy white button-down shirt, and a big brown leather belt, so I decided to go as a pirate.

I sat in the wee, cat hair–dusted living room, drinking beer after beer with old college friends. It felt heavenly—like being in Buffalo without the obvious disadvantage of being in Buffalo. Without being Helena's maiden aunt. Cracking wise and reminiscing before we went back out into the night and were minnows in a very large body of water again.

Really, the night needed for nothing. But then a man walked in—not a boy, like the ones from college populating the room, but a tall man in jeans and a sport coat, a button-down shirt. He carried a heavy-looking leather satchel with an embroidered patch on it. He had auburn curly hair and a goatee, and was wearing glasses and a hat that covered up the beginnings of his male pattern baldness. His name was Daniel, and he shook my hand. Instead of drinking beer like us, he took a diet soda out of his bag and opened it.

During the course of the night, we chatted. He mentioned that he published poetry zines, and named a lot of prominent poets.

We decided to go to Veselka, the Ukrainian diner near the Poetry Project. Another girl came with us, and I wasn't sure whether Daniel liked her or me. At some point during the evening, I had begun to care. In his car, he handed me his leather satchel and I held it in my lap. The exchange was wordless, and in his small, met expectation, the idea of us bloomed like flowering tea in a glass pot.

Deb and I talked for another few minutes, then introduced our friends to each other. When it came time to leave, we all walked across town together, because Deb had an East Village studio apartment that she used to share with her ex-girlfriend but now occupied all alone.

"It's filled with all of our stuff, all jumbled up," she said. "I'm supposed to be separating it out, but it's hard."

"How did you meet her?" I asked.

"She was my women's studies professor," she said, with hints of embarrassment and pride. "We were together for eight years."

Deb got my number and called me, and even talked about me to mutual friends. "She's so young," she fretted.

"Whatever! I'm mature for my age!" I told Helena.

"I know, but twenty-one and twenty-eight are so far apart in terms of life experience," said Helena, who was just then *shtupping* a fortysomething-year-old NYU professor who'd been published in *The New Yorker.*

"We have a date next Saturday," I said.

"Have you kissed yet?" she asked.

"No, not yet."

She fixed me with her huge, serious eyes. "You *have* to kiss her soon, because otherwise you're going to fall into the friends category."

I'd dressed for the date with the particular awareness that I was going on a date with a woman. I wore jeans and Doc Martens and a T-shirt with a puffy vest. I think I even wore a *hat.* On the park bench, I felt equal parts a) like I was playing a lesbian in a play and b) really fierce, really good in my skin. "Dashing," I said to my friend Rachel before I left.

Deb and I hadn't talked about my sexual history, and I felt so uncomfortably like a giant sham that I haltingly disclosed that most of my dating experience had been with men, although I was trying to change that. She chuckled when I touched on Pam, the straight roommate I was in love with in college.

"Both of those things are normal," she said. "I know so many lesbians who have short hair and glasses and wear rainbow jewelry and let on like they're gold star lesbians, but if you actually start talking to them, they've dated plenty of men in the past."

It seemed like there was a point at which these men-dating lesbians had shifted, crossed over to the land of official lesbian-dom—and me, I was just sort of wandering around, hoping to fall into that particular rabbit hole or find a missing slat in the fence. But sitting here with Deb was a start.

We took the subway back to the East Village. I gave her a hug and went on my way.

"Did you kiss her?" asked Helena.

"Not yet."

"Ugh! You have to! You're going to end up turning into friends!" This had a different speed. (And looking back, I really could have used a lesbian friend.)

For our next date, I asked Deb to come over for brunch. It was a worthy occasion to test out *Almost Vegetarian*. I'd been reading the cookbook like a book—because it wasn't just a compendium of "Chicken *or* Tofu Whatnot." Diana Shaw had taken the time to pack the book with helpful tips and definitions: fresh herbs and their flavor profiles. Cooking terms. What to do with unfamiliar vegetables and when they were in season. What made jasmine rice different from basmati, morels different from shiitakes, and how to cook them. Back in 1994, she advised me to buy organic potatoes so that I could safely eat their skins.

I decided to make the lentil salad with sun-dried tomatoes and feta cheese, and serve it with a crusty baguette and mimosas.

Once Deb arrived, I made nervous conversation denuded of any kind of substance because I was set on kissing her—not because I necessarily felt drawn to kissing her, but because it had been decreed. I had never been so bold as to kiss someone. I had always been kissed. I had no idea how to initiate. But I did. After our meal, I reached up and kissed her, my hands brushing her slim hips in their worn denim.

Nothing. I felt like I was kissing my hand—back when I was a kid and wanted to practice. Her lips were soft and not unreceptive, but there was just no charge.

The kiss did not tip Deb into lust, nor did it seem to repel her. She was so languid, so low-key, that I wondered if she ever reached the heights of horniness that I felt pretty much all the time. We spent some more time talking, and then she went off to study.

I did a mortified little dance after the door closed behind her.

Daniel called after our meeting to ask me out on a date to a reading at Poets House, and in the elevator on the way up to the room, he put his hands on my shoulders and kissed me.

"I'd rather get that over with so that I can relax and enjoy our date," he said impishly. I was caught off guard and charmed.

The reading was about an hour and a half, and he spent the entire time stroking my back. It was a gamble. Many people would have found it annoying or presumptuous or uncomfortable, but being touched like that puts me into a catlike trance of pleasurable sensation. I all but purr.

I think he must have spent the day reading advice books for inexperienced men, because in retrospect, his moves seemed rather contrived. Kiss the girl before the date really starts. Touch her non-sexually for an extended period of time, because it will turn her on much more powerfully than groping her like a lout. But his moves worked. I felt like a warmed bowl of maple syrup in his palms, ready to be lapped up. And the one most dramatic thing of all was something he had no way of gaming.

"When's your birthday?" he asked.

"December twentieth," I said.

His mouth dropped open and his eyes widened. Then he grinned.

"No way," he said. "Show me your driver's license."

"Why? What?"

"Just show it to me." I pulled it out, slightly embarrassed about the dorky photo.

"Oh my God."

I looked at him, still lost. He pulled out his driver's license and gave it to me. His birth date was December 20 as well.

We were in just the right ready-to-be-besotted place to see it as a very auspicious sign. He, like Deb, was twenty-eight . . . and did he worry about my being too young for him? No. And so I fell into the current of having a boyfriend. Finally.

10

The Way to a Man's Heart

THE VERY FIRST Thanksgiving I hosted was catalyzed by the thought of my mother spending the day alone. She had left Bill yet again, and although this was the third or fourth time, I wanted to give her a place to go. Daniel's mother, Esme, invited us to her house, but I was drawn to creating my own day.

So Esme gave me a frozen turkey that she'd bought the year before, right after Thanksgiving, for $5, and lent me her hardcover 1982 *Martha Stewart Entertaining* book, such a nascent depiction of the figurehead that the floral arrangement on the cover is bigger than she is. Her Gunne Sax dress, white, ruffled, and eyeleted, matches the tablecloth and napkin perfectly. She even bears one corner of the tablecloth aloft, as if to say, *Isn't it clever that we match?* Her book revealed very ye olde colonial indoor Connecticut scenes, all done in such oppressively "good taste" that you empathize with the rabidly drugging Brat Pack offspring her clients produced.

Although Daniel had initially been game to spend Thanksgiving with my mother, my sister, and me, the day itself found him bereft. I expected that he would pitch in and do the day with me, but "I don't cook on Thanksgiving," he said. "I watch football."

"I need your help," I said. I handed him a dust rag and a broom.

When I came in a few minutes later to check on him, he was sobbing. "I miss my family!" he said.

"Why don't you go to your family, then?" I asked. "Really, I can do this on my own."

"No, no," he said. "You're my girlfriend and I should be with you."

He did a purposely slapdash job of dusting and sweeping, and then plopped in front of the little twelve-inch television, surly.

I was beginning to understand what my mother had felt like on Thanksgivings past. I had a stack of things to do, a messy apartment, and worse-than-no-help help, and was on my third crying jag of the morning.

Since we were in our twenties and from terribly toxic families, Daniel and I called each other fucking assholes and then retreated to our different corners of the apartment (which were less than twenty feet away).

One of the beautiful gifts of a long career of preparing the Thanksgiving meal is the understanding that the more you do in advance, the more you will sail through the actual day. I had no concept of this, so I was behind, shot through with adrenaline and cortisol—possibly in worse shape than the cheapo, cryogenically preserved turkey, which at least was kosher. I wasn't blessed by any rabbis, and any Jewish blood that I maybe had was from my mother's father (possibly another of my mom's wishful-thinking family "facts"), which didn't count—and that made Daniel's mother very, very unhappy. She'd refused to meet me for months; it appeared she preferred Daniel terminally single to his being in a relationship with a non-Jew.

The stuffing I made that day was a radical departure from my grandfather Jimmy's bread-based stuffing; it was composed of basmati rice, shiitake mushrooms, diced apples, and fresh herbs. Outside of the bird, it was a passable pilaf, but cooked within the cavity, it was drenched with roasted juices, each grain swelled to the utmost, almost a risotto. The apples were no longer apples, as their flavor had been surrendered to infuse the whole, which had turned around and infused the apple bits with broth. And the mushrooms, which I appreciated for the earthy meatiness they lent to vegetarian dishes, now threw their robust weight behind the turkey.

Once the stuffing was almost done, I turned to the turkey. My first bird. Per Martha's instructions, I slid my fingers between the skin and the meat, cleaving each from the fascia. I placed butter and sage leaves in between the layers, arranging the velvety oblongs in a mosaic pattern.

I was aware of the barbarism of my gesture, as well as the sensuality and tenuous nature of each centimeter gained. I had to see with my fingertips. And given my callow inexperience, I did rend the taut, thin skin near the thigh.

I washed my slick hands and spooned the rice mixture into the cavity, and sewed the opening closed with special twine and hooks. At that moment, the idle thought went through my mind that I could have, with the right encouragement, become a surgeon. I slid the turkey into the oven, a reverse birth.

Now on to the cider. Martha had remarked that the lovely thing about mulled cider was that it scented the home, like a potpourri. I poured the cider into a stockpot and added the cinnamon sticks and whole allspice.

"Daniel, could you stud these apples with cloves?" I asked. He groaned.

Twenty minutes later, after peeling the white and sweet potatoes, I came back to get the apples. He was still on the first one. He had made a Fabergé-inspired design on the sole apple, choosing and placing each clove as punctiliously as if it would be featured on Martha's next television show.

"Why aren't you done yet?" I asked.

"I'm only doing this during the commercial breaks, if the commercials are boring," he said.

I grabbed the apples and cloves and finished the job myself inside of three minutes.

"Serve hot from a large earthenware bowl," Martha advised. My stockpot (and my boyfriend) would have to do for the time being.

By the time my mother and sister rang the buzzer, the apartment was tidy, the oven was at full capacity, and the air was perfumed with the vapors of mulled cider. They came in, wreathed in smiles, smelling of damp, cold New York autumn and bearing plump, shapely pies.

I hugged them both tightly to me and said, "I'm so glad you're here."

When it came time to make gravy, my mother performed her magic, passed down to her from Grandma Marie. Pull out the bird, put the roasting pan on two burners, and heat the drippings to a fare-thee-well. Then fill a tall glass with water, put in a heaping spoonful of flour, and whisk it until there are no lumps remaining. Swirl it into the pan, stirring, stirring, as the floury water blends with the broths and drippings—and becomes perfect, flavorful gravy.

Before long, we crowded around the tiny table, my mother said grace, and we took our first bites. I had done it.

"Oh my God," Daniel said.

"What?" we all asked.

"There's no vegetable."

I looked at the spread. Turkey, stuffing, sweet potatoes, mashed potatoes, and gravy.

"The potatoes," I said.

"There's no *green* vegetable," he repeated. He shook his head with a smirk. "I can't believe you forgot the vegetable."

My eyes met my mother's and my sister's. Just as Bill was ejected from our family circle, had I ushered in a replacement killjoy?

I knew Daniel would bring home this failing of mine to his judgmental family as proudly as a cat brings home a dead bird.

"It's fine!" my mother assured. "It's a perfect meal. You did a great job."

"Thank you, Mom," I said.

Future Thanksgivings would be busy and sometimes complicated, but they'd never again be fraught with the panic of the unknown, or the presence of Daniel.

After I broke up with Daniel, I lost weight by the handful. Like my dad, he had offered me ice cream and candy at every turn, and I'd eaten many a rich meal with his food-obsessed family. I picked up with all of the friends whom I'd neglected during my relationship, walked all over the city, and trekked to rooftop raves in Williamsburg, where I danced for hours. I could have gotten married to Daniel, moved out to the 'burbs, and given up. There were moments when it seemed almost tempting. But I had dodged that bullet. I was twenty-three, and I was free.

Before the breakup, Daniel's sister had helped me get a job at a start-up magazine run by young socialites, *Manhattan File.* On some level, it was a step down—from a corporate technical writer to a glorified receptionist, from the full complement of top-notch benefits to shitty, expensive health insurance. But I was much happier paying my dues at a magazine than at a dry, boring financial institution. And I did not have to dress up. The editors were mostly nice and threw me the occasional article. I was hungry to have some published pieces, besides the ones I'd written in college. I could use the clips to send to more editors, and hopefully get more assignments.

A constant stream of flower deliveries arrived for the leggy, gorgeous, Prada- and Gucci-clad editors tucked into nooks in the industrial-chic SoHo space. Thousands of dollars of couture on loan swung through the entry doorway on garment racks, and models dropped by for go-sees.

Eighties literary hotshots Bret Easton Ellis and Jay McInerney called and stopped by, and I yearned to register for them as someone besides the girl holding down the front desk, but felt that saying I was a fan would hardly distinguish me in their eyes. It was satisfying enough to see that they were human, with rain on their jackets or mussed hair. They did live on the same planet and were only inches away, at least geographically.

Following a tip from an intern, I requested an informational interview at Condé Nast. I didn't think I'd be hired, but I couldn't be hired if I didn't apply, and so I met with them. I also heard that another magazine was looking for a film editor. I called and snagged an interview with Jack Burton.

I thrashed around in my closet and finally chose a long black satiny skirt, an off-white shell, Spanish-looking black Mary Jane heels, and a black jacket. It was far from cutting-edge chic, but it was all I had.

Jack's cramped magazine offices were in Midtown and smelled of stale clothing. The young guy who buzzed me in had circles under his eyes and looked me over wearily, as if my bunnylike excitement were sweet but reminded him of more idealistic times.

Jack sat before his computer, paused, finished tapping out a sentence, shook his head, typed something else, and then hit send. He stood up, shot out his hand to shake mine, eyes piercing under thick brows, his straight eyelashes reminding me of the solemn yet endearing gaze of an alpaca. His nose had been broken, his teeth had never seen the inside of an orthodontist's office, but his lips were full and sensual.

He had a five-o-clock shadow and wore a suit and tie with the jacket off, and his office carried a faint whiff of pungent body odor.

"So," he said, "let's have a look at your clips."

I pulled the folder out of my bag and handed it to him, and then sat down in the chair opposite his desk, trying not to be fidgety or slack-mouthed, neither to slump nor to have artificially erect posture.

Before he began reading, he stared at me. "How old do you think I am?" he asked.

That was odd. "Twenty-nine?" I asked, hoping that was a good answer.

"I'm thirty!" he said incredulously. "I can't believe it." He turned to my folder of neatly photocopied writing. A few minutes went by, interrupted by the crisp turning of pages.

"Well, you can write," he said. "Now, what kind of music do you like?"

This was a test, I knew. He was not just some jerk at a party, trying to figure out if I was a poseur or not. He was a culture-mag editor who had the clout to give me a string of story assignments.

"Well, Pavement, Buffalo Tom, Sarah McLachlan, Liz Phair . . ."

I could see his eyes glazing over. I cast about, named a few more: "Tori Amos, Fiona Apple . . ."

The glaze was turning into hardened shellac. "Lisa Germano . . ."

He snapped to attention, a grin transforming his grim demeanor. "Old Lisa Germano? Yeah! I saw her in Texas. Interviewed her. She's *really* great."

"Isn't she? I love her." Weird that the very dysphoric and sylph-like singer's name would snap open the door to his coolness chamber, but it had. Singing along to Lisa Germano's music helped me to lighten the weight of my demons without actually taking them on.

I'd thought that telling Jack I liked Lisa Germano would open me up to gentle ridicule. It was goth music channeled through a slight female singer-songwriter who played the fiddle.

But Jack was enthusiastic about our shared appreciation of Germano, and he gave me an assignment that night. And then he invited me to a god-awful futuristic sci-fi movie preview and placed his hand on the small of my back as we walked to our seats. And I invited him to a *Manhattan File* party and wore a red cashmere polo sweater dress, and we got really hammered. We shared a taxi home, and I started making out with him. He jumped out at my corner, and we went up those three flights and had the very best sex I'd ever had to date—not to say that I came, because I didn't, although I faked it quite admirably—while listening to Lisa Germano.

I liked him, but inextricably mixed up in that was that I *loved* the fact that someone like him—a successful editor who had been imported to New York from Australia—liked me. Even if he just liked me enough to sleep with me.

Suddenly, I saw a future self I wanted to be. She was not this self. She was someone I envisioned Jack's dream girl to be. Slender, worldly, glamorous, tough, striding around in great boots, with shampoo-commercial hair. I had no idea where this vision came from, but I wanted to be her.

He spent the night, left cheerily in the morning after having a cup of coffee, and then even called me later that day to check on me. Promising.

We met for drinks a few nights later. I'd wanted to go to a languid Middle Eastern–style lounge near NYU, but he demurred and suggested a Hell's Kitchen dive called Rudy's Bar and Grill.

As we sat and drank pints at one of the booths, I noticed that Jack was nervous and shifty-eyed. We talked about writing and the magazine world for a long time.

"Listen," he said, after about three rounds, "I don't want to date you, Candace Walsh."

I blinked at him, in another sweater dress—this time camel-colored and short-sleeved—that I'd bought expressly for this rendezvous. *Stupid,* I chided myself.

He explained that a girl broke his heart when he was twenty-three, and that was the end of dating for him. He picked up the pack of cigarettes between us on the table and pulled one out. I lit it for him. "Candace, you make me want to smoke cigarettes," he said. "And you're damned sexy. But this isn't going to work out the way you want it to."

I wasn't convinced. He just *thought* he didn't want to be in a relationship for the rest of his life.

"Well, Jack," I said, "I never said I wanted to be in a relationship with you. Let's just have fun."

Jack grinned. "We shouldn't," he said. "Let's leave it where it is. I want to be your friend, Candace. I want to help you become a better writer. Nobody took an interest in me when I was young. I had to figure it out by myself, and it was hard."

"Okay."

But when we stood outside, next to the Rudy's pig, he took me almost sternly by the shoulders, looked me in the eye, and said, "I'm going to give you a chaste kiss goodnight, and there will be *no* funny business."

I smiled up at him, a slight bit unsteady on my feet. His lips touched my cheek, and then my mouth, and then we were macking like two junior-high kids after the school dance.

"You're a bad, bad, tempting girl," Jack said, grinning.

He took me by the hand, hailed a cab, and gave the driver his Upper West Side address.

With Jack as my lover, and not just my mentor, more than my words came under his scrutiny. He critiqued my underwear, preferred me with straight hair, liked me to wear black leather boots and subtle lipstick.

I felt like Eliza Doolittle, but instead of my diction being parsed, it was my style that was up for redaction. I didn't *mind*. I got my hair blown out more often and lost weight from sheer erotic nervousness.

In spite of the fact that he was molding me into more of a glam, urbane type, that didn't take away my urge to cook for him.

"I'll have you know," he said, "that I won't eat red things or round things."

I was so used to following his dicta by then that his odd preferences didn't faze me. Could feeding him wipe his ex out of his heart?

"You know what I'd really like? If you made me osso buco."

Osso buco? What was that? It sounded fancy. I hadn't a clue. And I wouldn't rest until I figured it out.

Luckily, I didn't have to go far. My mother had given me a cookbook called *Simply Stews* for Christmas the year before. Susan Wyler, the author, was formerly the food editor at *Food & Wine* magazine, and her well-crafted copy pulled me in. The book contained not just a recipe for osso buco, but dishes my grandmothers were known for— my grandmother Marie's chicken fricassee, my grandmother Migdalia's *ropa vieja*—although their modest recipes were doubtless different from Wyler's. Pages 98 and 99: osso buco. To this day, those pages are splashed, stained, and creased with the evidence of courting Jack.

Braised veal shanks. No more was I almost vegetarian. This dish would banish me forever from that nebulous category. Per the advice of friends, I called up Esposito's Meat Shop a few days ahead and ordered four pounds, cut into one-and-a-half-inch lengths. I rode my bike to Midtown and picked up the hefty order, wrapped in white paper by the polite and matter-of-fact butcher. I bought the vegetables at the Key Food on Avenue A, and as I paid, a handsome fireman behind me in line asked me what I was making. He had a cart stacked with dinner ingredients for his company. I wondered if I was going for the wrong type of guy, but then checked myself. I didn't want to be a fireman's wife, not so much because of the danger as because I wanted to leave my working-class background behind.

Back in my kitchen, I unwrapped the package, unsure what awaited my eyes. They were oddly beautiful. Pink, marbled, rosette-like meat clustered around a central cylindrical bone, sometimes slightly hollow, sometimes packed with creamy marrow. As the heat seared the bottoms of the disks, traces of blood crept up through the marrow and bloomed through the flour. Instead of being nauseated, I was mildly fascinated.

By the time Jack arrived, bottle of wine in hand, the osso buco was finished and I had dashed off to change clothes, wash my face, apply makeup and perfume, and brush my hair.

"Well, well, well, what have we here?" Jack asked merrily.

"Doesn't it smell good?" I asked.

"Didn't you know? I don't have a sense of smell." He didn't? Seventy-five percent of taste came from smell. That wouldn't help me win him over with food.

"So, how's the writing going?" he asked.

"Okay. I feel like I should be writing a single-girl-writer-in-the-city novel. I've been making stabs at that."

"A single-girl-in-the-city story? I don't think anyone would want to read that," he said, about a year before *Sex and the City* was published. "What you should do is write about your college experience in Buffalo."

Jack ate the osso buco with relish, thanked me for making it, and then put down his fork and knife.

"Come on over here and sit on my lap," Jack said. "You're a good one, you are."

I called him a week later, after I hadn't heard from him. He'd been fired, and told me he was going to disappear for a while.

"I'm going to write a bestseller," he said, "and sell it for a lot of money. But until I do that, I'll be underground."

"O . . . kay," I said. "Are you sure you don't want any cheering up?"

"No. Thank you, though."

I had asked to be Jack's recreational lover, no strings, but his disappearance from my life stung. I watched Bogart and Bacall movies, brimming over with almost pleasurable melancholy, and put away the Lisa Germano CDs.

A few months later, I got a call from Condé Nast. The German division, which published *Deutsch Vogue, Architectural Digest, GQ,* and other magazines, needed an editorial assistant.

11

Jack and Coke

I WORKED ten-hour days at German *Vogue*, but when I was home on the weekends, I cooked. I wasn't sure what to expect at my new job, but it was busier than anything I'd imagined. The New York *büro* served as an esophageal system for the staff in Munich, Germany —and they were one hungry stomach.

Along with the photo material, Munich requested art books and scads of clothing and accessories samples for shoots that needed to be called in, logged, sent over, and then returned once they came back. It was important to check the contents of boxes against return-freight lists, since it was common for editors to keep certain items and then play dumb when those items didn't actually come back in the box. And when that happened, assistants were the ones who got the old stink-eye.

I stood in the doorway of my boss, Katja's, office. I never knew what kind of mood she'd be in. She greeted my coworker Diane and me with either glissandos of happy hellos or a pallid, squinting scowl.

"Katja?"

"*Yes,* Candace." Uh-oh. Bad Katja was steering the ship.

"I just unpacked the *Fracht* from Munich, and the list doesn't square with the contents. There's a bracelet missing."

"Are you *sure,* Candace?"

"Yes, I checked it two times."

"What is the maker?"

"Noir."

Sigh.

"All right, call Beate and ask her to double-check, and if she doesn't have it, call Noir to find out how much we owe them for the lost bracelet."

"Okay, thank you."

During my interview, I'd been enthusiastic at the prospect of working for Katja. She was a tall, strong, handsome woman with kinky dark-blond hair and good cheekbones. But then Diane gave me the scoop about Katja's dark side over drinks after work. Diane was tall and thin, with a pixie cut, large brown eyes, and a tendency to wave her long arms this way and that when she got excited.

"The last two assistants couldn't take it! They quit! That's how I got the job, when Tara left. And you're here replacing Heike."

I decided that I'd make sure to keep up my honeymoon period with Katja. Maybe she was tired of losing assistants and had turned over a new leaf. But then Diane went on vacation and handed over the fashion-shoot responsibilities to me. She explained everything quickly, saying, "It's all in this binder, but you probably won't need to deal with it while I'm away. The shoot isn't for two weeks."

"Okay."

The Monday after that, Katja came rushing out of her office.

"Candace, *watsisdasdurchgelaut mit dem* shooting?"

I stared at her. My German, after a decade of disuse, was still rusty.

"What are you, *stupid?* Why are you looking at me like that? I have Klaudia on the phone. She wants to know about the Calvin Klein look for the double-face shooting!"

There were at least six shoots in that book, and each one had upward of twenty outfits. I pulled the binder out and turned to the shoot.

"Oh, *give me that.* Jesus!" She ripped it out of my hand, flipped the pages rapidly, found what she was looking for, and then slammed the binder on my desk with a bang and stomped back to her office in her black leather APC boots.

Whoa. I was shaking as I blinked back tears. *What just happened?* It was just like Diane had described. Maybe worse. And she did not apologize. She sulked for the rest of the day, and then the next day came in all smiles and trumpeting *Guten Morgen*s.

That was Katja. I never knew which one I'd get.

My college friend Effie always had stories about her coworkers, too. Her boss was a petty whiner, according to her, and she had bonded well with Tom, a tall, thin, blond, alt-musician-handsome guy who went to a live-music bar every day after work for happy hour. He was kind of like a less elongated, more acerbic version of Sonic Youth's Thurston Moore.

Effie didn't go too often because "the music is *awful*," she said, and the crowd tended to be really white and suburban. Effie was African American, but had been adopted by upstate New York WASPs as a baby. She had no time for hicks, especially in the city. But she talked about Tom a lot, and I wondered if she had a secret crush on him, or fought against it. Tom had a girlfriend—also African American, but unlike Effie she was tiny—barely five foot, small-boned, with long wavy hair.

"Tom does *coke*," Effie said at one after-work party, with a mixture of fascination and ironic disapproval.

"Really?" That seemed edgy, and yet a lot of people around us— in our work worlds, age groups, neighborhood bars—were doing at least one drug on a semiregular basis. It was a time when the city was like one big party, and Effie and I were trying to figure out if we were in the room with the cool kids or the goobers.

"Yes, he has a *dealer*."

Effie and I had already weathered the wave of heroin chic that had fallen on downtown like a giant outstretched manta ray. Heroin held no allure for either of us; it involved needles, disease, vomiting, and staring off into space with a slackened jaw. It turned people into junkies, and it was apparently near impossible to kick. The ex-junkies we knew of seemed to forever have a bleached, cadaverous look about them. "Just *no*," as Effie would say.

But coke had an altogether different reputation. It seemed folded into the nervy, go-go energy of the city. Wall Street people did it.

Moguls did it. Club kids, DJs, celebrities, fashion designers, writers, and socialites did it. I had even dreamed about it a few years before. In the dream, when I took it, I finally felt right inside—completely perfect.

In fact, one of the top jewelry companies had sent all the Condé Nast fashion assistants a silver coke spoon necklace as a holiday gift—which I didn't realize until Dave, the mailroom manager, pointed it out. I had thought it was just an abstract design.

"Wow." Effie and I were both thinking the same thing: If Tom had a dealer, then we could get it very easily.

So that Saturday, Tom scored for Effie and handed it over to her. We gave him cash and then went on our way.

My odd dream had been right. Whatever I was missing inside was more than restored by cocaine. We did a line in a bar bathroom, then went out and ordered beers. The beer became irrelevant, because, *slam,* we suddenly had so much to say, and it was all important. We *had* to tell each other everything that occurred to us.

The rest of the night became a blur of bar hopping, line doing, dancing, and jabbering. We smiled for so long that our faces hurt, but even the hurting-ness of our faces felt good. Everything felt so good, I was panting—like a rain forest jungle animal at the prime of my vitality.

A few hours after the last blast was gone, Effie and I emerged from a club and walked the twenty blocks to our neighborhood. As dawn crept in, I suddenly felt bereft and hollowed-out, as if a giant joke had been played on me: I was awesome and perfect, fascinating and capable of feeling really, really good.

Psych!

I was not. I was just another of the millions of New Yorkers, but one who hadn't gone to sleep yet, passing healthy, hale folks on their way to the gym or to a good cappuccino or a day of writing the next book of note. The sinking sensation inside me gained momentum.

"Well," Effie said, "bye." We were at the corner where she would go toward her apartment and I'd go toward mine.

"Oh. I kind of don't want to be alone," I said.

"Sorry, I'm going to go home and go to sleep," she said. "I'm tired."

"Okay." We hugged goodbye. I felt like an old person.

I walked to the corner newsstand and bought a Sunday *New York Times*. I craved its heft as an anchor. But I didn't want to go home yet. Not to the anxious cats, the dirty kitchen, the piles of laundry. No. So I walked some more and decided to sit down against a tall chain-link fence that bordered the community garden across the street. I flipped through the paper for a while but then realized how deeply ridiculous it was for me to be sitting on the city sidewalk at 5:30 AM, still in last night's clothes, earnestly reading *The New York Times*.

I hoisted my sore bones upward and went home. Through the big heavy wooden doors, up the stairs, and into my apartment, where the cats suddenly seemed precious, the best warm loving furry things a girl could ever have. I peeled off my tight, punishing clothes, unzipped the snug leather boots from my swollen feet, and climbed gratefully into mismatched flannel plaid pajamas. The top was from my mother and the bottom was from my father, and I entered them the way a prodigal child would enter the family property. Grateful, guilty, loved anyway. And sleep swept over me, blunting the rigors of the drug's peelout.

I woke up at 4:00 PM, famished. I'd skipped three meals since the beginning of my bender. I called up New Saigon and ordered Kung Pao chicken, steamed pork dumplings, and a soda. The food delivered right to my door was not only convenient, but a form of being nurtured—and I was at a very undernurtured time in my life. I was single in a city filled with other people who were looking out for number one.

I had no idea how to take good care of myself, besides generally going to sleep before midnight, bathing quasi-regularly, and doing my laundry when I absolutely had to (I often bought fresh underwear to delay the inevitable).

I also had a really hard time paying my bills on time—even though I usually had the money to pay them. I had inherited my parents' financial dysfunction, and the idea of getting on top of my money situation was too overwhelming.

I didn't work out, do yoga, or eat enough fruits and vegetables. And whenever I ate to the point that I felt too full, I made myself throw up. Just like in fourth grade, when I put my finger down my throat to play sick and get sent home, now I did it to press the rewind button on overindulgence.

This behavior went hand in hand with eating in restaurants, especially if my father took me out to dinner. I ate everything on my plate automatically, because he had forced me to do so all through my childhood.

I ate it all because it was one of the very few times that he wasn't stingy or withholding, and my whole being craved his benevolence. I gobbled up his treating me. And then the volume and the richness of my restaurant portion began to throb in my stomach, along with a sickened dread that I would blimp out.

But I didn't just do that when I was out with my dad. I also did it after work dinners, another form of complicated benefactor food-gifting.

Big deal, I thought—I wasn't bulimic. I didn't binge, outside of those particular circumstances, and how could a binge be one single meal, anyway? If I actually had an eating disorder, I'd be a lot thinner than I was—a diffident size 12, and in the fashion industry, that was downright grounds for an intervention. My mother's lifelong unhappiness with her postmaternity body, and my college classes about oppressive societal norms, made chasing thinness unattractive to me.

So my food thing was complicated, but not as bad as my spiritual life, which was truly anorexic. After casting off Christianity, I still retained the assumption that any other spiritual path was even worse, or creepily occult.

I loved writing more than anything but wrote sporadically, and the thought of pitching editors terrified me. I drank whenever the opportunity presented itself, and now I had become someone who had done cocaine, a really hard drug. And I had loved it.

I'd made it to the age of twenty-three without therapy—but then it became too hard to ignore that I needed it. I got a referral from a friend and began to see Dr. Morris. The day of my first appointment, I was so nervous—more nervous than before dates or job interviews. I felt like I was about to jump out of a plane. I got to the address early and then walked up and down Horatio Street like a stalker until the exact time.

I climbed the steps and rang the doorbell. Within a few seconds, Dr. Morris opened the door. She was a petite older woman with short auburn hair, well-sunned freckly skin, fine bone structure, and blue eyes. As soon as we reached the third floor and sat down, as *soon* as my butt sank into the soft cushion of the upholstered blue chair, I opened my mouth and, before I said one word, I started sobbing, much to my embarrassment.

It was as if an entire life spent pretending everything was okay had just been surrendered and we could at last get down to the business of salvaging and salvation. I'd wanted to see a therapist in junior high school, but my mother said no.

"What do you need to talk to a therapist for? You can talk to me."

Oh, great.

Dr. Morris was a strict psychoanalyst, not the kind of therapist who told me anything whatsoever about herself. Her office was a finished attic with glass jars of antique marbles, ornate Indian embroidered hangings encrusted with tiny mirrors, and tasteful paintings. She collected antique toys and dolls, including teddy bears that looked like they once belonged to Teddy Roosevelt.

Sadly, I often couldn't even get my act together enough to get there promptly, and then we had to spend what seemed like the whole session discussing the significance of my being late—which I thought was a further waste of time. When I did get there on time, we talked about the things that hurt me in my childhood. There was so much fodder.

"What would you say to your father if you could talk to him about that right now?" she would ask.

"What do you want to tell your mother?"

"How does that make you feel?"

She didn't think I should go on antidepressants. She thought that our therapy would resolve the underlying issues that were causing me to be depressed.

The one thing I could count on at Dr. Morris's house was that I would leave with a face so swollen and tear-stained that I looked deformed. In her office, I cried about whatever was bothering me in the present, and then I cried even harder about what it reminded me of from my childhood, and I cried as I hollered things at my parents, who weren't there, in Dr. Morris's attic, which was an admittedly powerful act even if it felt like a very uncool thing to do.

But there were no-fly zones in our sessions. I didn't tell her that I usually couldn't orgasm without a lesbian sex scene running in my head. And I vowed that I wouldn't tell her I had done cocaine.

My one hour a week with Dr. Morris was so important to me that I practically counted the minutes. The hour always flew by, and when I left, even though my face did look like a ruddy apple fritter, my soul felt washed, dried, steam-ironed, folded, and put away on a clean shelf, like a beautiful cotton sheet.

And then my real life pulled it down, dragged it through mud, and stomped on it. But at the end of the week, my session awaited.

As I waited for the food to arrive, the phone rang.

"Hello?"

"Hello there, it's Jack. How are you going?"

"Jack?"

It's Jack, it's Jack!

"Candace?" he asked.

"Yes," I said with all the stoicism I could muster.

"How are you?"

"Good."

"Are you grumpy with me?"

Yes.

"No. I'm just tired," I lied.

"At 4:30 PM?"

"It's a long story."

"Been up to some mischief, have you?"

"Definitely."

"Well, I've been experiencing no mischief. I've been writing, writing, writing. And I've finished my quota of chapters, and I'm ready to come out and have some fun."

My exhausted body still managed a little erotic jolt in response to that last sentence.

"Cool."

"So I thought, *I'm going to call up Candace and ask her to meet me for a drink.* I want to check out this place called Australia, the Bar. Can you imagine? It will be awful, but I really do have to have a look."

"We should definitely do that soon."

"What, are you busy tonight?"

"Yes, I have plans."

I normally wouldn't have put Jack off, but the exhaustion of having done cocaine for the first time trumped my desire to see him. And I couldn't exactly tell him that I was hungover from my first coke bender. Or I didn't want to.

Powdered Sugar and Spice

JACK AND I met for drinks about a week later, and we spent the night together. He seemed much more tender than he'd been in the past, and told me that he missed me terribly. I wondered if he was rethinking his decision not to properly date me.

But at breakfast, he confessed that he now had a girlfriend—a woman named Cullen he'd met at Australia, the Bar. He claimed not to have feelings for her—that he'd gotten together with her because she was the super of a Brooklyn apartment building and had offered to let him jump the list. But he knew that arrangement was contingent upon his turning what was probably a one-night stand into an official relationship. He assured me that I was the one he thought about constantly. "I really missed you, Candace. It was awful being apart."

I should have left him in his new Cullen ménage, but I had missed him, too. I'd felt haunted by his absence, seeing every movie as if I were channeling his reaction, dressing up to go out as if I'd be running into him. Now I had him back, but I was the other woman. It was initially exciting, but then I grew miserable. When he wasn't with me, I didn't just miss him; I pictured him playing the role of boyfriend with her. And so if I was on the train, or sitting on my bed, or on a park bench, or anywhere that didn't demand my attention, I went back in time and relived the experience of time spent with Jack. It was almost like spending more time with him and less time alone.

I told Dr. Morris about it. "I feel like I should fight it."

"Why don't you just go with it, instead of repressing it? See where it takes you."

Bad advice.

Once Effie and I popped our coke cherries, more opportunities came up. Upstate friends were visiting and wanted to do it. Diane and her club-kid friends did it, so work-related events with her became fair game. And when I let my new activity slip to Jack, his eyes lit up. "Count me in! Love the stuff." Coke wasn't just fun, it was one more thing I could use to lure Jack to me. I needed both to feel good.

Taking an Ativan as I was coming down threw a warm, fuzzy blanket over the harsh edges, and giving myself the next day to recover made the process less brutal. I slept for most of the day, ordered in food, and watched a movie or two, and then the next day was Monday.

My parents, of course, had no idea. And when I went home to visit my dad and stepmom, I was anything but a hard-drug-doing partier. I helped my father paint the attic, took my little sisters to the park, and pushed them on the swings. I cooked dinner for everyone, or sat outside with my stepmother in the backyard at dusk. We drank unapologetically sweet local wine as we popped boiled garbanzo beans out of their skins. I became obsessed with hummus after trying the stuff at Mamoun's Falafel Restaurant. It was nothing like the dense gunk I'd tasted at Buffalo's women's studies class potlucks; it was silken with tahini and olive oil.

We also went berry picking with my sisters and made shortcakes and jams. Although I wasn't fond of the cheesier aspects of hailing from Long Island, there were still stretches of rural splendor out there amid the strip malls and subdivisions. And there was something about working on a long, monotonous task with another woman that felt healing and timeless—as if we were carding wool together, or shelling peas. I talked to my stepmother about Jack, not telling her about Cullen or our tendency to get hammered and go on coke binges together.

"It's fun to hear about your adventures in the city, Candace. I'm an old married fogey with kids now, but your stories bring me back to when I worked in Midtown and used to party at the Limelight."

While she was living vicariously through me, I was beginning to notice a desire building steadily inside me. In the thickly forested backyard where I had played as a child, climbing trees, running on leaf-strewn paths, that desire asked to be noticed and spoken.

I wanted to settle down and make babies. And I wanted to do that with Jack.

Never mind that Jack was not the marrying kind, nor the fathering kind, nor even my boyfriend. Never mind that our idea of fun was to put a bag of white stuff up our noses and drink beer as if it were water, jabber about the famous writer Jack was going to be and how much he wanted to Pygmalion-neophyte me into something worthy of his sensibility—*his,* because I was too young to have one yet.

Despite my scorn for most of the kids I'd grown up with who graduated from high school and college and then got *married* and had *babies,* like mindless breeders, it turns out that I was the type of person who was only a few years behind them in the clamoring-ovaries department.

I wanted to be an urban mom—to take my kids to Tompkins Square Park and to Serendipity for Frozen Hot Chocolate, to fold little shirts and pants, and to let them run around in the Museum of Natural History, in the shadows of towering dinosaur skeletons. I could still write, I was sure, while they napped.

But my right brain didn't let my left brain ask too many other logistical questions. It was quickly becoming too flooded with estrogen to go there.

Canned and Green

ONE NIGHT I was at the Victoria's Secret Fashion Show at the Plaza, watching Naomi Campbell flounce by, mere feet away, her perfect bum barely covered in gauze, huge wings extending from her shoulder blades. After months of tears, recriminations, grandstanding, and nagging, I had managed to get Jack back from Cullen. He was legitimately my boyfriend, and I could call him whenever I wanted. He still lived in that building and she hated his guts, not to mention mine, but I sensed that she would not try to kick him out, and that he would not leave as an act of gentlemanlike repentance. No way! Cheap rent in New York has caused people to be far more unchivalrous.

I had just celebrated my one-year anniversary at German *Vogue* and been promoted to assistant editor. I'd visited HR to explore moving to something that was a better fit for me, but the woman I met with had been less sunny about my prospects, hinting that *Vanity Fair* was out of my league because I wasn't connected enough. "You really should let your current editor know before I can do anything for you. Once you do, I can start looking for something."

Katja didn't take it lying down. From that day forward, she looked at me with jaundiced eyes. And the HR chick didn't offer a single opportunity, which made me wonder if Katja had asked her to bench me.

But that wasn't on my mind at the fashion show. I called Jack and told him to come meet me. The drinks, the food, the people-watching—I wanted to share it with him. He threw on his second-hand pin-striped Paul Smith suit, jumped on the subway, and joined me. We canoodled and drank champagne and ate chocolate truffles, and then decided to leave. I was handed a goodie bag on my way out and knew the contents would be choice.

Back at my apartment, I pulled out perfume, moisturizer, a gift card, and a red see-through baby-doll nightie and matching thong. Just like the one Naomi wore!

I walked over to the top drawer of my dresser and pulled out my little tin of coke.

"Candace, really? It's a work night. It's not a good idea."

I was drunk on champagne; reason held no water. "Pshaw," I said, and offered him the first line. No more complaints from that corner. Next came me trying on the Victoria's Secret getup and dancing around to Blondie while he watched from the bed.

"C'mere," he said, smiling. I pounced on him, aglow.

"I love you," he said, for the first time.

"I love you, too!" I replied, flooded with a whole new array of good brain chemicals, on top of the dopamine. We talked and I danced, and we had sex and talked some more, and then fell asleep before dawn. The alarm went off at 7:30 AM.

"Oh, no, turn it off." I felt like I had been run over by a Zamboni.

"You have to go to work," he said.

"I have time. Katja has therapy this morning," I said. When we were chummier, I had turned her on to Dr. Morris. We got up slowly, got ready, and walked to Broadway and Bleecker, and I kissed Jack goodbye.

As soon as I got to my desk, I saw Katja beside it in battle stance, hair sproinging every which way, nerves jumping around in her jaw. I guess she didn't have therapy that morning.

"Candace, you are forty-five minutes late. What gives? You didn't call! This is unacceptable. What do you have to say for yourself?"

"I'm sorry. I overslept." Lame.

"You overslept? That's no excuse; you should have called."

"I should have. I'm so sorry."

"You took for granted that I'd be at therapy and thought you could get away with it!" Pretty much. I did my best to look penitent.

"This is bullshit!" She spun on her heel, went into her office, and closed the door. Then she opened it. "You know, Candace, if you want another job, you should just quit. I won't miss you."

Like I could afford to do that. The next morning, I had therapy with Dr. Morris. My stepfather came up. "What do you want to say to your stepfather?" she asked.

"I really don't want to say anything to him." He had tried to kill me, gotten away with it, had even taunted me afterward. I had never addressed it in therapy because it seemed too scary. I still remembered my neck, bruised by his handprints.

She prodded me until the boil popped open. Although I had hollered plenty of things at the brick walls of her office, nothing compared to this. I screamed. I cried. I shook. I pummeled the couch. I'd been beaten and berated, force-fed and shamed during childhood, but Bill managed to take one more thing away from me: the expectation that I would live out my life without being unexpectedly, fatally attacked by someone close to me.

I was in the middle of this fury when she said, "We have to stop now."

"But I can't! I don't know what to do with all of these horrible feelings. I have no idea how to function out there."

Ever the strict analyst, she looked at me levelly and said, "We have to stop now."

I got up, grabbed a wad of tissues, and said, "Thanks."

I always walked from Dr. Morris's office to work. I usually stopped at Magnolia Bakery to select a cupcake, a soothing post–doctor's visit treat more appropriate for a little girl, but this time, I didn't. My body was walking across town, but my spirit was still in my teenage bedroom, struggling not to die as the seconds ticked by.

At least work would distract me. I walked toward my desk and Katja came to her doorway, her eyes narrowed, face drawn.

"Candace, I want you to come into my office, please."

Fine. I put down my purse, walked into her office, sat down. She shut the door. Not good.

"Candace, I need to talk to you about your performance. I am not happy with you lately."

"In what way?" I asked, almost dully.

"The photo editors complained to me that their request for old pictures of Madonna was not adequately filled."

"Yes, Madonna *bought up* all of those old photos, Katja. There aren't any. I told them that. Call the photo agencies if you don't believe me. I must have called forty."

"And the Gucci shoes went missing from the return freight."

"Yes, they did. We all know that things get 'lost' every now and then in between Munich and here. You were there when I unpacked the duffel. And then we saw the paparazzi photo of Traüdel wearing the very same shoes at the Joop party."

"Damn it, Candace, stop making excuses!" She brought her hand down and hit the desk next to me. "You have some nerve!"

"No, Katja. I'm not the problem."

"What?"

"You're the problem. You're the one who can't keep your assistants. They've told me all about your episodes, your rages, your poor treatment, your instability. And I've also seen it firsthand. It's not appropriate to call people stupid. It's not appropriate for you to hit things and throw things and yell. You can try to make your problems into my problems, and you can keep going through assistants so that you don't have to be accountable, but I see the truth and so does everyone else."

She sat there still, eyes glazed with a sudden wash of tears, her mouth clenched like an angry child's.

"Will that be all?" I asked.

No reply.

"I'm going to go back to work now, Katja. We're on deadline, as you know."

Katja stayed in her office with the door closed for hours. My phone rang and I picked up. It was Ann Haxell, from human resources. Was this some amazing piece of fate? She wasn't the one I had worked with previously, but I was ready to think that I was being delivered from Katja's little fiefdom to another position, after all my hard work and forbearance.

"Hello, Candace. Would you please come and meet with me at 1:00?"

"I should be able to do that."

"Katja is aware that we will be meeting."

That wasn't quite so encouraging.

I got off the phone and walked over to Diane. "Ann Haxell wants to meet with me today."

Diane's eyes widened. She ran her finger across her throat. "She's the henchwoman of Condé Nast. You might as well start packing up your desk now."

And so my tenure there was cut short. No more sample-sale invites, five-party weeks, goodie bags, breakfast at Tiffany's, showers of holiday gifts, first looks at shoots, fashion show seats; no more being matchy-matchy with Naomi Campbell, no more oohs and ahs over where I worked.

And I had never been fired. I was surprised at how very devastating it was. I woke up in the morning and cried because nobody expected me. Work had been the one thing I'd been really good at. I'd been moving along, closer and closer to becoming a magazine staff writer, paying dues, trading up, but I had just been kicked down the stairs into the basement by Katja's boot.

I prayed that I would not see her in the city while on my bike, because I really didn't think I could keep myself from mowing her down.

The ifs. I could still be working there if I hadn't done coke, or if I had done coke but had called with some cockamamie excuse about why I was going to be late. I would still have my job if I had *not* followed the HR woman's advice about applying for a transfer after a year, if I had stayed put and let Katja think I still wanted to work with her indefinitely.

I definitely would have kept my job if I hadn't gone to work still unhinged from my therapy session—topic: my stepfather. So in a way, he had struck again—the poison of that day had shot into my current life and gotten me fired.

But now, as much as I was sad about not working for that company (I certainly didn't miss Katja), I at least had six months of unemployment checks queued up, and my apartment was so cheap that I could easily live on that money.

Katja had dealt me a deep blow, but she had also done me a huge solid. It would be like having a trust fund. This was my chance to write.

Oddly enough, another comforting thing about my shit-canning was that Jack and I now had that in common. It could bring us closer. And I'd have more time to spend with him. We'd both be writing.

"Walsh, it's time for you to write *Buffalo Stories,*" he said. He handed me a white binder. "Buy a ream of hole-punched paper, and every day, print your daily output and put it in the binder."

His surety was comforting. He really did believe that I should write up stories in which a guy who wanted to hook up with my friend Denise came over to her dorm room, drank liquor while on antibiotics, passed out, pooped in his pants, and had to be rolled up in a scrap of rug and carried out by his friends. Jack thought that would be a hit, along with the story of how Janie went from being cool to slutty after having sex with one too many guys, and then shaved her head and everyone forgot about the slutty thing and liked her again.

I wasn't sold, but I also didn't have any better ideas. So I sat and wrote for a few hours here and a few hours there. I also went to the gym a few times, and sat in Limbo Café drinking cappuccino and writing letters at 11:00 AM, and walked by the river, and wandered around the basement of the Century 21 department store, and visited my makeup artist friend Barbara at Bergdorf Goodman, where she gave me a free pick-me-up makeover. It didn't take me too long to figure out why all the nonworking trustafarians I knew were doleful and unsteady: Nobody expected them.

And I went to therapy.

"Dammit, I can't believe *Katja* comes here and sees you. I can't believe that after what she did to me, she pays you to listen to her say bad things about me. I can't believe she lies on this very same couch! I need to come here and get over this horrible trauma, but all I can think about is how you help her, too! In this room!"

It was like having to share my mother's breast with my worst enemy.

"She probably feels smug that she still gets to go to you even though she got rid of me."

"How does that make you feel?"

"No!"

"What do you want to say to Katja?"

"I already said it, every word. That's why I got fired. And I said it all because I was so messed up after our last session. You led me to this deep, dark, ugly place, I didn't have enough time to pull myself back together, and the repercussions were bad."

"We have to stop now."

I turned to her and looked in her eyes, pleading. She didn't say a word, but she looked grave, even regretful. She couldn't terminate Katja now because of what happened outside the walls of her office, but she could have declined to see Katja in the first place, as many therapists do when they don't want that kind of overlap. I'd given the card to Katja because I wanted her to get help and I knew Dr. Morris was good. I'd wanted to bring Dr. Morris a client because I wanted to please her.

I hadn't yet learned that if I didn't factor in protecting and pleasing myself, I'd have no one but myself to blame when things went wrong.

But fired, I had more time to entertain, which I made a point to do, since it cheered me up and kept me occupied. I even made a big pot of paella in an attempt to win over Jack's ex-girlfriend Danielle.

Danielle was red-haired, plump, and in her thirties. She was Jack's age, but she had been svelte once and hadn't had to cover her gray, hadn't had little lines and that English skin that seems to get thin and sheeny. I was so glad Jack wanted me to meet her. It felt like I was becoming more legitimate meeting such a good, old friend.

It would be wonderful to have an ally, a confidant, to ask for advice. I wanted her to like me. She wasn't prepared to, and she didn't miss a chance to throw catty pot shots my way, but she ate my food and drank my wine anyway. What a waste of shellfish and stirring!

Once I realized that providing an apartment full of friends with lamb chops and shellfish was unsustainable on my new fixed income, I went back to my grandmothers' Depression-era budget meals.

I made *ropa vieja,* not from my grandmother Migdalia's recipe, which I didn't have, but from the *Simply Stews* cookbook. I gave some leftovers to my stepmom to bring to my dad for dinner. "Don't tell him it's *ropa vieja,*" I said. "Just tell him it's beef stew." Now three generations of us women—my grandmother, my mother, and I—had participated in getting him to eat Cuban food without his knowing it.

I also made chicken fricassee, pulling every shred of chicken off the carcass, becoming intimately aware of all of its caverns and odd, dark bone nubs, adding white wine and plump halved bella mushrooms to the sauce. My grandma Marie was now in a home with advanced dementia, so I was glad that I had her recipe.

One day, Jack told me that he was going on a trip.

"I'm going to the Czech Republic for three weeks," he said.

"What?"

"Yeah, Danielle's friend Zusana went back home, and I need to do some research for my next book. You see, her dad was a big muckety-muck under the Communist regime, but after the 1989 revolution, they lost everything and now live very modestly. I really want to chat him up."

"Why are you going for so long?"

"Well, I might take the train into Paris. And check out Prague."

"How are you paying for this?"

"My mum agreed to fund it."

"Can I come?"

"No, don't be silly, I am staying with Zusana's family. I can't impose further by bringing you, too."

"Why don't we stay in an inn or something? It can't be very expensive."

"No."

"Why not?"

"Look, Candace, the answer is no." He shot me a truculent look and uttered the word that I knew was a kind of warning: "Settle."

Why did I have to be such a jealous, paranoid idiot? But I felt like Jack and Zusana had something going on. I felt it in my body, hairs standing up on the back of my neck. Zusana was even younger than I was. At twenty-five, I feared I was already aging out of his sweet spot.

To quell the beast, I wrote a self-reproachful essay about my jealous tendencies, but when my friend Raven read the essay, he said, "Candace, this isn't about someone being irrationally jealous. The stuff you describe would make anyone jealous."

I wanted to believe him.

14

The Cake Bible

THE DAYS LEADING UP to Jack's departure were hard for me, but I knew better than to be difficult about it. The night before he left, he came over for dinner. I wish I could say I made a meal of red things and round things, but no. Pork chops.

"I brought you something," he said. He pulled a vintage-looking hardcover out of his bag.

"It's old Nora Ephron's *Heartburn*," he said. "Now that I'm poor, I go to the Goodwills in Brooklyn and I steal books. And this book caught my eye. You know, it's really quite good. I thought you should read it."

"The story about how her husband cheats on her?" I asked. My mother saw the movie and expounded for days on the phone about how much it reminded her of her own life with my father. "*The betrayal!*"

She also felt the same way about *Terms of Endearment, The Piano,* and *Beaches*—basically, any tearjerker.

"It's good writing."

"Thank you." The cover art showed a big red valentine-style heart in a pot over flames, a little satyr-bottomed devil stabbing it with a pitchfork, just to add insult to injury.

A second book arrived after Jack's departure, this one from my cookbook-of-the-month club. It was *The Cake Bible,* by Rose Levy Beranbaum. To avoid thinking about Jack and Zusana, I threw myself into *Cake Bible* homeschooling.

It was a cinder block of a book—so much girth that its binding began to tear within a few months, due to my avid paging and how frequently I pressed it into use on my kitchen counter.

After cashing my unemployment check, I would ride my bike to New York Cake and Baking Supply and wander around the large space for hours, examining the stock: forty different kinds of colored sprinkles, cake pans in every size and shape, bowls, spatulas, spoons, and "buttercream" in dusty tubs.

Wedding cakes were constructions, and like anything that's built, they need the right tools. Cousins and college friends were getting married en masse, and I not only was in love but had baby lust. I wanted to have a wedding but could barely bank on a weekly date with Jack.

But I could bake wedding cakes. I bought a cake cutter, a handheld lathe that looked like a repurposed coat hanger with an adjustable bottom wire, to make surgically even layers. I learned that for piping borders and writing in script in frosting, a pedestrian plastic bag, snipped at the corner and combined with a good-quality metal tip, gets the job done just fine. Soon I was writing "Happy Birthday" in shaky Palmer Method script across the tops of my cakes. It was all in the wrist. And my friends were hardly tough critics.

My grandmother and mother used to make delicate, realistic rose bouquets out of clay with their bare hands, paint them, and fire them in a kiln. Now I was making frosting roses on the head of a flower nail, pressing fondant into molds, and cutting it with a little scalpel.

I loved getting lost in the complexities of cakes, but I also loved being surprised by simplicity when it showed up—for example, to make the world's best ganache, all you need are bars of bittersweet chocolate and sour cream. I always ended up with some left over, and I kept it in the refrigerator, a kind of Nutella that tasted amazing spread on a slice of baguette or licked off a spoon.

I admired Beranbaum's judicious use of sugar. I'd tasted so many cakes utterly wrecked by too much. To buy a buttercream cake was to participate in a lie, since the frosting contained neither. It was made up of Crisco, gritty sugar, and food coloring. It piped beautifully but tasted vulgar.

I learned how to make true buttercream, royal honey buttercream, described in the book as "mellifluous, subtly perfumed," which I enrobed my stepmom's birthday cake in before laying slices of strawberries across the top in a floral pattern. "I don't think it's sweet enough," she said.

I made my dad a chocolate cake covered in chocolate buttercream. You can add only so much melted chocolate to buttercream before it gets stiff, so the resulting color is more like wet khaki. I pressed his favorite candy, M&M'S, onto the top.

"You like it? You're happy?" I asked, instantly three again, craving his approval. He gave me the smile that I knew from that time as well. It telegraphed, *Settle down, you're getting on my nerves.*

I volunteered to make my friend Nina's wedding cake, a chocolate cake with vanilla crème anglaise frosting, adorned with pale purple rosebuds, layers separated by raspberry filling. I began the process with a Zen mindset, but things soon spiraled into chaos.

First, I realized that my bowls weren't big enough to contain the full volume of cake batter needed, so I had to make another batch separately. Then I ran out of butter, and by this time the supermarkets were closed, so I had to make do with salted butter from the bodega.

Whether it was due to stress or to tasting the batter or to some other thing, my intestines joined the haywire express. So I constructed, iced, and decorated the cake in between getting sick. Letting the bride down was not an option.

As the sun peeked over a smoggy horizon, I finished the cake, called the bride, and told her of my condition, and she arranged for her friend Amber to pick it up on her way out to New Jersey. After I passed it off, I went straight to the ER. (That marriage ended in divorce a few years later. But everyone, Nina tells me, still raves about the cake.)

I didn't make another wedding cake for twelve years, but I happily dashed off simpler cakes for other occasions. Baking brought me back to the best part of my childhood: standing beside my mother in our matching handmade aprons, flour-dusted, swiping cake batter when she wasn't looking.

I kept myself so busy baking that Jack's return surprised me with its imminence. I had to arrange for a car to pick him up from the airport, make osso buco, buy a bag of coke and, of course, beer.

My neighborhood car service had one driver with a Jaguar. I requested him and did my other sourcing. Veal shanks, cocaine, Heineken, Arborio rice, chicken stock . . . with that lineup, how could we fail to have a good time?

Hours after his return, when everything had been eaten, drunk up, and snorted, we rested in a pleasure-drenched pile on the bed.

"Jack, I want to marry you," I said happily. "I love you, we're good together, we're both writers, we have great sex, I want to have babies with your eyes, I want to do your laundry and cook your meals. Let's move to Bolinas and live near the beach and write and have an amazing life!"

Pause.

"C'mere," he said, and hugged me close. "Listen, I think you're really brave. Really, really, really brave. What you just did was show me the very inside of your heart, and I can't imagine doing that with anyone. I admire you. But we're not going to get married and have babies, Candace. I'm not that guy."

I was too high to feel bad about Jack's turning down my proposal, though I sensed that it was going to make me feel bad later. But having the suspension of the shower of sadness gave me space to think. And I realized that things couldn't go on this way indefinitely. I knew better than to hang around Jack for much longer, as I got to be older and less of a catch. I'd known him for three years, and I caught a glimpse of myself seven years from now—haggard, circles under my eyes, glaring at young clueless girls in his orbit, touching him possessively, bitchy, and thick-thighed.

I couldn't imagine ending our relationship when I'd finally clawed myself to girlfriend status. And adding a breakup to getting fired seemed unwise. Or maybe not—maybe it was time to get real about everything, since I'd bombed out of Condé Nast. Jack had spoken, and this time, unlike the time at Rudy's Bar and Grill, I heard him.

A few months later, in July, Jack and I went out to my dad's house for the weekend, to the annual Sound Beach Clam-B-Q, which we thought was both fun (lots of seafood, kegs of beer) and ridiculous (lots of suburban people with bad hair bursting out of their plus-size summer wear).

We got back on the train that night, and as it pulled out of the station, Jack said, "When we get back to the city, I'm going to say goodbye to you and then go underground. I don't know when you'll hear from me again. I'm not going to come back up again until I'm done with the book."

"So, no ballpark? Just, you're disappearing?"

"That's right. I'll call you when I'm done."

"Well, sorry, but I'm not going through that again. I can't just sit around waiting for you to call me for months, or however long. If you pull the underground thing on me, we're through."

"Then we're through."

Jack's timing sucked, because I began to cry in Port Jefferson and cried for two hours straight, all the way back to Penn Station. I wasn't loud, but I sure made a teary, snotty mess. There was no toilet paper in the lavatory. People stared. I was on a crying jag that would continue for several days, and I didn't have the slightest idea how to calm down, but in retrospect, I'm glad he had to sit there and witness my grief and disappointment, three years' worth of it.

He brought me back to my apartment, and we fell into an exhausted, dystopian sleep. In the morning when he got up and began to get dressed, his shirt was nowhere to be found. He became increasingly agitated as he hunted for it.

"Would you just give me my damn shirt?" he asked.

"Oh, now I'm someone who would hide your shirt after a

breakup? Sorry, I'm not *that* freak," I said through more tears, curled up in a ball on my bed.

Finally, he gave up and put on his socks, trousers, shoes, and undershirt, and then threw his jacket on and left. I never did find that shirt, and I wonder if some vengeful guardian spirit vaporized it—score one for me.

Although Jack had always talked the talk about supporting my growth as a writer, being around his outsize writer ego had shut me down creatively. It really seemed that there was room for only one of us in the relationship. In his absence, I felt tendrils of inspiration grow. I began to write stories based on my youth, around the time my parents split up. I shaped the material into a proposal.

My friend Jenny referred me to a prominent literary agent specializing in young-adult fiction. I made a cover letter and included the first chapter, biked it over, and dropped it off at the front desk, as if I were a messenger. And the agent called me that afternoon.

In just a week, I'd gone from being a pathetic, jobless, dumped loser to a writer working on my first book, with an enthusiastic literary agent urging me to finish it so that she could sell it.

I got to work. Every day, I woke up hyperventilating slightly from nerves. Then I got dressed, put on my sneakers, and walked or jogged around the East River Park's track. It was the only thing that toggled my brain out of panic and into writing mode, and the first time I'd exercised willingly and regularly, outside of high school sports teams. Then I made coffee and a smoothie and sat down and wrote for four hours. Sometimes more, if I was on a roll. I made sure that I wrote at least a thousand words a day.

The rest of my day was mine. I invited friends over for dinner, or met them at a bar or at their apartments. I still did coke occasionally with my friends, but I realized that without a boyfriend, coke was dangerous for me. I ended up going home with random guys. I wasn't myself, or not a self I wanted to claim. And yet my college friends did it. My writer friends did it. Even my makeup artist friend did it. Opportunities knocked.

"I think I need to go on a spiritual retreat," I told my friend Nina.

"You should go to Gita Nagari," she said. "It's a yoga commune where you meditate, milk cows, and do farm work all day."

I was tempted, but I wouldn't be able to write my book. The months went on, my word count grew, but I wasn't quite done with it by the time my unemployment ran out. So I got a job—working in my friend Debbie's vintage children's clothing store on Bleecker and Bowery.

I had never worked retail in my life, but the store was quiet and off the beaten path. I rang up sales, was nice to customers, and even bought stock in Brooklyn thrift warehouses like Domsey's. Debbie was extremely supportive of my writing and brought in an old laptop so I could write in between customers.

By February, I had not talked to Jack for four months. He sent me not one but three Christmas cards, filled with slightly manic, jolly, handwritten catch-up chat, but I didn't call him. I had a big black sketchbook that I used as my catchall for Jack thoughts, images, or anything I wanted to send him or show him, things that reminded me of him with all of the subtlety of a knitting needle to the heart.

Valentine's Day was difficult. I knew it was a stupid manufactured holiday, about as real as Betty Crocker, but I still felt like a seventh grader again, watching all the pretty, popular girls get roses and carnations. Only this time I was twenty-six, not twelve, and had yet to really have a good experience. My boyfriends never overlapped with February 14, except for Daniel, who handed me a necklace with a heart pendant, grumbling that he had to go to five stores to find it.

It was an easy opportunity to fall into a big, postbreakup, still-pining hole. I was unloved. Everyone else was being fêted, wined, dined, and made sweet love to. Not me. I was going to die an old spinster, in a garret overrun by cats. I was already in a fourth-floor walk-up with three cats. The only thing missing was a slanted ceiling.

I thought making beautiful handmade valentines and heart-shaped linzer torte cookies for all of my friends the week before the big day would karmically head this pity party off at the pass, but no, even though everyone loved them.

I called my mother, looking to be cheered up, but she was also crying. I asked her, "Do you think it will ever get better?"

She said, "Probably not."

Wow. The woman who had brought me into this world could hold out no hope for me. I ended that phone call rather quickly, as it was doing the opposite of what I had intended, and poured myself a glass of red wine.

My eyes fell on *Heartburn,* the book Jack had given me months before, with a big red heart on the cover. Yes, it was in a pot over a fire and being stabbed by a devil with a pitchfork, but it was still a heart-decorated paper item from Jack to me, as close to a valentine as I would ever get. I sat down and began to read.

A Will and a Way

DEBBIE'S STORE, Little O, was on a city block that was in the midst of a transformation. Steps from the Bowery, a wine bar, Von, was our neighbor on the left, a vacant space was on the right, and across the street was a big beautiful brasserie, meant to possibly lure people who couldn't get a reservation at Balthazar.

Although Debbie was lovely, the stock and clientele were adorable, and I had free rein to write, it was quite a fall from grace to be working in a shop just a few blocks from Condé Nast's international HQ.

But it was okay, because my book was almost done, and it would sell, and I'd make money and then get a three-book deal and be set. Katja would hate my success (so would Jack) and I'd be able to (whispered in my head: *buy more coke*) pay off bills, and go on vacation somewhere dreamy.

The day came when I finished the last chapter. In the book, Camilla Shaw triumphs over the mean girls when she's randomly picked as a PE volleyball team captain. Camilla picks all of the most uncoordinated, chubby, awkward, rejected girls to be on her team, shocking the jocks and popular chicks (and most of the geeks as well). She watches their faces register what it feels like to be passed over, with supreme satisfaction. And then, by a hair, Camilla's team wins.

I dropped it off at my agent's office and waited. Her assistant called me to ask that I come by. I took the elevator up, and sat down in the reception area, no longer pretending to be a messenger.

My agent came to the door of her office and beckoned to me, a smile on her face.

"I love it!" she said. "*You* are a writer, Candace Walsh. I'm sending it out."

I jumped up and hugged her. "Thank you for believing in me."

"Thank you for writing the book in three months!" she said.

Within a few days, letters began coming in. They loved the writing, enjoyed the character, thought it was funny, but. Was it a young-adult novel or an adult novel? It was too adult-y to be young adult, too young adult to be adult. One editor was interested, but needed to bring it to a meeting.

When I got the letter saying that publishing house was withdrawing its interest, I went upstairs to my apartment, closed the door, slid to the floor, and cried so hard I could barely breathe.

This process felt like another big practical joke—like coming off a bender. I had a period of feeling good, but really, I was garbage, and the proof rolled in with every letter. I was getting rejected, just on a far greater scale than ever, and after I had bared my soul and done my best (for once, outside of cooking, I had done my best).

But then, after I got more rejections, another house was interested, *if* I beefed up the adult Camilla's arc.

"Kind of like Judy Blume's *Summer Sisters,*" the editor said. "I want to know what happens to Camilla as an adult."

"Sure, no problem at all," I said. "I can do that; I just need a few months." I'd recast it—and in the meantime, my agent and I decided to stop sending it out.

One day at work, a couple of women walked in and I realized that one of them was Janine, a woman I'd met at Jack's apartment who bartended at a margarita bar. I'd been jealous of her, because she seemed to have an intimacy with Jack that made me suspicious.

The last time I'd seen her, I had at least been Jack's girlfriend. But now I was not. I didn't even talk to him anymore, and she probably saw him once a week at the margarita bar. They probably had sex in the back room against the wall.

Why did she have to come into Little O, of all of the stores in Manhattan, and torture me? I'd been truthfully having a few good weeks, Jack-free. I was beginning to realize that I *would* get over him, instead of just hoping.

I was so chafed that I closed the store an hour early and went next door to have a beer at Von. Debbie would understand. She would have to.

Luckily, Salem was bartending—a short, buxom, pixie-haired woman who wore tank tops all year long, the better to show off her unshaven armpits. She wasn't a hippie, but her display of taboo body hair, in a slick downtown bar, gave her an edge.

The bar was empty at that early hour, so Salem and I had the luxury of taking turns unloading our ex-boyfriend drama. I went first, given that I had just had The Encounter with Janine.

Salem was doing better; she'd started dating someone new. She was clearly one of those girls—relationships just fell in her lap. She was pretty in an unintimidating way, and was confident.

The door opened and closed, but I didn't look behind me.

"Would you like a glass of wine?" Salem asked the man staring at the chalkboard wine list intently.

"I'm trying to decide . . ." he said, "between the Syrah and the Shiraz."

I turned to look. Who was this person, who knew not only that Syrah and Shiraz existed, but also the difference between them? This person was a medium-tall, thin man wearing a suit and a nice overcoat. He had short brown curly hair, closely cut, and roundish glasses. He seemed so immaculate, and that and his wine knowledge made me think he was gay.

We introduced ourselves. His name was Will.

"So, you're a writer?" he asked.

I told him all about my book saga, and he told me about how he ended up in New York.

"I was helping out my dad in Santa Fe—he's an artist with a

gallery there—and we had a show in New York. My father's gallerist offered me a job on the spot, and so here I am."

"How do you know so much about wine?" I asked.

"I worked in a winery in California," he said, "in the Sierra Foothills, as the winemaker's assistant and tasting-room manager. I helped with the crush, scrubbed out the fermentation tanks, talked to visitors about the wines. I was this close to getting my master's, but had a bad breakup with my ex-girlfriend."

So he wasn't gay.

Salem drifted back, and we talked for another hour. Then I said goodbye, because I had plans to meet my friends. I wasn't ready for a relationship, but it was nice to know that someone like him existed. Hopefully I'd connect with that caliber of smart, polite, handsome man when I was capable of not scaring him off with my dumped, bereft energy.

Still, I made sure to mention that I worked next door. Just to give him one way to find me again, if that's what he wanted to do. I admired his wine knowledge and, as a lay food-obsessive, recognized that my zero knowledge of wine was a weakness. Maybe we'd end up friends.

The following Saturday, my friend Tina called me up at Little O to ask if I wanted to go have a drink.

"Meet me at work, we'll go to Von," I said.

This time, the bar was already crowded. We got drinks, walked to the back, and caught up for a while. I ran into Rick, a friend of the owners. I introduced him to Tina, hoping they'd hit it off. Then it was time to get another round, so we sidled up to the bar and I ordered another beer. I looked to my right and saw Will, just as he saw me.

Wow. There he was again. I hadn't been to Von in months, but I'd gone two times in a week, and so had he. The same times. I raised my glass to him, smiling. Later he told me that he turned to the guy he'd been talking to and said, "That's the girl I met here last week."

"Do you like her?" he asked.

"Yes."

"Well, then what are you doing over here talking to me? She just gave you the ultimate 'come hither'!"

He made his way over to me. I introduced him to Tina, and we picked up our conversation where we had left off—but this time, I touched his arm now and then, ostensibly to make a point, but really to flirt. I liked the way he smiled, lit up by the contact. Rick joined us, and I was glad, because it made Tina less of a third wheel.

After about another hour, Tina had to go, and I decided I should take off, too.

We all said goodbye outside.

"Hey, Will, I'm going to get a cab, and you live on the way. Do you want me to drop you off?" I asked.

"Sure, that'd be great."

"I'm going that direction, too," said Rick. I hailed a cab and we headed east.

Will got out at Second Avenue. We drove on.

"What's your stop?" I asked Rick.

"I'll make sure you get home safely and then walk to my place."

"Okay, thanks." Rather gentlemanly.

Rick got out when I did and walked up the stairs with me.

"Rick, I'm good," I said. "See you soon. Thanks!"

He seemed to nod, so I opened the doors. He followed me with a kind of swoop, pushing me through the second door.

"What are you doing?"

He grabbed me and kissed me, sticking his tongue in my mouth. With one hand on the nape of my neck, he pulled open his jeans and whipped out his penis, which was not only an unwanted gesture but also a sad specimen.

"Oh, baby, I want you," he murmured. "Let me make you feel so good." He grabbed my hand and tried to cram it onto his dick.

"Rick, no. I am going to scream if you don't let go of me. I do not want this. I will scream. Get. Out. Of. Here."

He continued to wrestle with me for another few seconds, and then I inhaled, in preparation to wake up the whole building.

"Okay, okay." He backed out of the doors and I watched him go down the stairs. Then I hotfooted up to my apartment, closed the door, threw both deadbolts, and made sure the windows on the fire escape were locked. And washed my hands, and my mouth out with mouthwash, and brushed my teeth. What a creep. And how dumb I felt for not being more cautious.

I knew that I wanted Will more than ever; he was the opposite of that sleazeball, and all of the sleazeballs I'd encountered for the last few years. Especially Jack.

But was I worthy? I'd been doing cocaine, hanging out in bars every other night, working at a job that started at noon, having pretzels and soda for lunch. All the while wanting to get married and have a baby. I planned to get my act together long before becoming a mother, so I decided to start now.

I opened my closet and started pulling out all the stuff I'd bought to appeal to Jack's smutty predilections. Purple satin pumps with silver heels. A white see-through sweater. The pile grew as I went through my hangers, shoe rack, and chest of drawers. I didn't spare the Victoria's Secret baby-doll set, hubris and regret trapped not in amber, but rather in red charmeuse.

If Will liked me—and I thought he did—he liked me sitting at Von in faded red corduroy bell-bottoms, a crew-neck sweater, and sneakers.

I wanted a fresh start, and it seemed like I might be able to have that with Will.

Will also seemed so different from Jack, and if I couldn't figure out how to avoid Jack and his ilk, I could at least guess at what the opposite was and head that way.

16

Inside the Gingerbread House

IT WAS 6:00 PM. The late-February night was dark and cold outside Little O. I recorded the day's sales and priced some new pieces. When I looked up, I saw street light glinting off Will's glasses, outside the door. He stood staring in at me with a smile on his face. I waved, and he came in.

"Well, hello there," he said.

"Hi! What a nice surprise."

"I was just walking home and I thought I'd stop by."

"I'm glad you did."

"I know you're at work, so I won't linger."

"Please linger." I laughed, blushing, noticing, to my mortification, that I felt a wave of warmth from head to foot and my upper lip was dewy with sweat. I wiped it surreptitiously. "I mean, it's dead in here, and I was just going to order dinner. Would you like to join me?"

"Sure."

I extended my arms. "Let me take your coat."

It was charcoal gray, cashmere, with a comforting weight. I hung it up and then pulled out the folder of delivery menus. "What are you in the mood for? Chinese, Italian, Thai, sushi, diner, Mexican?"

He threw up his hands with a smile. "It all sounds good. You choose."

"Thai."

"Great."

I picked up the phone and ordered two kinds of vegetable curry with rice.

While we waited for the food, we chatted easily about life, mostly childhood. The childhood-related conversational cues were everywhere, from the clothes to the furniture to the collection of vintage Fisher-Price neighborhood toys. I learned that he had spent time as a child living with his father's side of the family in France, and that he and his parents had traveled around the United States in a little red camper, going from art show to art show, selling his father's work. For most of his childhood, he thought that the PBS symbol was the face of God. He developed a love for classical music as a little boy, playing record after record on his grandmother's turntable, and he built his own collection of Beethoven, Mozart, Mahler, and Wagner records while combing flea markets with his uncle.

I joked about how my *Mr. Rogers* and *Sesame Street* habit was interrupted by my mother's overnight conversion to Jesus, and that by the time she relaxed about it, I found the shows babyish.

We didn't talk about the dark parts of our childhood, although later, we'd match each other story for story. His beloved dog that disappeared, though his dad searched for days. Getting whipped with a belt. His father's rages, his mother's torpor. Being force-fed.

No, that night was about creation and invention, discovery and anticipation. We were old enough to realize that you don't lead with the freaky. Not if you want to attract someone worthwhile.

The food arrived, and we sat down almost primly at the small desks, face-to-face. It was as if we had slipped off the realities of our childhoods, inside Little O, and were doing a kind of rebirthing, but as adults reexperiencing a much more idyllic childhood, Hansel and Gretel without the witch. Inside the gingerbread house, feasting on massaman and panang curries and possibility.

We left together well after seven. He kissed me on the cheek, with what seemed like a touch of formality, and then we parted, without making a plan to see each other again.

I found myself charmed by this fine-boned, old-fashioned young man. I felt the impulse to protect him, to keep him from harm. His love of classical music and opera, wine and German philosophers, made him seem like a romantic figure out of *Jane Eyre*. That he saw something in me made me feel anointed. No longer the tawdry girl that my sojourn with Jack had pummeled me into.

I didn't need to wait too long to see Will again. He came by the store a few days later, this time in jeans and a leather jacket, with coiled instead of courtly energy.

"You look different," I said. "Are you off today?"

"I got fired," he said with a terse smile.

"What?"

"I'm leaving town on Saturday, going back to Santa Fe. But I wanted to come and see you."

Leaving? That didn't seem right. It didn't go with the story that had been building.

"Wow."

"Can I buy you a drink?"

"Sure, I close up in a few minutes."

We walked next door to Von, sat down at the bar, and ordered pints.

"So, what happened?"

"Well, apart from my father's work, the gallery really sells shlock. And they wanted me to do this hard sell! I told them that they had to let me do it my way."

"I guess they didn't go for that."

He put his hands up, palms up. "They did not."

"You don't want to stay in New York?"

"I can't without a job. My father and stepmother lent me money to come out here, and now that I've lost my job, I have to go back there and work it off at their gallery."

"You could see . . ."

"I've already given notice at my place, ordered the UPS pickup, have a plane ticket."

"Okay."

I was starting to wonder if I was the job-loss catalyst of the dating world. As soon as I met Daniel, he dropped out of his PhD program and became a couch potato. Jack lost his magazine job after we started seeing each other. I lost my own job, and now Will had just been let go. But I didn't think I should mention that.

He was no longer cloaked in the mystique and the garb of an aesthete. He was in jeans, sneakers, and a sweater, injured pride coming through as something harder and possibly more authentic.

"So what now?" he asked.

"I have to go to my friend Casey's birthday party tonight at Joe's Pub," I said. "She's one of my best friends, *another* former White House intern for Clinton, can you believe it? From Little Rock. Would you like to come?"

"I'd love to."

We got to the party, danced, mingled, and sat down on a banquette, sweaty and happy. I looked at Will and realized that we were in the pre-kiss moment. After it, there would be no ambiguity. We'd not be just friends. We would be a different kind of unknown, with different stakes. I was ready.

If there's any question around whether I felt the titanic impact of kissing my future husband and the father of my children for the first time, let me lay that question to rest. I felt it. I forgot to breathe, everything else fell away, and all of my consciousness shifted into my mouth, my hands, and the places his hands rested.

And we stayed there for what seemed like days, kissing, not able to care that we were making out like fourteen-year-olds at a roller-skating rink. On either side of us, couples caught our fever and began to kiss and writhe. I barely noticed.

"I thought one of y'all was gone lose a lip," Casey said later. But as she and I had spent many a phone call bemoaning the difficulties of finding good love, she was fine with my lapse of good manners.

We ended up getting married, and had children who need to be spared the mortifying details of their parents' first night together. As do others. I want to leave it there, back in 1998.

But I do recall my thoughts. He seemed perfect. But he was

leaving. I was beginning something that would be an obstruction, should Jack come calling. I was glad. I wanted there to be
an obstruction. I'd had a dream—I was married to Jack, and he
ordered me to get a ham sandwich, in a high-handed yet caveman
manner. "That's what it would be like," my sister said. "He'd be the
writer, the man of the house, and you'd be hating life, making ham
sandwiches."

Will and I made the most of our last few days together. I had no
idea what would happen after he left; he'd made noises about not
wanting to be in a long-distance relationship. The morning of his
departure, I walked him back toward his apartment, past Tompkins
Square Park. At the corner, we hugged and kissed goodbye. It was
too cold to get worked up. I turned and walked back to my place,
numb. The apartment comforted me with its familiarity and the
residual charge of Will's presence.

Before I could even begin to think that I'd lost big-time love
in a new way, Will called and we talked for hours. And the next
night. And the next. I pulled out *The Cake Bible* and made him a
lemon-poppyseed cake, brushed with lemon syrup I composed in
my kitchen by dissolving sugar into warmed fresh-squeezed lemon
juice. Dulcet in the way only things baked with cake flour are—and
sent it to him in a small box with letters I wrote him at Little O
while not working on my book revision.

"I want you to come visit," he said on the phone one evening,
and he sent me a plane ticket.

Santa Fe. I knew nothing about it, except that usually, on whim-
sical maps of the USA, a cowboy hat or chili pepper served as its
symbol. Ever since my trip to Germany, I'd been a confirmed travel
bug, my jaunts limited only by funds. Now I'd get to see a new part
of the country and, more than that, reunite with Will.

When I met him at the gate, he gave me a restrained kiss hello,
but then pounced on me in the car, removing any of my worries
about his ardor.

We drove up I-25, through a peachy-earthed landscape ringed
by bee-stung, piñon-studded foothills that looked like soft mounds

of chocolate chip cookie dough. Silvery and sage grasses waved and glistened.

Santa Fe struck my sea-level eyes as a series of low-slung sand castles, edges softened by exactly one gentle wave—just like the adobe church that started melting when Aaron's LSD took effect back in Buffalo.

Will took me to Tomasita's restaurant for dinner. Across the table, we smiled nervously at each other. Were our feelings for each other like fog that socks you in but then burns off as the sun climbs in the sky? Time would tell. The deck was tilted toward our resuming or inhabiting our idea of what we wanted—a relationship.

I loved Mexican food but was wary of anything spicy. My idea of Mexican food was bare-bones—Taco Bell and other drunk-munchies joints, or, at home, a can of refried beans with browned ground beef and a packet of seasoning, chopped lettuce and tomatoes.

But this wasn't Mexican food, it was *New* Mexican food. (And the Mexican food I liked wasn't Mexican food either, but that's a tangent for another time.)

My meal arrived on a large oval plate. It contained a taco, a burrito, a chile relleno, and posole, with a small bowl of green chile on the side. The chile relleno was a whole green chile, stuffed with cheese, battered, and fried. The posole was a kind of hominy stew, something I had never eaten before: large starchy cornlike kernels, white, curvy, and indented, like molars as seen above the gumline. It had a musty taste that didn't grab me.

"Taste the green chile!" Will urged. "It's amazing!"

I gingerly poured a glug of the pale green liquid over a bite of burrito and tasted it.

Slightly salty, earthy, with a touch of heat.

"What do you think?" he asked, beaming.

"Maybe it needs to grow on me," I said. "Right now, I don't really get the appeal."

My tongue had yet to develop the correct taste buds to register it. It would be a journey to increase my threshold for spicy food. I'd one day ask for my New Mexican food to be "smothered," a term used to describe a plate awash in chile, preferably "Christmas," with garnet red chile sauce on one half and the pale pea green stuff down the other side. But not yet. My commitment to New Mexico was minimal—I was there because Will was. If he'd been in New Orleans, I'd have gone there and eaten jambalaya.

Will's father had rented a big house in the South Capitol neighborhood, right across the street from the Roundhouse, and it was there that Will stayed, in a sparsely furnished bedroom with an inflatable mattress on the floor. The living spaces were packed with paintings, and his studio had several works in progress, bright wood panels drunk with colors and curving lines.

The kitchen was small, countertops and walls covered in rustic, arched-back talavera tile, yellow and blue hand-painted floral patterns, and thick joints filled with grout that showed a few decades' worth of age. As I cooked breakfast the next morning—cheese omelets, sausages, and toast—Will sat on the counter, talking as the sun came through the old small-paned windows.

He had to work at the gallery, so I kissed him goodbye and got directions to the closest grocery store, as I'd offered to make his dad and stepmother dinner that night. It was my attempt to make a good impression, given that he'd already described them as being tough to please. I planned to make chicken fricassee, and decided to serve vanilla frozen yogurt with a fresh berry sauce for dessert.

All day long, I simmered the chicken with vegetables, then completed the familiar steps of pulling the chicken off the bones and making the sauce. I put it in the refrigerator and simmered raspberries and blueberries in a simple syrup. Once Will arrived, we packed the food into the car and drove over.

As I walked in, Will's stepmother exclaimed, "So you're the woman person who's been hanging around with William!"

"Hi," I said. *Woman person? Okay.*

Will's father was diminutive and sulky. Getting dinner ready gave me something to do in the midst of the awkwardness. I could tell that Will didn't feel any more comfortable than I, and my heart went out to him. These people were strangers to me, but they were his family.

"Do you have any rice?" I asked. "I should have picked some up at the store, but it slipped my mind."

"I have this rice," she said, pulling out a box of boil-in-bag Success rice.

Success rice? Was that specifically marketed to career women who not only dressed for success, but riced for success? Or people who feared the making of rice so much that they needed to be guaranteed success . . . in the form of ricelike husks that cooked up in a plastic baggie?

I'd grown up on delicious, perfectly steamed rice-cooker grains doused with butter. But this stuff would have to do. As I plated the food, Will said, "Wow, I feel spoiled. This is my third home-cooked meal of the day!"

"Oh, God! Christ rose again; you can get off the cross, too," his stepmother exclaimed.

"What?" I asked.

"Set yourself free from the kitchen!"

I paused as her meaning set in. She thought I felt like I had to cook, and was doing so out of some sense of unshirkable duty.

"If I can't choose to cook for fear of seeming like a martyr, isn't that a form of slavery?" I asked. "I love to cook."

"It's true," Will's dad said.

"So," Will jumped in, "this is Candace's grandmother's recipe."

"Yes, chicken free-cass-ay," I said, self-conscious in front of Will's French dad, "although my Irish-German grandmother pronounced it 'chicken fricass-ee.'" I laughed, but they just stared at me as if I had admitted that I grew up amidst hobos. Will laughed with me, bless him.

I was happy to leave.

The next morning, we left Santa Fe, driving off in Will's old BMW sedan to explore the state, driving to Georgia O'Keeffe's Abiquiú, *The X-Files'* Roswell, Billy the Kid's Fort Sumner. We stayed in cheap roadside motels, my tri-state eyes agog at the

$25-per-night rates. We were supposed to head back but, caught up in the road-trip momentum, continued on to Carlsbad to see the caverns. That meant that Will would not be home in time to resume work as planned, but we felt immune to responsibilities, aglow in love and landscape.

Will called in to the gallery, but his stepmother wasn't feeling our vibe. She chewed him out so loudly that I could hear her across the room. "Okay, I see your point. You're right. Okay, bye."

After he hung up the phone, he turned toward me. He looked stomped on, defeated.

"That wasn't cool," I said. "She has no right to talk to you that way. Either she's your boss and she has to maintain a certain civility, or she's your stepmother and she still has to recognize that you're an adult, not a bad dog who just pooped on the rug. This isn't healthy."

"But what can I do? I owe her money and I have to work it off."

"You can work it off in New York. Come live with me; you can split my cheap rent, get a job, and send her money. Indentured servitude is against the law."

"Really? You would let me do that?" He jumped up and wrapped his arms around me.

"Well, you don't *have* to live with me. I don't want to put too much pressure on what we have. But we could at least play it by ear, or you could stay with me until you find a good job and apartment."

We held each other in the little motel room and imagined our future.

In the morning, we got on the road and had breakfast at a road-side café. Eggs, red and green chile, and fresh sourdough buns that I'd never before encountered and haven't since: soft, tender, with a tangy flavor, with yeasty, airy insides, and the glossy, smooth exterior of a hot cross bun.

Wedding, Bella

I FLEW BACK to New York by myself, but with the knowledge that Will would join me in a few weeks. A stack of messages from Jack was waiting for me. While I was in Santa Fe, he had come back to New York (I hadn't known he'd left) from Australia and left messages on my answering machine, notes for me at Little O, and even called up Effie.

"Candace is in Santa Fe with her new boyfriend," she told him with immense satisfaction. "Too little, too late, Jack!"

"Right, cheers," he said, and hung up.

He turned up at Little O and asked if he could please take me out to dinner.

"I have a boyfriend, Jack," I said.

"I know," he said, a little nervously, looking drawn around the eyes. "I respect that. I just want to catch up with you. I'm in town to meet with my agent about a book deal."

I said yes. At dinner, it came up that he needed a place to stay that night and was flying back the next day. High on the fun of enjoying Jack without there being a fraught romantic component, in conjunction with having terrible boundaries, I assented. That night, after drinking more wine, he predictably tried to put the moves on me, and I very *unpredictably* shunned him.

"No more of that. I'm with Will now," I said, grateful that I had Will as a shield. I couldn't have been so principled on my own. Besmirch my beautiful love for Will with dodgy Jack? Yeah, right.

I'd learned my lesson when I lost Aaron, and wasn't going to make that mistake twice.

Jack fell asleep on the floor, good-natured about my new-found integrity but clearly befuddled that his plan wasn't coming together—me, at his beck and call, signed up for more drama and misery down the road.

I didn't see fit to tell Will about any of it—I thought he would be distressed, and although I had done nothing inappropriate, why plant seeds of doubt? Why jeopardize our very good thing? Will moved in a few weeks later, and our life began. Sure, it was crazy to move in right after we'd met, but it felt normal. Not just normal. Perfect. Together, we were a team.

I called him from Little O, a few days after he arrived. "Hi!" he said cheerfully. "I'm washing the windows."

"You are?" I asked. I instantly felt embarrassed. I should have thought to wash them myself, but it had never occurred to me. "I'm sorry."

"Not at all," he reassured me. "I like washing windows."

Inspired by New Mexico, I decided to make breakfast burritos with tortillas, eggs, and beans. Will pulled a small bottle of liquid out of his pocket. Melinda's XXX.

"Habanero hot sauce," he said. "The good stuff."

"And?"

"I want you to give spicy food another chance," he said.

I ate spicy food for the first time back in college, by accident, when a burrito I ordered as "not spicy" was switched with a brutal one. It turned me off, I thought for life.

"Let's just put one drop on your burrito," Will said, "and I'll pour you a glass of milk. That way you can temper it if you want."

The red drop against the pale eggs reminded me of Sleeping Beauty's pricked finger. When I placed the bite in my mouth, I chewed a few times and then winced a little. Melinda's *was* hot. But the heat was sinuous and I could sense its boundaries. When it faded, I felt eddies of pleasure roll in, along with a flush in my cheeks. I giggled.

"Notice that?" he asked, a bit of the revival-tent soul-saver about his eyes. "Endorphins."

Midway through my breakfast burrito, I was a convert.

Will needed a job, so I created a killer resume and cover letter, and he sent them out to the three best wine stores in New York and got offers from all of them. He picked the one with the best pay and highest potential for advancement.

I got a job just a few blocks away, working for a book packaging company headed by a slave driver with fake boobs who was always trying to screw freelancers out of their pay, but luckily paid her staff every two weeks. It was not glamorous by any means, but paid better than retail and was in the editorial field.

Between my new, brain-sucking job and living with Will, I found it hard to revise and add to my book. I spent a few hours here and a few hours there, but was chagrined. The editor wanted to know what happened to Camilla. I was living that. The story was far from finished, unless I wanted to make it up. And when I tried to do that, I floundered.

At lunchtime, we met in the middle, he took my hand, and we sat in Central Park and ate our brown-bag sandwiches, or once in a while, we stopped by Tony Dragonas's food cart to pick up pillowy pitas stuffed with seasoned chicken, lettuce, and tomato and drizzled with creamy yogurt and hot sauce.

Dinners stumped me, though, because I was very good at making impressive, time-consuming, epic meals, but not quotidian suppers. I needed to come up with quick, nonfussy dinners that were still delicious and enough of a challenge to hold my interest. That's when I borrowed *The Working Stiff Cookbook* from friends who also worked long hours—and had two small children.

Once I had a routine, I could shop and plan for the week. Will knew what I was making that night, and bought a wine (employee discount) that paired well with it. Over dinner, he told me about the wine's region, varietals, and characteristics.

He did the dishes afterward, which was a welcome change after David's and Jack's lack of sink chivalry. Will was different! So different from those louts, and also different from my father and stepfather, who sat down to home-cooked meals each night but didn't even clear the table, let alone do the dishes.

"What do you like?" I asked.

"Linguini with clam sauce," he said. "The canned kind."

I made it, appreciating how little effort it took. Boil pasta water, open can of sauce, heat up in separate pan, cook pasta, toss together. He ate it enthusiastically.

The next week, a few nights went by without his doing the dishes. I did them once, then left them in the sink, irked but nervous about bringing it up. The second night, I made another turnkey linguini-and-clam-sauce dinner but was so cramped for space that the hot water from the drained pasta leaped up and burned my hand. I jerked, and the bowl of clam sauce fell into the sink.

"Fuck this!" I yelled, and dumped the pasta on top of the spilled sauce and the dirty dishes and stormed out of the kitchen.

"What the hell is going on?" he yelled back.

I threw myself on the bed. It was really hard to storm off and sulk when there were no doors to slam, and I was just a few feet away from him. I curled up in a ball and waited for my heart to slow down. Not only had I just acted like a total jerk, but it was exactly the kind of thing my stepmother would do. Now that I was living with Will, would I helplessly turn into her and/or my mother?

"I think we just had our first fight," I said, smiling contritely. "I'm sorry."

"It's okay," he said.

"I got frustrated because you stopped doing the dishes, but I shouldn't have dumped the food."

"I'm sorry, I was just consumed with studying about different wine regions for work."

We kissed, made up, and went out for Indian. I felt comforted that we were able to recover from our argument so easily. But I never made linguini with clam sauce again.

My mom loved Will, my dad loved Will, and so did my stepmother. We spent more time at both my dad's and my mom's

WEDDING, BELLA **181**

houses, and I could feel my father exhale with a sort of complicated relief. He and my stepmother didn't like David and they
hated Jack.

When I got a big freelance check, Will and I bought an old
sailboat with a small sleeping berth. We spent weekends out at
the boatyard, just a few blocks from where I was born, sanding it,
priming and painting it, and tinkering with its different workings.
Buying a sailboat together was a pretty big step, but I think buying
Bella together really meant more.

One day, I got off work early and browsed around in a kitchen-
goods shop, waiting for Will. There, in the back of the store, stood
a cherry-red KitchenAid mixer, on sale for $150, more than 50
percent off.

"Excuse me," I asked, "is there anything wrong with this mixer?"

"No, we just put it on sale because it's red and it hasn't moved. All
of the white and gray and black ones have sold, but not this one."

People didn't like it *because* it was red? I especially loved it
because it was red. Who would want a plain old white one? I'd
coveted a KitchenAid mixer for years.

But I needed to ask Will. I only had enough money to pay for
half of it. I walked to a pay phone and dialed him at work, filled
him in, and asked him to meet me.

As he walked in, I smiled, proud that this handsome man loved
me. He caught sight of me, and then the mixer, and broke into a
smile. "Yes. We have to get it." He circled it, touched it, played with
the tilt head and knobs. "What a classic."

Not only did it mean so much that we were buying this together—
it meant so much to *me* that Will totally got it. He wasn't humoring
me, acquiescing to my female enthusiasm for kitchen objects. He
wanted it and loved it too.

"I think she needs a name," he said.

"Bella."

"Perfect!"

There we were, in the foodie version of a Tiffany commercial,
arms around each other, staring moonily at the KitchenAid. We

nodded to the salesman, and he packed it up, and we paid for it and took a taxi home, Bella between us.

December 1999, I stopped impulsively in front of Tompkins Square Park, where Christmas trees were being sold. I'd never bought a tree for my apartment before, but with Will, I had a home, not an offshoot. I picked one out, and the vendor roped it to my bike. I walked it home, my nose full of the fragrant piney smell, my heart warm. Will was already home, and I pressed our buzzer.

"Hello?"

"It's me. I have a surprise."

"I'll be right down!"

Will bounded down the stairs. "Wow! This is great!"

We untied the tree, I locked up my bike, and we carried it up the stairs. Although it seemed huge on the sidewalk, it was short enough to put on my filing cabinet, in a pail. I wrapped an afghan around its base and then stopped. I had no ornaments, and didn't want to run out and get any when this moment with Will felt so good.

"I know," I said, and opened up my jewelry box. I pulled out handfuls of costume jewelry and draped the necklaces, bracelets, bangles, and earrings on the branches.

Will took a bottle of champagne out of the refrigerator, along with cheeses from a recent trip to Gourmet Garage. "Our first Christmas together," he said. "That's cause for celebration."

We sat down in front of the tree, flickering candles on the table throwing light around the room, cuddled, and drank bubbly. We decided to get married that night, in the course of a conversation, intoxicated by our first experience of trimming a Christmas tree without the overwhelming weight of noticing how idyllic it wasn't. I noticed at that moment that I wanted the Christmas tree trimming to be the official story, but really, the month before, my period had been late, and we talked about what that could mean for us.

"Well, we love each other," he said. "If you're pregnant, we'll get married."

But then I got my period.

"Why don't you get married anyway?" asked Dr. Morris, in a shockingly uncharacteristic break of her blank-slate demeanor.

Between the pregnancy prompt and my therapist's potent suggestion, it was in the air. Sitting in front of the Christmas tree with glasses of champagne just gave it a perfect moment to land.

I had lunch with my dad the next day, as he was in the city to see a client. "Let's meet at Maggie's Place," I said, thinking he would like the traditional, old–New York Irish restaurant with framed prints on the polished wood-paneled walls. I walked the few blocks to meet him, and then we hugged and sat down, just like any father and daughter would.

After some small talk, I told him. "Dad, Will and I got engaged last night."

He smiled. "Congratulations. That's great, honey. I'm happy for you. Will is a good man." I watched his eyes fill with tears.

He dabbed at his eyes with his cloth handkerchief. He always had one on hand, soft from being washed hundreds of times.

When I found out that my stepmother would be leaving to spend New Year's with her ailing father in Florida, I volunteered to come with Will and celebrate with him and my half sisters. They were just out of toddlerhood, and although Will and I had long planned to celebrate with my friends, the frenzy around the millennial New Year's Eve, along with my newfound sense of my "good daughter" persona, influenced me to want to go to them. Family was important.

"Sure!" Will said, when I asked him. "Who needs to go party with a bunch of drunk people in a bar?"

"You don't have to do that," my dad said.

"No, we want to. You'll be all alone out there."

So we got on the train with a bottle of Veuve Clicquot, I made us dinner, and we watched the ball drop from my childhood home.

Five months later, we were married. On our wedding night, we took a car service to JFK International Airport and got on a plane to Paris, by way of Reykjavik, Iceland (Priceline tickets, height of the Internet bubble, $150 each).

Being engaged was lovely. My stepmother and my mother paired up to throw me a shower at the Long Beach Historical Society. My father parted with three grand without even losing his mind (probably because I didn't ask him to pay for the whole affair). My boss took the whole office out to lunch to commemorate it, and Will's coworkers clapped him on the back and invited us over to dinner.

I had wanted to get married ever since I'd sat in my childhood backyard, popping garbanzo beans out of their husks, a few summers before. That's why I'd stopped fighting for Jack and waited to meet someone who could fill the role of husband-to-be. But I had no idea that getting married would be such a publicly rewarding experience.

Not everyone was ecstatic. When I told Effie, she said, "I think you and Will will always be friends. But I don't think he's the one you're supposed to marry." I was wounded by her response, but told myself she was just being weird.

I loved being involved in every facet of the wedding planning. I loved event planning (or do all brides feel that way?). I loved designing the invitations with my friend Frank, and handwriting the addresses on thick Italian paper with raw edges, and using a wax seal to close each one. And of course I would make the cake.

"Oh, no!" everyone said. "You can't! You'll be too busy!"

So I conceded. I was overwhelmed. My mother knew a guy. He made beautiful wedding cakes. We should order it from him.

I had a series of conversations with this baker named Ryan: "I just really can't emphasize enough that I don't want my cake to be too sweet. Can I give you a recipe from *The Cake Bible?*"

He acted as if he were a surgeon and I had offered him my own personal scalpel with which to remove my appendix. "I have thousands of recipes," he said. "No need to give me yours."

My "wedding cake picture" shows me taking a bite and unsuccessfully masking a grimace. It was far too sweet. Tongue-stinging, teeth-grating sweet. But I also had an awareness that, as the bride, I had to act like it was delicious. Or at least palatable.

It was a bitter moment. Will, not a fan of sweets no matter how dulcet, supported me in my pique. We went up to the roof of the catering facility and flipped our pieces off the china plates and into the New York sky.

We rejected what wasn't good enough for us, and it felt redemptive. And then we ran back down the stairs to dance.

My mother, grandmother, and sister got a ride home with Mom's old friends Mary and Carl. The hot postreception gossip in that car was all about my dear friends Frank and Scott, from Buffalo—that they were a couple. This needed to be picked over by the passengers, although Frank and Scott had a relationship about seven thousand times more healthy and edifying than any my mother or Mary had landed. My sister roundly debated their perspective, bringing up her lesbian best friend, Nadine.

"No!" Migdalia piped up. "No, you're too old! It's okay to go with your girlfriends when you are young, but when you get older you have to go with the mens!"

You could hear a pin drop in the car. Mary quickly changed the subject, asking everyone what they'd ordered for dinner. "The chicken, the salmon, the prime rib?"

18

Lune de Miel

AS OUR WEDDING RECEPTION wound down, our party shifted from dancing and dreaminess to brass tacks. We paid the caterer, shlepped our wedding presents down to the front steps, and noticed that the rainy forecast, which had held its breath all day for us, let loose with every drop of power that a daylong rain squeezed into a few hours could exert. Will hailed a cab and began loading the presents into the trunk, with my brother's help. I gathered up my dress's voluminous skirts and sloshed down the granite steps and through the flooded sidewalks' gritty urban runoff.

The cab driver took off with a jerk, not happy for us in the slightest. The car seemed to tilt back under the weight of our wedding presents. We headed down from the Upper East Side's grand silhouettes to our grotty Alphabet City block. And somewhere in between the two, we began to argue. I don't remember what it was about. But what I do remember is that Will grabbed my jaw with his hand and squeezed it, hard, for several very long seconds, saying, "Stop, just stop, be quiet!"

"I can't believe you just did that! That hurt. Why did you do that?" I dissolved into frantic, exhausted tears. He had never done anything like that before. Was it just a freak occurrence, or had I just married one of those men who began to act abusive after the wedding, after I was trapped?

"Don't make such a big deal out of this," he said. "I'm tired, we have been under a lot of stress. I think this is just having such an effect on you because of your issues with your stepfather. Can we please have a good wedding night?"

I couldn't even talk, I was crying so hard. Especially because I didn't know what I was supposed to feel. Either I was having an appropriate reaction and my future was ruined, or I was overreacting because I was damaged goods and, as such, was ruining the wedding night for myself and my husband. The car pulled up to the front of our building, and I rushed up the stoop, opened the doors, and waited for Will in the vestibule. He stood in the dark deluge in his wet tuxedo, pulling boxes out of the taxi's yellow trunk. He looked like a boy. In the door's glass panel reflection, I looked like a Halloween bride, mascara running down my cheeks.

You idiot, you thought you could escape this. Not special. Not normal.

I picked up the box of Pottery Barn "Emma" plates, balanced a centerpiece on top, and made my first trip up the stairs. As soon as Will pulled the last box out of the car, the taxi driver gunned it, doubtless eager to get away from our dénouement.

As we brought the last things into the apartment, I looked down at my white-garbed body. I needed to get this rig off. How? I'd been helped into it. Slowly, I found the zippers and hooks and left it in a heap on the couch. I stood there in my underwear, unwilling to put on the special bridal peignoir set that I had received at my bridal shower. It mocked me. I grabbed an old flannel nightgown and got in bed.

"Candace, Candace, Candace," Will said, out of his suit as well. "Come here." He opened up my arms, put his chest against mine, and stroked my hair. "It's okay. I'm so sorry. I didn't mean to do that. I wish I could take it back. Can we just have a do-over? I don't want this to be the way we spend our wedding night."

Slowly, he stroked and soothed me, and because it was so early in our married life, I was capable of shifting from sorrow and panic to a sensuality that felt not only healing, a "making up," but also oddly more charged and passionate by far than regular sex ever was. This hand here, that opening there, this breath here, that advance there, make it all better. It erased what he did, and it erased my response.

It meant that we could go on, and go on happily. That was what I made it mean.

Every morning of our honeymoon, Will and I stopped off at Didier and Sabine's Burgundian auberge for breakfast. Sabine was petite, wiry, consummately engaged, no-nonsense, with boldly etched dimples like parentheses that bordered her mobile, full mouth, which was always smiling or frowning or making stretchy Gallic faces of *who cares?* or *why not?* or *who can say?* They had two daughters, reminiscent of a fairy tale: one grave, beautiful, and responsible, the other silly, young, and plump.

Fresh from a good night's sleep, flushed from our latest round of babymaking efforts, we sat down at a table for two.

"Bonjour, les nouveaux mariés!" said Didier, dropping a basket of stout little rolls, fruit confiture, and local, grassy beurre. *"Vitamine?"* he asked, referring to the citrusy juice he served in small glasses. *"Du café, du thé?"*

"Café au lait, s'il vous plaît," I said.

My three years of high school French could have benefited from a refresher, but I was content to let Will take the communication lead. When we weren't at *marchés* scooping up beautiful produce, Will and I spent our days driving around the vineyards with wine appellations that sounded like angels' whispers: Pernand-Vergelesses, Nuits-Saint-Georges, Arnay-le-Duc, Chalon-sur-Saône, Aloxe-Corton, Chassagne-Montrachet, Gevrey-Chambertin, Pouilly-en-Auxois. We parked the car and walked up and down sleepy limestone streets.

Will's work connections also got us private tastings in the cellars of Louis Jadot and Faiveley. François Faiveley himself sat down to lunch with us, tall and handsome in a crisp Façonnable button-down shirt. Faiveley had a sailboat, and regularly sailed across oceans with his small crew.

"Does your wife go with you?" Will asked.

"Oh, no, she meets me on the other side," he said.

"If Will decided to sail across the ocean, I would go with him," I said.

"Why, because you love to sail as well?"

"Not really. I think it's dangerous. But if I couldn't talk him out of it, I'd have to accompany him, because if his boat went down, I'd want to go down with him. I couldn't imagine living without him."

Faiveley and his PR man sighed and cocked their heads in appreciation of my fealty. I wasn't putting on a show, or even that aware of the impact my words would have as they flew from my mouth. At the time, that's how much I loved him. Our lives were inextricable.

Oftentimes we'd finish a lunch and then realize that the reservations we'd made weeks ago for a hard-to-get-into restaurant were scheduled for a few hours hence. Although I didn't sit down to dinner ravenous by any means, soon, the sheer novelty of the chefs' creations overrode my near-satiety. We were in France! At La Bouzerotte in Bligny-lès-Beaune, I was served an appetizer within an eggshell, the top gently lopped off. A mousse of foie gras, egg, and cream rested within, the ultimate grownup's Easter egg.

We made sure to keep an empty stomach for Lameloise, the Michelin three-star restaurant in Chagny. As soon as we sat down, amuse-bouches began arriving: gemlike little layered cubes of smoked salmon, Comté cheese sticks, beef tartare topped with rosettes of avocado, and other exquisite canapés that demanded to be consumed. The thought of the tiny sculptures being thrown out . . . impossible. By the time I was finished with the rest of the courses, I knew that I had to go to the restroom and bring it back up. My stomach was groaningly full. I tried to be quiet. When I finished, I went to the sink and rinsed out my mouth thoroughly, looked at my eyes. My lower eyelids were pink, a bit of a giveaway. But Will never seemed to notice when I did this, so, after splashing my face with water and patting it dry, I returned just in time for dessert.

"Why do you want to have a baby right away?" Will's coworker Marty had asked. "That's nuts. You gotta enjoy each other for a couple of years. Have fun. Having a baby is a lot of work, and it changes things big-time." Maybe for him. I knew having a baby would just bring Will and me closer together. We were going to love that baby so much.

When we flew back to New York, we brought red cast-iron skillets from Déhillerin in Paris, a set of Laguiole knives, eight tall juice glasses printed with red cherries, a silver roll-top sugar bowl and a box of wrapped sugar cubes, Noire Velours coffee for Frank and Scott, our cloths and napkins, and, although I didn't have the nerve to weigh myself, at least ten new pounds on my frame. So what? It was well worth it.

19

Bun in the Oven

AFTER SIX MONTHS of trying unsuccessfully to get pregnant, Will and I stopped paying attention to my supposedly fertile days and returned to just having sex for the fun of it. The following month, I conceived.

My mother and stepmother had both had highly medicalized births. My mother had four cesareans, and my stepmother two inductions.

"What is your practice's cesarean rate?" I asked my OB, a new doctor who was tall, young, rushed, slim, and brunette. I had ended up with her because I was new to the practice (which came highly recommended), and so was she. She literally never made eye contact with me, and made me wait in a paper robe for about forty-five minutes every time we had an appointment.

"Oh, hard to say. Why do you ask?" she said, while riffling through papers.

I explained that I didn't want to have a cesarean.

"We don't give women cesareans unless they *need* them, and if you end up with one, it will be because you *needed* it," she declared, finally looking at me. "So, you'll be with one of the seven doctors here, and you'll probably get a chance to meet with each of us before your birth."

"But I've already met with you four times in a row. So how am I actually going to meet all of them?"

"It doesn't matter, because you end up with who's on call anyway."

"A perfect stranger?" Not like I felt safe with her, and I'd spent the most—well, all of my—time with her.

"Trust me, you'll be in good hands."

I reasoned that Dr. Twit was probably very nice underneath her horrid bedside manner. She was just awkward, or so brainy that she didn't know how to relate to people.

But then I heard her chatting up the nurse's aide outside the door of my examination room. I'd already been waiting for a half hour, but she stood there, pretty much kissing this woman's ass. "I love your pants! Oh, you got them at T.J. Maxx? Oh, I love bargains. I'm going to go there after work and pick up a pair! I'm so low on trousers. Good for you! Yeah, they really look pricey. Right on, sister!"

Really? She could be that nice to the nurse's aide on the topic of *slacks,* but she couldn't be bothered to be nice to me, her pregnant patient?

Evenings after my appointments with Dr. Twit, I sat on the couch, catatonic and weepy. I had such a bad feeling about staying with her. And I felt so responsible, yet overwhelmed.

"What is wrong with you?" Will asked. "You're just so distant."

"I'm upset and scared about my obstetrician situation," I said.

"But why do you have to be like this? I just came home from work and I was looking forward to spending time with you, and it's like you're not even here. I feel like you don't see me."

"I'm really upset, and I don't know what to do, so yeah, I am not very present."

He got up in a huff.

"Why are you mad at me because I'm upset? Why can't you comfort me? That's clearly what I need." I cried harder. "I can't believe that you're acting like this."

"I could say the same thing about you!"

He went into the other room. I was on my own.

I decided to find another doctor. I called office after office. "What month are you in?" the receptionists asked, as if they were all the same receptionist at some central switchboard.

"I'm in my fifth month."

"Sorry, we don't take transfers after the first trimester."

"Why not?"

"It's harder to bill, for insurance purposes." Or, "It puts our doctors in an awkward position. We try not to steal each other's patients."

"Nobody is *stealing* me. I'm not happy where I am."

"Sorry, that's just the policy."

I paged through my insurance practitioner directory one more time, but I'd exhausted every option. Then I saw "midwives." Midwives still existed? And my insurance covered them? Weird! Come to think of it, I did remember that my writing-group friend Jenny had homebirths with midwives. She was also a model of hip, beautiful, vibrant motherhood I'd never before encountered: She breastfed and was slim and energetic, with glowing skin and well-adjusted children.

Sylvie Blaustein and Lynne Chapman. Upper West Side. I called and left a message with the receptionist, who did not appear to care that I was in my fifth month.

Within the hour, the phone rang. "Candace?" a woman's voice asked, all chocolate babka and tea with sugar. "This is Sylvie." She had me at hello.

I transferred to her practice after one consultation. Sylvie had a huge, loving smile, and that nurturing, bliss-inducing voice, and just sat and beamed at me as she asked all of the right questions and didn't hesitate to answer mine. Lynne, the other midwife, was athletic—a runner—and slightly more businesslike, but still very warm.

Their receptionist faxed Dr. Twit's office to request my records. The phone rang the next day. "Hi, this is Dr. Twit. I just got this request for your records. You're transferring care? I would think that you would have talked to me if you weren't happy." Her voice was shrill.

This was her attempt to woo me back? By scolding me? She was probably getting her narrow ass chewed out by the senior doctors over losing a patient.

I could have read her a list of reasons, but I was unprepared, and my formerly sassy brain was in a bath of unhelpful estrogen and oxytocin. "Oh, it's not you, it's me. I just need a more warm and fuzzy experience."

"Oh," she said, as if I had just said that I required a warm walnut oil perineal massage at every appointment. "Well, good luck with *that!* Bye!"

After I connected with Sylvie's practice, my pregnancy took a hard right turn into happy land. I stumbled upon an online pregnancy forum, HipMama.com, and connected with other women across the country who were also due in my birth month, July. They often were also the only pregnant woman in their circle. Many of them were also working with midwives, and had to deal with sometimes grumpy partners, strangers grabbing their bellies in the supermarket, and obnoxious relatives forcing unwanted advice and *stuff* on them.

I felt so connected to my baby. I was reading an anthology of essays by pregnant women, and just as I read the sentence that talked about the writer's feeling her baby move for the first time, my baby moved—almost as if she knew what I was reading, or got the message from my thoughts.

Our childbirth preparation classes began at the Elizabeth Seton Center, where every Wednesday Will and I sat in a circle with several other couples. Our teacher, Jessie, was sweet and knowledgeable. We watched childbirth movies. We shared complaints and highlights, and every week a different couple brought the snack. When it was my turn, I spent the day baking: two different kinds of cupcakes from *The Cake Bible*—vanilla cupcakes with white chocolate–cream cheese buttercream, and chocolate cupcakes with bittersweet chocolate–sour cream ganache.

"Wow!" said one of the pregnant women, Daphne. "These are *amazing.* I'm afraid I'm going to have to send John to get me another one!"

"Don't be afraid," I said. "You should absolutely have another one. That's why I made sixty."

"I'm going to make flan next week for everyone," she said.

"Oh," I said, "great!" I had never eaten flan but was wary, since my sister had told me that she'd recently had some at a restaurant with a friend, and they'd decided that it tasted like penis. Was that really what a bunch of superpregnant women wanted to deal with? But the next week, Daphne brought it, and it was like heaven. Creamy yet light. Caramelized but very richly vanilla. Sitting in an amazing delicate syrup.

Daphne and John had Will and me over to their beautiful Park Slope flat and grilled butterflied chickens in the back garden. Daphne, who was Dominican, made a beautiful assortment of salsas for our soft tacos. We filled the homemade tortillas with the chicken, sliced cabbage, and tomatoes.

I realized that Bastille Day was July 14, and it would most likely be the last time I'd be able to throw a big food-centric party before the baby came. Will thought it was a great idea—and was soothed to see that I hadn't lost interest in entertaining. I invited my friends, including Daphne and John, and Will's foodie friends from work.

Since it was such a hot summer day in my non-air-conditioned apartment, I made three chilled soups: blueberry-yogurt, white vichyssoise, and red gazpacho, then poured them into shot glasses and arranged them on a large rectangular tray in the design of the French flag.

I also made Spring Potatoes with Caviar and Chives—from the *Cooking with Daniel Boulud* cookbook. First I hollowed out the mini-potatoes, then baked them, covered, in a chicken-broth bath. After they cooled a little bit, I stuffed them with the crème fraîche–chopped chives mixture and topped them with briny caviar. Fruit salad, a green salad, endive leaves stuffed with herbed chicken, and another tricolor-themed food—a rectangular tart, of pastry crust, filled with pastry cream, and covered with rows of raspberries, blueberries, and, in the middle, whipped cream. The apartment was wall-to-wall happy eaters, wine and champagne cocktails flowed, and I felt like our worlds were mixing up to evolve along with our new life.

I had hoped that I would go into labor at the end of the party, as if this bounty of (mostly) French food would call forth my little girl. It was almost like a dare. Will and I had decided to name her Honorée, a feminine form of an old French name that I saw as part of the BOULEVARD ST. HONORÉ signs in Paris. (Later, I found out that Honoré is also the patron saint of baked goods, which was a lovely surprise.) But that wasn't the case. The party ended, and she didn't arrive.

July came and went. My due date came and went. I was huge, tired, cranky, and swollen. My thighs chafed when I walked, unless I had on prophylactic bike shorts. My ankles became cankles. My nose widened and I developed a double chin and back fat. My butt, which had always been a flattish Walsh ass, turned bubble-round. I wore ugly floral cotton *shmattes* that my mom picked up at yard sales for me, because I was unable to deal with spending any more money on ridiculously overpriced maternity wear. Hell, I no longer fit into the maternity wear. My feet were so big that I bought a pair of men's knockoff Birkenstocks from a sidewalk sale and wore those every day, along with a zebra-print tube skirt that fit me like a sausage casing and a Motherhood Maternity T-shirt.

I knew that many women went to the beauty parlor and got pedicures when they were pregnant; I clearly wasn't one of them. They didn't turn into sweaty, bloated, unkempt slatterns who didn't give a hot damn.

During my second trimester, I had rashly promised to send two of my July mamas (who had gestational diabetes) brownies as soon as they gave birth and could go off their no-sugar diets. Well, they had given birth. And I hadn't. In August, a million months pregnant? I kept on waiting to have the baby so that would be an excuse not to make the brownies, but I began to wonder if I wouldn't have the baby until I fulfilled my promise.

So I got to baking. As sweat pooled in the hollow of my clavicle, I mixed up chocolate brownie batter in Bella, and then made the frosting. I baked the brownies, took them out, let them cool, and spread the frosting on top. No contractions.

I left to go uptown to my fetal nonstress test. Even though I had midwives, they didn't want to let me go much further without inducing me. I was seven days past my due date. I knew that an induction could easily turn into a C-section, and that the due date was an approximation anyway. I had read my Ina May Gaskin.

As the tech tested my belly, she kept up an unremitting stream of patter. "You really need to just go have that baby. There's no reason to wait."

"Well, is there any indication from the test that I need to go in?"

"No, but you're overdue. You should go. She's ready to come out."

I thought that if she were ready, my body would be acting like it. I left the hospital and walked to the bus. I'd been having Braxton-Hicks contractions for weeks, so I didn't pay much attention to those. But by the time I got off the bus at Fourteenth Street, I had to pause every few steps. The contractions didn't hurt at all, but they were intense.

I took the bus down Avenue C and then slowly home. Once I got inside, I began to feel real contractions. I called Will. "It's time," I said.

"Okay!" By some miracle of traffic, he was home in ten minutes. I also called my mother.

"Go to the hospital!" she said. "What are you waiting for?"

"It's so early," I said. "I'm fine." I knew that going to the hospital too early could derail labor. I called the midwife's office. Lynne was on duty. "I'm in labor," I said.

"How far apart are your contractions?"

"About eight minutes."

"How do you feel?"

"Great! I'm just making a salad."

She laughed. "Okay, well, if you're feeling good enough to make a salad, you've got a ways to go. Call me when it gets more intense."

She was right. This was my first birth. I probably had hours and hours to go. We ate the salad, and I decided to take an aromatherapy bath. Will lit candles and began to play our birth mix tape.

Once I was in the bath, the contractions turned from bearable things to burly slaloms of pain only a few minutes apart.

"We have to call Lynne," I said, crying, as I stood up, naked and wet, looking like a monster seal in a child's nightmare. I held out my arms to be helped out of the tub. "This is really intense!"

I called Lynne.

"How are your contractions?"

"Agggghhhhhhhhhhh! They're so much more painful!"

"Okay, it sounds like you're ready to meet me at the hospital."

Will called a car service; we grabbed our bag, the mix tape, and the little tape player and headed down the stairs. I had only one contraction on the graffitied stoop before the oddly beautiful, extra-fancy town car pulled up. Now I had to worry about my water breaking on this guy's buffed, cordovan leather, pride-and-joy seats, instead of in one of the usual beaters that the Lower East Side Car Service sent our way.

I was hugely pregnant and looked distraught, we had a big bag and a car seat, and we were headed to the hospital, but somehow the driver didn't seem to snap to the fact that I was in labor. He drove fifteen miles per hour up Avenue C, singing along to the radio in Spanish.

"Could you please hurry?" Will said, as I grabbed the shirt handle and had another big contraction.

"Counterpressure!" I yelled. "Oh God, press on my back!" The driver stepped on it and about fifteen minutes later pulled up in front of Columbia Presbyterian, Allen Pavilion, at the northern tip of Manhattan.

I'd preregistered, so I was confident, in between more contractions, that they'd get me into a room. But when I walked up to the desk, the bored clerks told me to go have a seat next to three other pregnant women, who didn't seem too happy but were not yet at my state. I looked at the clerks, dropped my bag on the floor, bellowed, and fell on the floor on all fours.

"Get her in a room," one said. And that was that.

Lynne came rushing in as I walked back and forth in the room. "Hi, Candace! Are you ready to have this baby?"

"Oh God, yeah." I had on one of my cotton *shmattes*.

She checked me. "You're at nine centimeters. And you're having back labor."

"What?" I was expecting to be at two. I'd been checked the day before, and hadn't even been at one. Back labor was supposed to be way more painful than regular labor. It sure seemed that way.

"Get that thing off. It's time to get naked and have this baby." I'd always wondered why, in the childbirth videos, the women were always naked. Why did they have to give birth naked? But now, it seemed like the best possible idea.

"Oh, Lynne, I feel like I need to sit on the toilet."

"That's fine."

I had a few contractions there, and they were beyond what I ever thought I could imagine pain to be. "I want drugs!" I said. "I said if I was going to have back labor I'd have drugs. And I'm having back labor." My team looked at me.

"You're so far along. Just have one or two more contractions, and we'll see where we are. Let's get you in the shower."

Will jumped in the shower, fully clad, and turned on the water, soaking himself in the process. He didn't care. "Come on, honey. We can do it."

I had another contraction, he gave me counterpressure, and *blooooooosh,* my water broke as the baby came down my canal. It felt like I had just popped a water balloon with my vagina.

"Come back over to the bed!" Lynne commanded. She got in my face as I began to walk that way. "Pant like a dog!" She stuck out her tongue and demonstrated. I obeyed. Naked and panting like a dog, why not. "It'll give you a few extra seconds," she said.

A few more steps, and I was there. I dove sideways onto the bed, and Lynne had Will lift my leg up.

"I have to push!" I said.

"Try to take your time," Lynne said.

"I can't!" Out came Honorée, and Lynne lifted her up and put her on my chest. Her round, urgent eyes, her wet mop of black hair, her cherry-red lips. "Ohhh," I said. "Baby."

I fell in love with her immediately. I knew her, and she knew me. She moved her head to my giant purple headlamp of a nipple and opened her mouth. With one shockingly strong tug, this little being claimed me. And I was not just a creator of this tiny, avid human. Now that she was in my arms, I was the creator of her food.

As she sucked, I felt another contraction come on. "It's your placenta," Lynne said. "You just need to deliver that, and then you'll be all done pushing." It slid out like a raw pot roast.

"Look," Lynne said, "isn't it beautiful? Can you see the tree of life?"

I did. It had a central trunk and beautiful symmetrical branches. Lynne turned and put it into a plastic bin.

Will pulled out a bottle of Nicolas Feuillatte rosé champagne. He put a drop on Honorée's tongue. "Just like in France."

After a few minutes, the nurse took Honorée away to be weighed and tested across the room. Will went with her. She cried piteously. Will sang to her and spoke soothing words, and held her little hand. I looked at Lynne. "Wow."

"Not bad for your first baby. What was it, five hours?"

"Maybe seven, if you count the mild contractions."

"You did great."

I'd spent my whole life feeling ashamed of my body. In gym class and in sports, I'd been slow, clumsy, graceless, and uncoordinated. But it turned out that I was a natural gold medalist in the Birth Olympics. If the goal-scorers and ribbon-breakers and baton-twirlers and ball-dunkers and break-dancers could cry out in triumph, high-five, and swagger, so could I. But right now, what I really wanted was a big juicy hamburger and a chocolate shake.

20

Baby Food

In the first few weeks of Honorée's life, we took her to the Union Square Greenmarket, City Bakery, and Tartine. I sat with her in Tompkins Square Park, looking forward to the time when she'd be big enough to clamber around on the jungle gym and ask to be pushed on the swings.

I brought her downtown when she was three weeks old so that she could help me pick out birthday presents for her dad at Century 21 department store. We got him a tie and some new socks. I also wanted to get him a book on sailing, so we walked across the street and down the escalator to the Barnes & Noble below the North Tower of the World Trade Center.

I was eager to hang out with Daphne again, this time with our babies on the outside. I called her up. "Want to have a playdate?" I asked jokingly. The babies were only a month old.

"Sure, that would be great. When were you thinking?"

"Next Tuesday morning? I could come out to Brooklyn with Honorée."

"Um . . . well, let's see. I was going to go into work with John and show off the baby to his coworkers."

"Oh, we can make it another day."

"No, let's do it. I can go into work with John some other time." We agreed to meet up at 10:00.

It was fun to bop around and visit people with Honorée. I had lunch with friends downtown, and took the 7 into Long Island City to meet my dad for lunch another day. We decided to make a weekly ritual of it, and I imagined Honorée looking forward to it, moving from our arms to a high chair, then a booster seat. I imagined writing a story about it—the healing reunion of two alienated souls, father and daughter, through the granddaughter.

Will and I spent a restorative three-day weekend with my mother in Long Beach. Monday night, it was time to go. "I feel weird," I said. "I really don't want to go back into the city."

"Stay!" said my mother. "You can take a walk on the boardwalk, we can go to lunch . . ."

I thought about it. Staying there while Will went back didn't feel right, either.

"No. Will has to go back in, and I don't want him to go without us."

"Okay, suit yourself. You know I just want more time with that perfect baby! I can't wait until she gets old enough to visit with Grandma all by herself and you can have some time to relax and go get your hair done, whatever."

That Tuesday morning, I took a shower before Will left for work and sent him off with his usual egg sandwich. Honorée enjoyed being held by him while I did my thing—after her morning top-off, of course.

He called me a few minutes after 9:00. "A plane just flew into the World Trade Center," he said. "Can you see it from the window?"

I turned and looked out the window at the building, which was two miles away but in plain sight. The tall gray rectangle had a dark pockmark marring its face, with smoke pouring out of it. "Yes, oh my God. Oh my God."

"They think it might have been a Cessna."

You know the rest. The other plane hit, and transportation on and off the island of Manhattan was shut down. Will began to walk home from the East Sixties, people crowded around parked cars to listen to their radios, they queued up outside ATMs, and they walked home to the boroughs over the bridges. The hipster guy who lived upstairs, the one who bragged about having seven dates on Valentine's Day, ran up and down the five flights of stairs, screaming, when the first building fell, and we all went up on the roof and looked at the hole in the skyline, and up at the lean fighter jets banking above in the blue sky. I held Honorée, and one of my neighbors told me that her son was in the school across the street, which was on lockdown, and she had to wait for him to be returned to her.

"I'm sorry," I said.

I called Daphne. "I have to cancel," I said.

"Candace," she said, "I was going to take the baby in to work today with John, and if I had, we would have gone in early." John worked in the World Trade Center.

"Is John okay?"

"He's on his way home," she said. "Walking."

"So is Will," I said.

"You saved us," she said.

"I just asked for a playdate," I said.

"Well, that playdate kept us out of there. I have to go. I'm getting a lot of calls from friends and family."

"Sure, talk to you later."

Frank also worked in the World Trade Center, but he and Scott were on vacation at a cooking school in France. Everyone I knew was okay. The footbridge that I used to walk over every day was dangling in the middle of the air over West Street, and the World Financial Center's Winter Garden Atrium was a shattered shambles.

And every minute, the air darkened.

"We have to get out of here," I told Will when he got home. "I want to go to my mom's."

"I have to go to work tomorrow," he said. "The other managers weren't happy that I left."

Two days later, I packed a bag with baby clothes, diapers, my own clothes, and toothbrushes and left with Honorée. The hardware store on Avenue C was out of face masks, so I draped sheer scarves around our faces. Our neighborhood had been requisitioned as a parking lot for aid vehicles, and we had to show ID to get in and out of it. I walked past fire trucks, and trucks sent by chain supermarkets, filled with donated food and supplies.

I walked all the way to Twenty-Third Street, where we caught a bus to Penn Station. I looked up, hearing applause, at one of the stops. A man in a hardhat, covered in ash, had just gotten on. I clapped, too, with nothing approaching celebration in my body. I had to get out with my baby. Penn Station had been receiving bomb threats, and it was far from a safe location, but it was the only way to get to Long Beach.

Once I left, I didn't want to go back. I would have, if I weren't a mother. I would have jumped on my bike and ridden down there to see if I could help. But I had to get Honorée to clean, fresh ocean air.

I sublet our apartment. Will and I started looking at apartments near my mother. As luck would have it, the house next door had an upstairs apartment that the owners were renovating at that very moment. The price they quoted us was clearly inflated, but we weren't in a position to be too particular. I thought about my mother growing up next to her grandparents in Sheepshead Bay, and wondered if this horrible tragedy couldn't offer some slender fringe benefits.

We spent weeks sleeping on my mother's foldout couch in her living room, and I spent my days sitting on it reading "Profiles in Courage" in the *New York Times* and crying as Honorée watched me with worried little eyes. I walked on the boardwalk, when I could motivate myself. I hadn't lost anyone, but I'd lost my life as I'd expected it to unfold, and lunches with my father in Long Island City, and afternoons in Tompkins Square Park. And I worried about Will as he took the train into and out of the city amid anthrax scares and bomb threats. We clung to each other at night, disoriented.

Once we signed the lease, setting up house in the apartment next door was a welcome and absorbing distraction. The apartment was beautiful. It had freshly polished hardwood floors, high ceilings, and a front patio, just like Migdalia's in Bay Ridge so many years before. The kitchen was huge compared with my last one—with lots of counter space, and even a pantry. Bella looked beautiful against the blond wood. I furnished the place cheaply with under-appreciated midcentury-modern furniture sourced at estate sales, and filled in the blanks during trips to IKEA. I cooked at my mother's house and at my own, while my brothers took turns holding the baby. It was nice to have a break, and to make meals again.

My mother was busy and hard to pin down. I'd thought she'd be around more, to help me with the baby and even just keep me company. I'd helped her so much with my siblings when I was a kid. Now that the shoe was on the other foot, I felt ripped off.

But she did help by doing loads of our laundry and lending us her car. "Why don't you try Weight Watchers?" she asked. "They meet in the synagogue on the corner."

"How much weight do you think I need to lose?" I asked her. Big mistake.

"About sixty pounds," she said nonchalantly.

"What?" I felt like she had punched me in the heart. If I lost sixty pounds, I'd be the same weight I was when I was sixteen, exercising two hours a day, on a diet of grapefruit, salad, and chicken breasts. That's how far I was from what she thought was acceptable? Sixty pounds?

In spite of her skewed perspective, I began the program, to lose the *twenty* pounds of baby weight that I'd gained. It didn't help that nursing made me crave sugar in a way that I never had before. Bored and noshy, I made batches of snickerdoodles on a regular basis, or snacked on cookies from Trader Joe's. It took weeks for even one half-pound to drop off, even though I was obsessively compliant with the plan.

Over three months, I lost ten pounds total, and then gained back two. I gave up. It was too frustrating. Will loved me the way I was, and I didn't have any diminished sexual interest, although I kind of wished he did. I was touched out after day after day with the baby, but he seemed to need sex as a form of reassurance or as a source of pep.

Maybe if we had followed Marty's advice and waited, we would have been better off—or maybe we wouldn't have had a child together. The jaw-grab that happened on our wedding night was not the last bad thing between us. Maybe the commuting, or the post-9/11 trauma, the long, six-day workweeks, the pressure from his bosses, and our utter lack of time together as a couple, were to blame.

On his birthday, a year after I shopped for him at the World Trade Center Barnes & Noble, I made the latest *Bon Appétit*'s cover recipe, a Bolognese sauce with homemade pappardelle pasta. Unlike the red-sauce Italian stuff I grew up with, this recipe had an intriguing assortment of ingredients and steps that promised to add up to something special.

Honorée blessed me by taking lots of naps that day—her birthday present to her dad. And then my brother Jimmy came over to visit and play with her. By the time Will came through the door, my mother, brothers, one-year-old Honorée, and I were waiting to fête him. He was jolly and had wine bottles in hand.

We sat down around the small table, crowded and happy. Although the dinner looked like a million other pasta-and-sauce dishes, the pasta was soft yet delightfully stretchy, and soaked up the sauce, bits of meat and vegetables nestling in its folds. The Bolognese was complex, starting off with tomato, then deepening into wine and the savory browned-meat and bacon flavors. For dessert, we had *The Cake Bible*'s vanilla cake with whipped cream and berries.

Will was all smiles and opened his presents. After everyone left, I took a very overtired Honorée to bed to nurse her to sleep. I started to doze off after a few minutes.

"So, you're just going to bed?" he asked, with an accusing tone.

I opened my eyes and saw the silhouette of his outline in the doorway.

"Um . . . maybe. I'm tired. Why?"

"Well it's just that the kitchen is trashed, dirty dishes everywhere, and I'm gonna have to do them even though it's my birthday?"

"No, you don't."

"Well, if I don't do them now, I'll have to do them in the morning, and that's not the way I want to start my day, before going into the city for ten hours."

"I'll do them tomorrow."

"No, you can't, because it's so hard for you to do them with the baby, that's what you say, anyway, and then they'll be here when I get home . . ."

So that turned into a long, miserable argument that I tried to end, but he wouldn't stop arguing if he wasn't ready. I knew that by now.

It seemed like the slightest thing would set him off, and he'd rage for hours, following me around the house, yelling at me about how the house wasn't clean enough, the money wasn't spent right, or whatever it was. One time, after I took Honorée into her room and closed the door, he followed me and forced it open. I picked up the Boppy pillow and swung it at him, and it ripped right along the inner center seam.

"Look what you did!" he yelled. "You ruined her pillow! What's wrong with you?"

I didn't have a very good answer, standing there with the mangled Boppy. He certainly appeared to have the moral high ground.

Another time, I decided to leave and go next door to my mom's. Why not? She was right there, and this discord wasn't good for Honorée to witness. So much for our desire to do things differently so that Honorée's childhood would be lovely and harmonious. I picked her up and started down the stairs.

He leaped down to the landing below. "Don't leave me."

"I'm going. You won't stop, you won't calm down."

"Well, too bad!"

"No."

I kept walking until I crossed the foyer and stepped over the threshold. Just as both feet landed on the other side, I felt his foot on my rear. He had just kicked me—albeit gently, more like a nudge—but it threw me a little bit off balance, with an infant in my arms. How was that even remotely okay?

This was my sweet boy, my rescuer, my sensitive lover of Mozart and first-growth wines, screaming himself hoarse over my failings and flaws. It broke my heart.

❧ ❧ ❧

And then my mother told me she was getting a gastric bypass.

"What?" I said. She had been on every fad diet that came along, but this had serious risks attached to it. She was fifty-three, and lately *had* been heavier, but she ate like crap. I'd been watching her. She brought home pizzas, fried chicken, polished off bowls of nuts, chocolate, sleeves of Chips Ahoy cookies in one sitting.

"You're not heavy enough for that, Mom," I said. "That's for obese people."

"I'm almost there, and when I am fat enough, my doctor says that he will get it approved by my insurance company and do the surgery."

"You're purposely gaining weight in order to qualify for a gastric bypass?"

"Right!" she said, smiling, as if I had just guessed that she had a winning lottery ticket.

"It's a terrible idea," I said. "Why don't you just stop eating junk food and exercise?"

"I can't diet," she said. "And I can't exercise, either. I'm allergic to sweat."

"Seriously? How can you be allergic to your own sweat?"

"I don't know. I get itchy."

"You're making a huge mistake. Please reconsider."

"I've made up my mind."

My sister and I spent a lot of time on the phone and researching online, freaking out about it.

"She's getting the irreversible gastric bypass."

"It has a one-in-ten mortality rate."

"She's going to kill herself this way."

"This is just another example of her eating disorder."

"She has a surgery fetish."

"This causes a lot of illnesses down the road that are life-shortening."

"If she eats the wrong thing, or too much, she'll spend hours in pain, vomiting."

"This is the stupidest thing she's ever done."

All of the time we'd spent watching my mother hate her appearance—covet skinny women's bodies, and even look critically at our own bodies no matter how thin we were—hit us like a sledgehammer. We cried together. Worst of all, I imagined the loss of the rest of her culinary life. She wouldn't be able to eat many foods, and the ones she could eat were going to be limited to a few spoonfuls. Would she stop cooking?

"You should be happy for her," one of her friends told me. "She wants to feel good about herself."

"That's my point," I said. "That's not going to come from a surgery," I said. "That has to come from inside herself."

The whole thing made my stomach hurt, and it continued to, as she went through with the surgery and spent weeks recovering next door. I let her friends take over; she knew I didn't support her decision, and the sight of her bandaged, origamied stomach, drainage tubes, and drugged-out demeanor were too upsetting.

Will's stepmother called up one spring day. "How about I fly you out to New Mexico for your father's birthday?" she asked brightly. "We can surprise him!"

We didn't have to think twice about that proposal. It would be great to visit Santa Fe. But as we packed and prepared, we had no idea that it would lead to our moving there.

The thought stole up on us separately, and lingered in the air between us. Will and I looked at each other. I don't remember who uttered it first, because both of our brains were reverberating with the same message: "We should move here." And when it was said, the other blurted out, "I know!"

When we were younger and in our twenties, Santa Fe had seemed too slow, too remote. But now that I was married and a mother, it felt just right.

If we moved to Santa Fe, we'd be able to buy a house sooner, and I was sure Will would be happier and less short-tempered, the sanguine man I had met instead of the unpredictable, angry person he'd been lately.

I'd be sad about leaving New York, but not overwhelmingly so. My fantasy about being a part of an extended family hadn't exactly panned out. My mother was busy. My father was his usual self. Having a child didn't prevent old patterns and hurts from resurfacing.

The night before we left Long Beach for good, we stayed up late finishing the odds and ends of packing and went to sleep on an inflatable mattress that could be tossed into the back of the Ryder truck that would take us across eleven states. It was hard to fall asleep, even though I was tired, because I was keyed up. But finally, I began to doze off, and as I did, I dreamed that I was watching my life progress as a straight line. I felt the sensation of a finger-thin tree root rip from the earth, small hairs tearing away from it, as the line turned sharply at a ninety-degree angle and moved steadily away from the original vector and whatever might have awaited me.

We left at 5:00 AM. Bundled up in the darkness, we rang my mother's doorbell. She opened the door and brought us into the kitchen. There she hugged each of us fiercely, sobbing, almost doubled over in our arms.

After all of the months of wanting time with my mother, I was sad that our time as neighbors had been so unsatisfying, and that the passion she clearly felt for us was coming out only now. The power of the scene—daughter leaving daughter with own daughter in arms—was strong, and my tears surfaced as well.

But I wasn't distraught. We were going someplace where the disappointments (as well as the joys) would be unpredictable and new, not a deepening of lifelong grooves.

21

Wine and Chile

As we arrived in Santa Fe in late October, I wondered what we'd do for Thanksgiving. My instinct was to have our own, small gathering with the three of us and maybe Will's dad or his stepmom (they were no longer married). But my father-in-law invited us over, and that was that.

"Don't worry about it, just show up," he said. "I'll take care of everything."

"Can I bring pies?"

"We'll have everything. Just bring yourselves."

This was new for me, but what wasn't new? Why not? But I still couldn't resist picking up a few Thanksgiving-themed food magazines. A few days before Thanksgiving, Will called his dad, "So, how are the preparations going?"

"Good, we have everything we need: turkey and vodka."

"How big is the turkey?"

"Oh, the cook from the Green Onion is bringing over turkey."

The Green Onion was his dad's bar.

"What else?"

"That's it. We don't need anything else. Oh, Ellen's making mashed potatoes."

Ellen was Will's dad's girlfriend—a tall, lanky blond who was both a vegan and a good listener. Together, they were deeply metaphysical—into channelers like Abraham, countless gurus, and creating your own reality. She loved animals and small children, and regarded them both as if they were fascinating emissaries from the land of pure love.

It made me bristle that I could never complain to Ellen and get a satisfying response—she'd always pause thoughtfully and reframe the situation in such a way as to present a teachable spiritual moment, were I willing to accept it.

And it made me bristle that I bristled, that I wasn't angelic and evolved, more like tart and bitter, and that being in the presence of people like Ellen made me want to be sweet and soft: pasta left in the hot water just a few seconds too long—when really, I was not just al dente, but *fra diavolo*.

Yet she was one of the five people I knew in Santa Fe, and she was a kind of family, and she was kind, so I had reasons to be patient, and even appreciative.

"What about gravy?" I had Will ask.

"Ellen's making Tofurky gravy," his dad said.

I fell onto the couch sideways, pretending to gag.

"Tofurk that!" I proclaimed when Will got off the phone.

We were in a strange land, for sure.

Turkey from a bar, vodka from Liquor Barn, and gravy from a tofu company. In my quest to escape my own family's dysfunction and start a new life with my immediate family, I was headed toward a loosey-goosey, patched-together, PETA-friendly, French-artist-expat, booze-soaked, New Age Thanksgiving.

And the "turkey and vodka" menu was all the excuse I needed to spend the next two days cooking my ass off. It was my medicine.

I made homemade blue cheese crackers with cranberry chutney (insight: Crackers are just savory cookies!); pumpkin and apple pies; parmesan scallion mashed potatoes; turkey gravy; Grandpa Jimmy's stuffing (which was back on the menu, thanks to my newfound nostalgia); ancho chili compound butter; sweet-potato gratin; and green bean casserole.

Watching everyone dig enthusiastically into my food was deeply gratifying, and when Ellen broke her vegan vows to eat a blue cheese cracker, I felt more than a little bit smug. But the best feeling was knowing that I might have left the dysfunction back in New York, but I had kept the presence of handmade and memorably good food.

We moved, sight unseen, into a house with shiny, stippled walls painted month-to-month-tenant white. The talavera counter tiles rose and fell, glaze worn away at the edges, grout stained and pitted. The house's drafty walls were made of "penitentiary brick," created by New Mexico state prisoners and then covered with adobe. Given the draftiness, the central forced-air heating system was both noisy and ineffective, and the house never did warm up. Our front yard was fenced, and Honorée toddled around safely among the trees and patchy grass in her camel wool toggle-buttoned coat and red lace-up boots. But the fencing itself was strange to my eyes. It was made of long, variegated shavings of thick dark tree bark, the kind of fence a Black Forest witch would lash around her hut.

We didn't have a car, we were new to town, I had no friends and no job, and Will worked long hours. On good days, I'd take my daughter for open-ended walks around town. On bad days (and these came in stretches), I stayed home day after day, glued to the Internet or a book, serially popping our only two kid videos into the VCR, making desultory lunches, and nursing.

Moving did not magically fix our marital problems. Will was under a lot of pressure at the gallery to make sales, and he was working for his stepmother—again! I had once offered him a way out of that life, but we had circled back, this time with more pressure: a baby to raise, and our belief that it was time to hunker down, get our financial act together, and buy a house.

I turned thirty in Santa Fe. The night before, something set Will off, and so I spent my birthday with a face swollen from crying, wanting to die. I was the wrong woman for him, because I cared. The hopelessness of it made me so frustrated and hurt that I wept for hours. It reminded me of my father. I hadn't chosen my father, but I had chosen Will.

When Will was in a good mood, I could appreciate it, but I could no longer relax enough to really enjoy it. And with every angry spell of his, I liked him less, although I loved him. There was still passion, because I believed he could stop this behavior. There was passion in the arguing, in the penitence. There was engagement. There was the dream that began on Bleecker Street, and there was my pride.

About five months after we moved to Santa Fe, Will went back to New York to meet with the gallery owner who was currently showing his dad's work. I wanted to go with him, of course, but we didn't have the money. He made arrangements to stay at my brother's apartment.

I stayed home, got bitten by a rare cleaning bug, and scoured the house from top to bottom. That night, I went to sleep cuddling with Honorée. And when I woke up, I felt different. Something was missing. I felt lighter, but I also felt adrift. As I walked into the kitchen to make Honorée her breakfast, I passed a framed picture of us that my mother took on our first Easter with the baby: Will, handsome in a suit; I, with milk-swollen breasts crammed into a printed rayon dress, feeling self-consciously bovine. Honorée, tiny and alert, looked perfectly turned out in a lavender sweater dress and black patent Mary Janes.

Will, handsome in a suit. And I didn't love him anymore. Like sticking my tongue in the hole where a tooth used to be, I scanned my heart for a shred of feeling, but found nothing. I called my mother, crying, to tell her. "That happens," she said. "The love will come back. Just wait, and pray." And I did. And thought, it's just the way that love changes over time. How did people go on?

So, I didn't love him anymore. That wasn't a reason to rip my family apart, to what? Be poor, or move back to New York and live with . . . who? Nobody had room for me, nor did I want to be a burden. I didn't want to put the baby in day care, and even if I did, working *and* paying for childcare would mean that I would make hardly anything. I just had to deal with my life as it was. I just had to stop triggering Will's anger. Every argument we had seemed so random, so preventable—if I could just see it coming.

Even cooking for Will had become joyless. What made it worse was that he insisted that I do it. If I didn't, his low blood sugar made him even more likely to lose his temper. To make matters worse, he refused to feed himself. Every once in a while, he made a tomato sauce that was actually quite good, but that was rare, and he had to be in the mood.

So I made uninspired food—dinners of the defeated. Trader Joe's simmer sauces, with chicken tenderloins, spinach, and garbanzo beans thrown in, over rice. Elbow pasta mixed with beans, broth, and frozen peas. Pasta and sauce. Breakfast for dinner. Grilled cheese sandwiches. My depleted cooking jones went along with my depleted libido, the geographic disruption of my freelance writing career, my zeroed social life. It was all gone, but I assumed that most new moms felt like I did—disenchanted and yet stoic.

We drank wine every night, though. Wine had gone from being the catalyst of our relationship to the crucial anesthetic of our unhappiness. (Lest you think that was part of the problem when it came to Will's angry tantrums, he did stop drinking a few times, but that didn't prevent them.) I put on weight, and I didn't care. I lost more interest in sex, and that made Will even more unhappy.

But it seemed normal. Most of my July-mama friends, running around after their one-year-olds, were indifferent to sex, and did it out of duty if they did it at all.

"I mean, if you asked me whether I wanted to have sex or a piece of really good cake, I think I'd go for the cake!" my friend Karen exclaimed.

We did make some friends in our new hometown, and invited them over for dinner. In that way, I began to find a way to take pleasure in cooking again. It was a relief to have guests, because I knew Will wouldn't lose his composure in front of other people.

We had an open house on our first Christmas Day, and I made a big pot of turkey chili with a side of rice, and toppings of chopped green onions, jalapeños, lettuce, tomatoes, sour cream, and grated cheddar. It was really good and a crowd-pleaser, but instead of paging through my stash of cookbooks and cooking mags or spending an anticipatory hour on Epicurious.com, I just followed the recipe on the package of ground turkey.

In the spring, my July-mama friend Karen came to visit us with her husband, Mike, and daughter, Ella. The girls played together happily, and Karen and I grabbed snatches of conversation, not really able to sit and let our hair down with husbands around—and that was kind of a drag. But oddly, by the end of the trip, I didn't see Mike as a third wheel.

Mike was like a subtle, creamy sauce that you first mistake for cream of chicken soup from a can. Instead, slowly, with each spoonful, you realize that it's in fact a velouté made from chicken stock simmered and skimmed for days, with garden-grown celery, carrots, and onions and well-built white wine.

Mike was gentle and portly, with blue eyes, dark hair, and glasses. He was somewhat nerdy about music and writing, and given to dropping witty asides that you might miss if you weren't paying attention. He loved to cook and insisted on making dinner one night.

A man who cooked? Its rarity was affecting, and as I watched him bustle around in my kitchen, an erotic jolt flared in my otherwise quiescent pelvic region. Mike was making pesto from scratch, and I of course wanted to watch. Frank and Scott had introduced me to pesto back in Buffalo, but it was one of those simple things I had yet to make.

A small mountain of basil, a bowl of waxy, fragrant pine nuts, freshly grated parmesan, olive oil, salt, and pepper. Into the food processor they went. Mike hit the button, and the sturdy machine whirred the ingredients into a vibrant green paste.

He had pasta going, and when it was ready, he tossed it with the pesto, working the ratio so that each bite yielded a whopping hit of pesto's creamy-bright-sharp-nuttiness. Once all of the portions were plated, he squirted a lemon wedge over them to heighten the brightness.

"Doing this makes almost anything taste better," he said.

I agreed. The lemon juice italicized each mouthful. I couldn't have Mike, but I could have his pesto—and now I had his recipe, too.

22

Down the Hatch, Up the Stump

Santa Fe slowly stopped feeling shockingly new to me, as we bought our first car, continued to make friends, and hosted visits from family. My mother came; she was a mini version of herself. She'd lost almost half of her body weight, and she looked good, although a little gaunt.

I hugged her when she arrived. Tears sprang to my eyes as I noticed the loss of her amazing bosomy embrace. It was one of the things I loved about my mother, that I'd taken for granted since birth. She'd always been comfortingly buxom, and now she was gone.

My body, on the other hand, told on me. It was upholstered with the accumulated effects of wine, seconds on dinner, and not giving a rat's ass about looking attractive. I didn't want Will to pay me any extra attention, nor did I want anyone else to. I was much too unhappy to turn down a chance to feel good, so I kept myself camouflaged behind extra pounds and baggy clothes. Will and I had also been eating our way through Santa Fe's restaurants as a way of getting to know our new home. I often went for New Mexican combination plates: beef taco, chile relleno, chicken enchilada, and lard-laced beans, all covered in chile (lately red was my choice) and melted cheese.

That's what I ate as we sat in Castro's restaurant. My mother picked carefully at her food and shared some news.

"I'm getting married to Tony."

"Really?" She and Tony hadn't known each other for very long, and I feared that my mom's crush on him had more to do with her obsession with *The Sopranos* than with any real love. Her Tony talked like a gangster, too, and she hinted about his connections as if that were something impressive.

"Don't try to talk me out of it . . ." she began, and I waved my arm.

"I would never try to talk you out of anything."

"I know, I'm a stubborn idiot. But I'm doing this."

"Okay."

"And I want you to be my matron of honor. I want my whole family there. Tony has tons of miles; he'll fly you all out."

Sweet.

"I can't go," Will said.

"Why not?" I asked.

"I have to work at the gallery. I can't get the time off."

"But it's a free trip to New York! Why can't you take a few days off?" I pressed.

Will, who loved travel, was oddly staunch about it. He must have felt so insecure at work. Mom bought the tickets and I bought a matron of honor dress, feeling sick at the thought that I would look more matronly than my damn sylph of a mother, pressed into her tableau vivant of a role reversal.

I decided to spend a week in New York—I had no reason to rush back to Santa Fe. I even stopped by Will's old wine store, eager to show off Honorée. I wanted to say hi to the managers and, of course, some of the staff who had seen her as a baby. Most sat in a room right behind the sales floor, handling the phone orders.

As soon as I walked in, the two managers, who were by no means small men and, come to think of it, played college football, swooped together, blocking the doorway to the back room.

"Hi!" they said, with giant grins. They proceeded to chat me up, and I picked up a very strange energy. They all but escorted me out.

"Will, they were really weird," I said later on the phone. "I wanted to say hi to Eric, Spencer, and Bob, but I felt like they were physically repelling me from going any further."

"I don't know," Will said. "Those guys can be really strange sometimes."

I let it go. I couldn't make sense of it but felt relieved to shrug it off.

Up at the altar beside my mother, I felt betrayed by my flesh, by my utter lack of attention to what I looked like—because somehow I had bought into the belief that I'd never need or want to look good again. In every wedding I'd gone to, there was at least one heavy woman in the wedding party, clearly hating life in a dress that looked great on the skinny chicks around her but grabbed every bulge she had going on. I'd gone from being the flower girl to the bride, and now I was the heifer.

I wanted to feel like I was awesome and beautiful with what now truly were sixty extra pounds, but those pounds were not goddess-y goodness or my natural body type. They were slapped onto my form in response to pain, loneliness, and disappointment.

Little did I know that my extra pounds were about to be the least of my worries. The day of the wedding, it seemed like my sister was giving me bad vibes. Was she feeling superior because I was so heavy? At the reception, I had a few drinks and got angrier with every sip. Finally I confronted her. "I need to speak with you privately. Why are you giving me such an attitude?" I asked as we walked to the foyer.

She spun on her heel, eyes blazing. "Grandma Marie died. Daddy told me this morning and said not to tell anyone."

When I'd been back visiting around Mother's Day, my brother Peter and I had taken an impulsive side trip to visit Grandma Marie at her nursing home. She seemed nervous and certainly didn't give any signs of knowing who we were, and she didn't speak. I sat beside her with Honorée in my arms, and said, "This is your great-granddaughter."

Suddenly, her eyes came online and she said, "That's a cute baby." She touched Honorée's fingers, and they wrapped around her translucent, veined, bony finger, trustingly. Marie's ring finger still held Jimmy's wedding band, although it hung on loosely, thickened with Band-Aids.

We stayed for about half an hour, and then an aide told us that we should probably let her rest. I began to gather my things. We said, "Goodbye, Grandma."

"Goodbye. I love you!"

Pete and I looked at each other, smiling. She must be in there somewhere.

"I love you, too, Grandma Marie." I hugged her gently, Honorée between us.

That was the only thing I had to cling to; I had been given the gift of saying goodbye, of hearing her say "I love you" one more time, even though I thought that was impossible. But it didn't stop the crushing pain of knowing she was dead. I hadn't expected to feel it. I spent my whole childhood fearing that she would die, because she was frail, in her seventies, and smoked and drank heavily. People like her weren't supposed to live into their nineties. But she had.

And instead of feeling like I'd lost a woman who was ancient, out of it, and clearly unhappy, I found that I was grieving the Grandma of my childhood, red-haired, beaming, wry, and adoring, who pressed dollar bills into my hands with a wink. The one who walked out to the end of her driveway every time we drove away, to throw kisses until I couldn't see her anymore, and to catch mine. The one whose gaze telegraphed the following message: *You are special. You are smart. I am proud of you.*

Later, I'd wonder why my father saw fit to tell this to my sister, and no one else, on the morning of my mother's wedding day. He clearly could have waited until the next day.

Knowing Grandma, I believe her spirit chose to move on that day as an "up yours" to my mother's wedding. Not because she didn't love my mother, but because she did, so very much. It might have also been her attempt to derail the wedding, since my mother's marriage to Tony turned out to be such a god-awful experience and, as a parting gift, granted her the dodgy status of three-time divorcée.

It also could have been because we were all together on Long Island. I wouldn't have been able to make it to the funeral if I hadn't already been there. Will and I didn't have the money to buy last-minute airplane tickets.

That night, I felt the combined pain of my grandma's death, finding out the news so savagely, and missing Will.

I sat in my mother's kitchen nursing Honorée. My brothers and sister were out. Mom came in to grab her luggage, because she was about to leave on her honeymoon. I put Honorée down on the bed and came back to see her off. I thought she knew about Grandma, so I mentioned it. I was mistaken.

"What? What?" She stood in the small kitchen.

"I thought you knew. I'm so sorry."

"No, I didn't know." Her face crumpled. I leaped up to hug her. We held each other in the kitchen, and sobbed together, our chests heaving. Then she pulled back, her arms ramrod-straight on my shoulders.

"Okay, okay. I have to go. I can't deal with this right now. Tony's waiting for me in the car."

"Okay," I said. "You're right. You're going to have a good time. I promise. I'll be fine."

"I have some Ativans in my top drawer," she said. "Take one before you go to bed."

I went to bed, but not before looking in my mother's top dresser drawer for the Ativan. *Shit. Gone.*

I went to bed and fell into a brief, merciful sleep. But then I woke up at 3:00 AM, feeling unhinged. The last time I had slept here had been right after 9/11, with Will and my infant. Now I was back, alone, with my almost two-year-old, who was so much more aware of my emotional state, and if I was a mess, it would distress her. I closed my eyes to shut it all out and imagine I was somewhere else.

But the backs of my eyelids seemed to be made of a fabric, and the weave was loosening, letting in the light. I felt like I was having a nervous breakdown. I called Will.

"Will, my grandma died," I sobbed. "My heart literally *hurts* . . . I feel strange . . . I'm scared . . ."

I was in so much pain that it dwarfed the pain of my marriage, and I needed comfort so much that I let him comfort me. He stayed on the phone, sleepy-voiced, just like when we used to spend every night talking until we fell asleep. I cried, and he soothed. Although I wished he were there and I could cry in his arms, it was the next-best thing. I missed him—only something like Grandma's death could make me.

And so my mother's wedding trip turned into my grandmother's funeral trip. I put my stupid matron of honor dress on a hanger and pulled a black outfit from my mom's closet for the next day's wake—a thick, stretchy skirt and top with a white-trimmed scoop neck. I'd helped her buy it years ago, when she had gotten a new job and needed a sophisticated wardrobe that worked with her then-fuller figure. Now I was the one who needed stretchy black crap to wear. And we had no idea, that long-ago spring Manhattan afternoon, that we were buying my outfit for Grandma Marie's funeral.

That night was the worst. I felt all of my grief at once—and it was almost too much to bear. But then it was done, and I began to feel a sense of relief that she was no longer trapped in her wasted body and old, broken mind. She was with her father, her husband, and her two sons, Jimmy and Gregory (I hoped), and the thought of that reunion gave my spirit a boost.

Being with Will again, in my grief, felt more like pleasure than I'd felt in so long—because he was my husband, and he was familiar, and he held me as I cried or just sat, heavy-hearted.

"Will, I think we should try to have another baby," I said. "I feel like my grandma is telling me I should." She had five. Aunt Carole had six. My mother had four. I had one. Even though she was gone, I could fulfill one last request of hers, and in the process create a new life. Thinking about it felt like a salve on my pain.

"All right," Will said. We had a bunch of unprotected sex, even though I didn't even bother to check my cycle to see if I was fertile.

A week later, Will had second thoughts. "We should really get you back in the workforce first and buy a house," Will said. "Otherwise, it'll be another three years before we can do that. Honorée will be five, and we'll still be renting."

"Let me check the calendar," I said. "Ah, don't worry. I was so not in the fertile zone. Not even close."

"What a relief."

It was true. I was a good ten days away from ovulation. A few weeks later, I bought a pregnancy test and took it anyway.

"It's hard to tell," I said, showing Will the slightly shadowy spot where the second line would be. It was more like a thought than a line. Another week, another test. This time it came up so strongly that if there had been a church bell around, it would have clanged throughout the valley.

Will and I hugged each other, grinning. "Here we go again," he said. "At least now it's not the great unknown."

A few days after that, he came to me. "Why doesn't it make sense, in terms of your last period?" He seemed worked up.

"I don't know, Will."

"Did you cheat on me in New York?" His face was flushed, his eyes wide and unblinking.

"Um, *no,* that's ridiculous." I laughed. Fat me, in orange velour yoga pants, in New York during my mother's wedding and my grandma's funeral, with my two-year-old on my hip—finding time to meet a chubby-chasing orange-yoga-pants fetishist and then get laid?

"Well, it doesn't add up. It doesn't add up!"

"I cannot believe you're accusing me of cheating on you and carrying another man's baby. Sign me up for a paternity test, but in the meantime, you really need to drop it!"

I had an explanation. It was my grandma's miracle. She'd pulled some strings to make it happen, even though the week of my supposed ovulation, Will gave me a wide berth. Or, if that was crazy talk, the stress of that week disrupted my cycle.

A few weeks later, he came back to me with the same expression on his face. "What about you going to work?" he asked. "You need to go to work, even if you're pregnant."

"Um . . . where?" By this time, I was back in morning-sickness hell.

"I don't know—it's up to you! We had goals! Now you're pregnant!"

Who was this person? It was Will. And he was making it impossible for me to forget all of the reasons so much distance had grown between us before my grandma's death.

Unlike the first pregnancy, which Will thoroughly, tenderly nurtured, this time he did not want to touch me, to rub out the aches and pains that occurred as my ligaments loosened, my bones ached, my skin stretched. And I had a two-year-old who wanted me to be good company. Instead, I dozed all day, exhausted, dragging myself upright just to feed Honorée or rewind the Maisy videotape. Racked with bad-mama guilt, I drove us three blocks to the park, and as she played, I threw up under the slide and then covered up my puke with sand.

I could barely keep any food down (that is, if I got it past my lips), and I was not just growing a baby and maintaining my own body's needs, but I was nursing. Three lives. One ghost of a diet. It was time to wean.

In New Mexico, midwives didn't have hospital privileges; they only did home births. I was a little nervous about that, and Will was even more reluctant, but we met with a trio of midwives and they put us both at ease. Like Sylvie and Lynne, they were lovely women and had decades of experience between them, except for Caroline, who was an apprentice. She reminded me of my college friend Pam—slightly gappy teeth, preppy blond bob, from New England. And she pulled off wearing long cotton dresses with cute Converse low-tops. I wondered idly if she was gay, but after a few appointments, she mentioned her boyfriend. Not like it mattered—I was not only married, but sitting there next to my husband, pregnant, with a daughter who was bouncing around the room.

I gained only twenty pounds with that pregnancy; there was so much already on my frame that could be of use. When I was pregnant with Honorée, I craved berries, sorbet, Caesar salad. This time, my cravings were completely different. The local Indian restaurant was my second home. I craved its rich lamb, chicken, goat curries, spinach-packed *saag paneer,* roasted cauliflower, puffy naan, and dipping sauces, all washed down with mango lassi.

We moved to a bigger house in my eighth month of pregnancy—a rental in Eldorado, a suburb one exit farther north on I-25. My urban self hated the idea of living "outside of town," but the house was amazing. It had a huge kitchen—about twenty times as much counter space as my Manhattan nook, with a big bar counter that overlooked the dining room.

My father emailed me and let me know that he'd bought plane tickets to come visit in early April, after the baby was born. I was due in mid-March, so I figured that would work out, but the due date calculation didn't account for my screwy cycle during the month of conception. On my supposed due date, the baby hadn't dropped at all, I wasn't dilated, and I hadn't had any contractions. The midwives changed the date to April 1, based on the date our actual sex had occurred.

That meant that my father would be showing up not when the baby was in my arms, but possibly when I was about to pop. I felt nervous. Would my body want to give birth with him around, given our history? Once again, I sailed past my due date. Honorée had been eight days late. I hit my eighth day, and again, the midwives started to talk about plan B. After fourteen days, they could no longer work with me at home. I'd need to go to the hospital, and they'd be there, but the doctor on call would be the point person.

On top of being so overdue, I also felt a lot of pressure to have the baby before my dad left.

"I'm sorry," I said to him about two days before his flight back. "I wanted you to be able to meet the baby."

"You could get induced," he said.

I stared at him, aghast. "No, I'm not going to get induced." I couldn't let my father's departure date dictate my child's birthday.

At 3:05 AM on April 8, I woke up to the sound of Honorée whining and moaning in her toddler bed next to ours. She did that when she had to pee but didn't want to wake up and actually go. Growly and exhausted, I hoisted myself up and took her hand to lead her to the bathroom. Then I felt a contraction. A big one.

"Will, I think it's time."

"Okay," he said sleepily. "Did you have a contraction?"

"I just had a whopper," I said. "And . . . ooohh."

"Okay, let's call the midwives."

Will called them, and I went and knocked on the guest room door.

"Dad, I'm in labor. I need you to take care of Honorée."

"Okay," he said, half asleep but excited. "Come on, Honorée, let's go read some books."

I sat on the yoga ball, legs apart, and bounced gently, to encourage the labor to progress. The skies opened up in an odd spring desert storm, and rain pounded on the roof like it was trying to bore holes in it. Thunder and lightning boomed and flashed.

Caroline arrived first. She checked me. "You're at eight centimeters!" she said happily.

"Really? I've only been in labor for an hour. I should have babies for the whole world!" I said, giddy.

A few contractions later, I was not singing the same tune. They were monsters. Caroline's strong, pleasingly cold hands applied counterpressure on my lower back this time, until Will took over.

I rolled on my side and lifted my leg. Caroline held it up, my water burst, and they whisked away the soiled chucks and slid in clean ones. Nathaniel came out at 5:03. Unlike wee Honorée, he was a big-headed nine-pounder with a chubby butt and boy parts. And we were in my bed, which meant I didn't have to go anywhere. We were home. Nathaniel latched on to my breast, just like his sister had.

"Do you want us to get your dad and Honorée?" Caroline asked. I nodded.

Will covered me up, and then they came in. Honorée walked in slowly with her own baby doll, eyes as wide as saucers, and climbed into bed beside Nathaniel and me. She curled up next to my body.

"This is your brother, Nathaniel," I said. She reached out and stroked him tentatively, while clinging to me at the same time. I put my other arm around her and held her close.

Will climbed into bed. "I'm making an Honorée sandwich," he said merrily. My father sat on the floor, smiling ear to ear.

"He made it!" he said. "He wanted to meet his grandpa."

"Thanks for your help, Dad," I said.

"It was my pleasure."

Later, I would wish that I could always make my father this happy. Instead, it was just a moment of happiness, amid years of mutual misunderstanding and disappointment. But that didn't occur to me then. Right then, he was in my world, aglow in the presence of my baby boy. I was so high from my birth that there was no doubt in my mind that my father and I—and my husband and I—had turned a corner.

In the morning, my friend Catherine drove out to Eldorado and made us a huge frittata in a cast-iron skillet, studded with chopped green peppers, tomatoes, scallions, and diced chicken, and dotted throughout with toasty gouda cheese. I ate hungrily, Will took Honorée to the park, and Catherine crawled in bed beside me as I nursed, happy and tired.

Home Cooking

"There have always been many things you can do short of actually ending a bad marriage—having an affair, having a baby and buying a house are the most common, I suppose . . ."
—*Nora Ephron,* Heartburn

JUST WHEN I thought that moving to Santa Fe had killed my career, I heard about a part-time job at *Mothering,* a national magazine that just happened to be headquartered in my town.

"They need someone to fulfill store orders, and you can bring Nathaniel," my friend Ana said.

It was a pick-and-pack job, completely manual, but that appealed to me. I could get my foot in the door, and not only would not having to leave my ten-month-old be precious on an emotional level, but I'd also keep the money I'd normally have to pay a sitter.

I loved working again. Nathaniel toddled around the stockroom and slept on his blanket after he fell asleep. The staff was a delight—new, bright friends. And the editor had me do product reviews and write bulletins as soon as she realized how much experience I had.

That bit of extra income lifted us up to the point where we could qualify to buy a house, and we started looking. When I saw the third house, I knew it was the one. It was a three-bedroom with a beautiful location: up at the top of a hill, entirely invisible from the dead-end lane. Following our realtor, I drove up a long, winding driveway, which I later measured at one-tenth of a mile. The lot contained almost three acres of rolling terrain, lots of piñon trees, and a little clearing beside an arroyo. The house had a large, high-ceilinged living room with a fireplace, a den, and a big, gorgeous kitchen with a wall of windows looking out onto a flagstone patio with a low adobe wall.

It was definitely a fixer-upper. The floors were covered in puce-colored shag carpet, except for the kitchen and dining room, which had terra-cotta Saltillo tile. The living room walls were yellow, a color that might have looked better in a cozier space, if at all. The aqua blue bedroom opened up onto the dining room.

We gave the owners a low offer and then settled on something in the middle. And then we got to work. Will and I ripped out the curtains, stained the concrete slab, and picked out vibrant paint colors.

Once it was finished, we couldn't wait to entertain. Will and I had gotten pulled into some gourmet dinner party round robins with other oenophile couples who dropped hundreds of dollars per dinner on wine (or, more frequently, went down into their wine cellars and pulled out bottles that would pair well). We had a small wine fridge, but it was usually empty. When it was our turn to host, Will drove out to New Mexico's answer to Sherry-Lehmann: Koko-man Fine Wine and Liquor, in Pojoaque, a very shabby-looking warehouse near the Cities of Gold casino that nonetheless had a great selection, and he spent more than we could afford to host the group in the manner to which it was accustomed.

I was also in a whole new hot seat. I was responsible for creating multicourse dinners for six, plus a kids' meal (because, let's be real, they wouldn't touch our food). Although it was fun the first few times, I didn't feel much of a yummy connection with the wives or the husbands. (A good crush would have spiced things up a bit, but no such luck).

Now, instead of providing sliced baguettes and a few nice cheeses (a blue, a Brie, a manchego), an entrée, and dessert, there was a series of courses: a starter, a salad, a soup, an entrée, and then a dessert course (where the cheese resurfaced, per French tradition), all presented with different wines.

We wives were along for the ride with our men, who were pouring, swirling, sniffing, and slurping the wine with the seriousness of neurosurgeons in the operating theater. We could have gotten all geeky with them, but I was too exhausted from the cooking, house preparations, and child tending to give much of a damn about anything but the ability of the wine to sock me in the brain with a well-needed buzz.

For the soups and main courses, I often turned to Daniel Boulud's *Café Boulud Cookbook* and *Cooking with Daniel Boulud*. Curried Cream of Cauliflower and Apple Soup, Oyster Mushroom Soup with Walnuts and Red Wine—and I discovered, through trial and error, that a dash of dried thyme, stirred in at the end, could really bring a blah soup to life.

After everyone left, I went to bed and Will stayed up, high on the experience, and washed every dirty dish, wiped down the counters, and put the empties into the recycling bin.

Perhaps as a corrective for this kind of entertaining, I decided to throw a Tacky Hors d'Oeuvres party, and invited everyone at *Mothering,* as well as my other friends. Guests were instructed to bring a tacky hors d'oeuvre and dress the part, if desired—in vintage cocktail-culture garb.

Susan brought rumaki. Carolyn brought Little Smokies sausages, bobbing in a mini-Crock-Pot of grape jelly mixed with barbeque sauce. Ana made a booze-injected Bundt cake, dotted with plastic palm trees. I made what looked like a pastel-frosted seven-layer cake but was actually a few loaves of sliced Pepperidge Farm white bread, crusts removed, the slices spread with smoked salmon and pimento spread, all frosted with pistachio green–tinted whipped cream cheese. Someone brought a punch bowl and made a very fizzy, boozy punch topped with rainbow sherbet islands, which was an excellent chaser for Kimber's tater tot casserole composed of niblet corn, cream of mushroom soup concentrate, and cheese. There was a lot of ridiculous food, and most of it tasted surprisingly good.

Outside of theme parties, one Boulud recipe that worked equally well for the fancy foodies and my own friends was Hot and Crusty

Chicken My Way. You take a cut-up chicken and marinate it in a mix of wasabi, lemon, coriander, ginger root, garlic, honey, and olive oil. Then, much like an haute Shake-n-Bake, you dredge the pieces in flour, then dip them in an egg-and-soy sauce mixture, then in fresh bread crumbs. The chicken is then baked until done, and then—wow. Spicy, sour, earthy, sweet, salty, juicy, and savory, too. It's great with bitter greens and my own mashed potato recipe.

I made this chicken when I had my *real* friends over. The kids had a parallel party, playing throughout the house, and we adults stood around in the big kitchen and dining area, drinking wine, laughing, and talking, sometimes all in one big conversation, sometimes in smaller groups. I found some of my friends' husbands appealing, and flirted with them, although there was a line that I never crossed. Knowing that a crush object was coming over gave me a reason to put on makeup, change my outfit, and spend a little more time on the menu.

It felt, at those times, that I had successfully made the transformation to being a legitimate grownup. I was sorted out (except for my unpredictable husband, but I didn't choose to focus on that right then). There I was, in my kitchen with the Viking look-alike stainless steel stove, the big fridge, the bar stools pulled up to the counter. Outside, there was a beautiful sunset, and no other houses visible for acres. My husband was handsome and smart, and he was making a lot of money after his gallery promotion. I had a job, a daughter in preschool, and a toddler boy. We owned a cute, sporty station wagon. I cooked for people I loved, and they were passionately appreciative. My life looked like a success. If I didn't feel satisfied or happy, that was my problem.

Unlike the wine folks, my real friends brought drinks or dessert to lighten the load. Kimber in particular assembled exquisite salads and taught me how to make a killer vinaigrette.

After dinner, Will put some records on the turntable connected to his tube amplifier and the rest of his audiophile sound system, and we danced. I could have kept going in that life, because it often felt full. Will was even having fewer rages. Fewer. But they hadn't disappeared. A few months after I began working at *Mothering,* he had one in the morning. I had to call in sick that afternoon because my face was swollen from crying and I just couldn't be seen by my coworkers.

"I realized that I can't do that anymore," he said, "now that you have a job and you have to go to work. I'm sorry."

It was galling that his big epiphany had nothing to do with his desire to stop attacking me with words. It had to do with preserving my income stream and keeping up appearances. But I took what I could get.

Now, if he got mad, it happened on Saturdays. Sundays, he was contrite. I found ways to go places those Saturdays. When *Sunset* magazine began assigning me stories, I was given a reason to take the kids and the double stroller and explore nearby places.

Because these seemed like such spells, or attacks, for him, I sat around thinking up ways to derail them.

"I'm going to videotape you the next time it happens. So promise me that you won't break the camera."

"Okay," he said, looking grave. "I promise."

On Saturday mornings, I packed the kids in the car with my double stroller and a bag of diapers, snacks, and sippy cups. I got on I-25 and drove an hour south to Albuquerque's Nob Hill neighborhood. After years of turning my nose up at this city—this airport with a city attached, as far as I was concerned—I became aware that my urban soul could go to a place where city block after city block stretched out, packed with cafés, record stores, galleries, boutiques, vintage-clothing stores, bookstores, restaurants, bars, chic houseware emporiums, and even a small art cinema.

I was so attracted to that neighborhood. It was almost erotic. Yes, me, bopping along with my double jogging stroller, my preschooler, and my one-year-old still on the boob—I felt as expectant as a girl at her first dance. I maneuvered the stroller through the narrow aisles of a brutally curated record store looking for bands that Karen's husband, Mike, had mentioned.

I sat with the kids at Flying Star Café and took notes for *Sunset* article pitches, while making sure my monkeys didn't fling their macaroni and cheese across the room, all the while people-watching, hungry to soak up college-kid style so I could give my own boring mom wardrobe a shot in the arm.

In Objects of Desire, a home decor shop, I lingered during the double miracle of two kids asleep at the same time, and bought a few dreamily intricate Christmas tree ornaments.

Then, I drove back, late-ish, in time to make Will an omelet or something equally quick.

"I'm not hungry yet," he said when I got home. "Maybe in a little while."

A few hours went by, and I put Honorée to bed and got in my own bed to nurse Nathaniel to sleep. I fell asleep.

"You're asleep? I thought you were going to make me an omelet."

"*Mmmf.*"

"Candace, I'm hungry. I thought you were going to make me an omelet."

"You're seriously waking me up at ten o'clock to make you an omelet? Why can't you make your own omelet?"

"I don't know how to."

"You crack two eggs, whisk them with a fork—"

"Never mind, never mind, I'll fry an egg." He walked off in a huff.

This was just about as bad as my dream about Jack's demanding that I make him a ham sandwich, although I doubt even he would have woken me up to do that.

Ellen, Will's dad's girlfriend, had become more of a confidant and peer during our first few years in Santa Fe. She had her own problems with Will's dad's rages, and she shared with me about how she was creating her own reality. Every morning before she got out of bed, she created her day by speaking it out loud in the present tense. So I tried it.

"Today, I love my husband. Today, we get along beautifully. Today, I am patient and content with the children. Today, I do household chores without feeling dread. Today, I have a great time at my job and get everything done on my list. I go to the store and get groceries, and the people at Whole Foods are kind and friendly to my children. We are able to get in and out quickly." And so on, until I had created that I tucked my kids into bed and had great, connected sex with Will before falling asleep.

It was actually . . . sort of working. I felt so good about it that I told friends who had borne witness to years of my unhappiness. But even affirmations couldn't sustain the next time Will let me down.

It worked in other areas of my life. One morning, feeling especially cheeky, I "created" that I would receive a big money windfall that day. And that afternoon, I got an email from a publisher asking if I would ghostwrite a book with a local stone artisan. Ellen also told me about something else she had learned. It was called releasing.

"It's ridiculously simple," she said. "Whenever something comes up that bothers you, ask yourself this: *Would you release this? Yes. Could you release this? Yes. When? Now.*"

I tried it with some smaller things, like being irked by a coworker, or even my dislike of housework, and it did make me feel lighter, less beleaguered.

So when I began to feel an attack of depression come on, while I was driving down Rodeo Road, I asked myself if I would release this sadness. *Yes.* Then, *Could you release this sadness? Yes! When? Now.*

Within a fraction of a second of my *now,* the word dislodged a memory and a knowing that hit me so hard that I pulled the car over, as my body seized up with an instant sob.

As a toddler, I'd been molested. *When?* I asked myself.

Sitting on my uncle's lap as we drove around the Poconos, Pennsylvania, and he gave me an ice cream cone: "Don't tell." Don't tell about his letting me steer the truck, the ice cream cone, and other things.

I felt anxious about this insight. Was it even true? How would I ever know? I was relieved that he'd been dead for decades, which removed the option to confront him. He took his own life. But since it came up so powerfully during that releasing, I thought it would be foolish to dismiss it.

If Ellen's method worked, then my desire to release depression had morphed into a revelation of the reason for my depression. It had marred my ability to feel joy for my entire life, leaching into every moment. And I could only blot it out by numbing myself with food, drink, and, when I was younger, cocaine.

If I was sexually abused, the many symptoms I manifested, such as disordered eating, gastrointestinal symptoms, depression and anxiety, and purging, could also be shed.

I talked to Will and my close friends about it. I felt like I was walking around in a fragile amniotic sac pulsating with pain. I absolutely lost any connection to sexuality. I felt sore, exhausted, and almost paralyzed with heaviness. When another relative saw a piece I wrote about it, he told me that Jimmy had molested him, too.

Now that I had asked my body to release it, I had to participate in getting it all the way out. I made an appointment with a therapist, but I kept forgetting the appointment time and losing the piece of paper. I finally made it, though, thanks to this woman's patience.

The night before the appointment, I had a dream. In it, I was in bed with Will, but our bedroom was not our bedroom. It was the one my parents had when I was four. An invisible force picked me up and threw me across the room, as if I were a rag doll. I curled up in a ball and it came and did it to me again. This time I landed on Will, who was completely asleep, and I grabbed on to him for safety, but my strength was low and I knew he couldn't protect me.

I remembered what my mother taught me when I was small: Whenever I had bad dreams or night fears, she taught me to say, "I rebuke you in the name of Jesus," and keep on repeating that until I felt safe. I was thirty-five and far from a Jesus lover at that point, but I hadn't found any replacement. Through the weight of a big heavy hand clamped over my mouth, I kept on repeating it, though my words were slurred, until I could actually say it clearly. Then I was awake, but still drenched in the fear of that experience.

Something was trying to intimidate me. Maybe it was something inside me that wanted to preserve the status quo, but it reminded me of the older males in my family, beefy, ham-handed, and domineering. It could have been my uncle's spirit, trying to intimidate me into not telling, trying to silence me. It matched his energy, which I remembered from when I was a child. Back when I was a little girl you could throw across the room.

Will couldn't protect me—I had to grapple with this with a therapist, and myself. He could be there for me, and he had been, but he couldn't fix it. I would go to my appointment that day. The dream monster terrified me, but it would not stop me.

When I stepped out of the car and walked up the flagstone path in front of the therapist's office, I felt like I'd just staggered across the finish line. Her office was dim blue, dusty, punctuated by ethnic pillows and trays of small toys. I imagined that the chair I was in would become a familiar cradle as I healed. She began to take down my information, and when I uttered Will's last name, she looked up.

"I can't proceed."

Was she kidding? It made me giggle nervously. "Why?"

"I know your husband's family socially."

I burst into tears. "A referral, then?"

She started nodding as she looked at me. "Trauma," she said.

"Excuse me?"

"I can tell that you have undergone deep, deep trauma. You forgot the time of our first appointment, you forgot the directions to the correct entry, and your wide-open eyes—classic signs. I am going to refer you to someone who does what I do in that situation."

My tears turned into sobs. Although I understood her reasoning, I felt vulnerable, sussed out, and rejected. It was like my dead uncle won.

"Here's her card. Her name is Céline. You'll call her?"

I nodded, but I wasn't sure. I felt so dejected. She handed me Kleenex.

"Call her in the car before you leave. I will also call her to tell her to expect your call."

Dutifully, I called and left a message before I began my drive home. Her outgoing message revealed a dusky, French-accented voice.

As I turned up my street, my cell phone rang.

She, just like my midwife Sylvie, had me at hello.

24

Soul Food

WILL'S MOM came to visit, and she smiled mischievously as she flashed a small envelope.

"I got us tickets to Benise," she shared excitedly. "He's coming to perform in Albuquerque. And then we'll stay at a hotel and come back the next morning. It will be a girls' night out!"

Although I had never heard of Benise, I was happy for some respite. Roni Benise turned out to be a really great example of a positive-thinking world-music beefcake, regularly featured on PBS—the sensitive, intellectual woman's kind.

All evening long, Benise and his entourage exhorted us to live our truth, be genuine, enjoy the magic all around us, and seize the day. I'd never liked a singer this positive. Sting was about as happy as I could go. But although Benise was inarguably cheesy, it was the kind of top-notch stuff my soul needed.

Women of a certain age filled the audience. They panted and strained to get his attention, but I was just happy to be out of the house with Peggy, distracted from my healing process. So when Benise decided to throw his guitar pick out into the audience as a good-luck token, I wasn't really paying attention. There was a flurry of expectancy on either side of me, and then the little plastic pick lodged between my breasts. Benise smiled and winked at me, then ran across the stage, sweat droplets glistening in midair as they flew from his mane.

Looking back, I want to believe that he was a kind of emissary from the spiritual world, that the pick, steeped in his mojo, was a talisman of transformation. In that regard, all signs pointed to yes.

I really liked Céline and her office. I didn't realize how much the rustic French-countryside decor I remembered from my honeymoon overlapped with Santa Fe's viga ceiling beams and plastered walls until I was in her space. After the abruptly aborted session with the other therapist, Céline was much more welcoming—and was also more maternal looking. She was full figured, with the round eyes, full lips, and high cheekbones of an antique doll. Even her hair formed curves. In passing, I noted that she mentioned her partner and referred to her as "she."

Céline introduced me to a kind of therapy called somatic experiencing, which involved noticing sensations in my body, and the relationship between sensations and traumatic memory, and releasing the trauma.

Since I'd moved to Santa Fe, I had noticed people saying, "She's really in her body" or, "I'm so not in my body right now," and I had no idea what on earth they were talking about. I began to get it. I'd spent my whole life dissociated, and touching down into my body felt as juicy as landing a plane on a lush tropical island. In the ensuing sessions, I felt like we were really getting a lot done, and afterward, I was completely exhausted and even felt sore sometimes. Will wasn't too pleased with how much I needed to crash, but he managed.

One Saturday morning, I drove with the kids back from our morning jaunt to the farmer's market, idly thinking about how wonderful Céline was. Her warm smile, the way she offhandedly inhabited her body, her sweet smell and eyes that brimmed with empathy. I really felt like she *saw* me, and that was an unfamiliar sensation. Thinking about her made my whole body feel good, and I let myself continue to do so, like a cat who cozies up to the radiator. It was because of the somatic experiencing therapy—she was my guide, and when I thought about her, my body remembered the healing sensations, too.

Just then, I saw a sign next to the Center for Contemporary Arts: RUMMAGE SALE—FUNDRAISER. I impulsively pulled over and parked. It was worth checking out.

I put Nathaniel on my back, in a soft cloth carrier, and took Honorée's hand. The space was large and packed with all sorts of items. My eyes roved hungrily through the objects on tabletops, and my hands flipped through the stacked canvases and prints while Nathaniel jostled and played with my hair. Honorée wandered over to a table and picked up a crone mask.

I found a plump celadon ceramic turtledove, reminiscent of Jonathan Adler's work, about the size of a large pomelo. Two dollars—it was so mine. And then there was Céline, in front of me, smiling. She seemed to swim out of the crowd.

Wearing makeup! Her hair done! With a pale green, fitted fleece vest and jeans, not the scrubs she wore in session. I introduced her to my children, flustered and pleased. Honorée placed the mask on her face and stared at Céline through the eyeholes. I, tremendously self-conscious, my pulse beating in my eardrums, looked down, surprised to see the turtledove in my hands and to feel so bashful. After the flutter of initial chat happened, I couldn't think of what to say next, although I desperately wanted to continue the conversation. She seemed to sense that I was abashed and said goodbye, leaving me with pinked cheeks and a spinning heart.

I probably fell in love with her right then, bird in the hand, boy on my back. My feelings had been growing, under something like a rock, but seeing her out in the world—in my world, for a moment—gave my feelings the kind of oxygen they needed to *boing* up into being, like a cheeky weed in a manicured garden, forbidden but exuberant.

It meant something. I had been thinking of her, and I decided to go to the tag sale, and there she was. It was a sign.

That night, I woke up in the middle of the night. I felt a lot of pressure in my pelvis, as if I were turned on. I thought about masturbating, but I just couldn't focus. I vaguely remembered something about kundalini and feeling more confident about body sensations, I decided to see what would happen if I tried to move the energy up my spine.

I felt it gather and redirect. It moved up, and then it seemed to stop just past my lower back. Just getting it to the middle of my back took at least a half hour, if not more. But I had nothing to distract me. It began to feel like it had a life of its own, creeping up my spine like warm fingers. It started to itch at the base of my neck but it really itched when it got to the top, and it felt like the whole top half of my head was covered in itch. I scratched it.

I felt euphoric. Since I felt so aware of my body's sensations, I decided to do some somatic experiencing therapy right then. I felt hot in a specific spot, or a pang of pain, and then brought my attention to that spot and waited for images to come up, memories of hurtful things. Instead of trying to think them through, I just observed the memory and the sensation. It turned from heat or pain to a tingling sensation, which Céline said was a sign that the trauma was being released from my body.

Would you release this? Yes. Could you release this? Yes. When? Now.

That simple series of questions had set me on this path, and here I was, lying next to Will, who slept innocently beside me while energy flowed up my spine and I tingled and shuddered.

I did this for about two hours. Afterward, I got up to try to understand what had happened. It seemed linked to Céline.

"Oh, I know your therapist," I remembered my friend Jeannette saying. "I see her in the park, doing yoga." They did live in the same neighborhood. "And I've seen her at the meditation center behind the Toyota dealership."

I looked it up and found out that Céline was most likely a devotée of a guru whose teachings centered on "moving kundalini energy." *What? Shaktipat,* or the laying on of hands, caused it to rise, and when it did, a great deal of affection and gratitude arose from the recipient to the guru as well. Although this guru didn't appear in public very often, people could still receive *shaktipat* by looking at her picture, or through another devotée.

Had Céline given me *shaktipat?* She'd hugged me at the tag sale, and in sessions she sometimes put her hands on my knees, or her feet on mine, "to help you stay grounded."

I stayed up for the rest of the night, although I rested in bed, expecting to fall asleep. It didn't happen. The next day, I found that I was jittery but happy.

At work, Kimber asked if I wanted to go to a new dance exercise class with her. I normally would have said no, because I didn't consider myself a dance exercise class type, but today was different. I was anything, everything, but not my old self anymore.

"Sure," I said. I hopped in Kimber's car and we drove up to Studio East, a funky old space off Canyon Road. It had a dinged wooden dance floor, mirrored walls slightly warped in places, and white Christmas lights strung around the ceiling. It reminded me a little of the Buffalo apartment I shared with Pam. The teacher was a small, trim, but still curvy-bodied person with a mass of orange curly hair—kind of like a lion's mane.

"Welcome to my Nia class. I'm Susana," she said with a husky-voiced British accent and a cute, gappy grin. "When I'm about to make a change of movement, I'll call out. You just have to watch me."

She began the music, and to my enjoyment, it was Sinéad O'Connor from start to finish. As she led us in spirals and figure eights of the hips, I lost my mind for an hour, and found my body. I felt sexy and warm and juicy, and sweaty, too. And I wanted more. That week, I went to three more classes. After that, I was one of Susana's regulars.

I learned how to meditate, and I found that it calmed me down and settled my energy after the kundalini awakening. More than that, I heard voices and helpful messages, and things that seemed like problems before the meditation session were no longer important afterward. I felt like I was in a fascinating metaphysical-adventure movie.

I also spent days eating hardly anything. Food seemed irrelevant. I had a bite here and a bite there, but meals? Whatever. I also had no taste for alcohol or anything but simple, fresh foods. It was like all of my appetites had been reset. Over the next few weeks, weight dropped off.

"I'm not cooking anymore," I told Will.

"What?"

"I'll feed the kids, but I am no longer going to make dinner unless I feel like making something specific. You're on your own."

He stared at me as if I had just grown an extra head. But it felt so good to quit that job. I used to love to cook, but I didn't anymore; it had been compulsory for years. And now I had decided that it was not compulsory. Who knew it was that easy?

I looked forward to my next session with Céline. I spent a long time planning my outfit, doing my makeup and my hair. I'd never dressed to attract a woman before. The very thought of it caused my body to react. Between the kundalini energy coursing through my body and Nia's pelvic rotations, I'd never felt so aroused—from my sacrum to my thighs, I felt like my insides were made up of warm, silky crème brûlée.

And I was also insatiable. Sex did nothing to diminish my desire, although it made Will happy. Nor did getting off on my own. Moving the erotic energy up my spine helped, when I remembered.

It was so strange that this process of healing from sexual abuse would create so much sexual energy. Maybe because I was reclaiming my body, kicking out these old, dirty, violating energies? I could feel myself.

I knew all about transference and countertransference by this point. I'd ordered several books on the topic and read them furtively. People transferred love from parents to their therapists, and then the therapists could alchemically manipulate this love energy, facilitating catharsis, a fresh start. That was all very well and good, I thought, but I also thought that we had more going on.

It wasn't the best time for Céline to be taking a six-week vacation. I sat on the couch, across from her.

"Speaking of abandonment issues, I am going to be away for some time. How do you feel about that?" she asked.

"I'm too cool to have abandonment issues," I said.

"You *are* cool," she said.

I grimaced jokingly, the way my generation does. We know admission of being cool instantly invalidates that status.

"What?" She smiled.

"I was just joking, but thank you for the compliment."

"It's not a compliment. You *are* cool."

I shuddered for a second, overwhelmed but glowing. "Thank you."

She laughed. "I may be away, but that doesn't mean I won't be thinking about you. . . ."

"Same here," I murmured, right before my chest became an exploding-firework-champagne-bubble-warmth expanse.

"And there is email."

It was getting a lot harder to think that these feelings were one-way only.

After she got back, I said, "I really feel like I wish we could be friends, and not just . . ." waving my hands around the therapy office.

"Well, we have work to be done now, but that will be finished soon, and then we can be friends. I really enjoyed seeing you out at the yard sale with your kids when we ran into each other, but for now, I believe in preserving a safe place for us to do our work here."

As she led me in a meditation exercise, she said, "I notice your breasts . . . "

I started giggling.

"I mean, *breaths,* getting fuller. I'm sorry, it's that *th* sound."

"You might want to work on that," I said. "I don't mind it, but some others might."

She continued laughing and blushed scarlet.

In November, I gave her a Thanksgiving present: Époisses cheese, the wonderfully pungent-smelling stuff from Burgundy. It came in a delicate little wooden box, almost as thin as a wood shaving, stamped with a château's tower and sundry official markings.

"Oh, thank you!" she said. After strict Dr. Morris, I felt extra giddy with how much Céline seemed to let me in. I'd offered to make her a CD mix of my favorite songs, and she had accepted it enthusiastically. She told me that she enjoyed listening to it in between sessions. Not only was the fact that she was transgressing the boundaries of an appropriate therapeutic relationship exciting, but I was totally okay with it.

Yep. My French honeymoon, now fodder for the wooing of my therapist. The dinner parties I hosted with my husband—I was leveraging that gourmet knowledge to select gifts for her. In the short span of four months, I'd gone from being a quietly miserable wife to a blubbering adult child of sexual abuse to a scheming, seductive, Sapphic client—who was also, by the way, hammered on *shakti* and no longer cooked dinner.

I began to gather information for an article about somatic experiencing therapy, and made other contacts in that field who were colleagues of Céline's. When I found out that two of the women would be in Santa Fe for a conference, I decided to have a dinner party for them and invite Céline as well. I doubted that she would go for it. That *had* to be against the rules. But she agreed, without hesitation. I felt a little nervous about Will's meeting her, but not nervous enough. It turned out, though, that he had a work-related event to host.

That morning, Will began arguing with me. He wasn't happy that I wouldn't be by his side that night, and he also thought the house was a mess. How would I pull things together in time?

Will usually picked fights with me right before we had company —it was one of the most predictable times for him to have an outburst. This time, I had assumed that I would dodge that bullet, but here he was, picking the fight in the morning because he wouldn't be around to pick it later.

"Why is the house so messy? How are you going to clean everything? I thought you were going to do laundry. I'm low on socks. And you still have to go shopping! You always do this!"

"Stop it."

He continued. I snapped. I picked up a featherweight red plastic colander from IKEA and threw it at him. It fell on the floor. "You threw something at me? You *threw* something at me?"

"I'm not doing this. I'm going to get my iPod and put the earphones in." Will had given it to me, had it engraved with my name. Now I would use it as a barrier between me and an argument.

Bam!

Our big, thick cutting board ricocheted off the wall, inches from my neck, leaving a large gouge in the plaster, in the paint that we had just chosen a few months before.

"What the fuck!" I yelled, and ran at him, fists flailing. "You could have paralyzed me!"

I beat his chest as if it were my own. He grabbed my fists, screaming at me. I screamed back. Nathaniel watched TV in the next room. Honorée was down the hall.

He was late for work, mercifully, so we disengaged and I went back to preparing for my dinner. But all of my excitement and happiness was gone. I felt like I had so many other times, depressed and demoralized, especially since it was the first time I had ever struck him. Our fights were never going to get any healthier; they would escalate as I got stronger, trading out my weepiness for ferocity.

I was a little bit subdued when my guests arrived that night, but by the time I'd had a glass of Lillet, and then champagne, and white wine with the soup course, I felt wonderful. Céline came early, "to help," and brought me a gift: a pink bougainvillea plant. She was in my house, drinking my wine, eating my food, exclaiming over my art and decor, and stroking my children's hair. I was about to faint from pleasure. She smelled so good. She looked so good.

I kept on looking up in the middle of cooking tasks and catching her eyes on me as she smiled. She was always ready to help me— anticipating my needs for an extra hand. And I thought I overheard her telling one of the other women that she and her partner were breaking up. Between the ugliness of the morning and the beauty of the evening, my next step was crystal clear.

The day after the dinner party, Will and I had our first divorce discussion. It was almost like we were kicking around a beach ball on the sand.

The subsequent conversations were far from calm.

"You've got to be interested in someone else," he said. "Women don't want to leave unless there's someone else. They're too attached to security."

"There's nobody," I lied.

He snooped in my office, and even though I had stashed diaries and deleted computer files, he found a scrap of paper with my doodles on it. Enough to connect the dots.

That's when he wrote me a letter telling me he was setting me free, because he knew that I loved Céline now, and not him, and he wanted me to be happy. I almost thought that I was about to have the most anticlimactic divorce in the history of civilization, until I read the next paragraph.

He confessed that when he went back to New York to meet with his father's gallerist, back when Honorée was one and a half, he was unfaithful to me.

He went out with his old coworkers from the wine store, and a new employee came along—a single woman. Everyone left, but they stayed, drank more, and began making out, and he went back to her apartment.

"I couldn't perform," he said. "I was too inebriated. But I've felt terrible about it for years." He went back to my brother's apartment on Long Island and crashed.

Click. That was the weekend I fell out of love with Will.

Click. When he returned, he looked around at the oddly immaculate house, and said, "Is everything okay?"

Click. The wine store managers executing a block formation, barring me from entering the back. I had to love them for it, in retrospect. They protected me from seeing her *and* being seen by her. Or maybe they thought I was there to make a scene.

It did hurt. Whether I loved him or not, or loved Céline or not, I retroactively felt the grief of being that young mother with the baby on her hip, who had just moved across the country and left her family, friends, and career behind, believing in the soundness of her family.

I'd never questioned his fidelity, but now I had reason to wonder if other indiscretions had occurred.

I didn't know it, but Will also cc'd Céline on this letter. He meant to scare her, and he surely did, but he also lost me forever. I don't really blame him for doing it. It was creepy and invasive, but he was trying to salvage his family, and if I had been trying to salvage my family, I would have probably done a similarly desperate thing. I was not trying to do so. I was trying to salvage my life. I couldn't have both.

Céline told me about her copy of the letter when we met in the park near her house. I'd made a pot of chai and brought a thermos for us to share. "I'm going to be in the neighborhood," I'd emailed, "if you want to have some chai with me."

My son climbed on the jungle gym, my daughter twirled in dance class down the street. My body curled into the fetal position on the park bench.

"Well, it's all part of transference, anyway," she said.

"I've read six books on transference. I know all about it, and . . . I just can't dismiss it that way. There's a part of it that is, but I don't dismiss it that way. I hope you don't dismiss it that way."

"Nothing is dismissable," she said.

Nathaniel called out to me, and I ran to help him. She followed me, and we stood there together.

"So . . . are my feelings viable?" I asked.

"Probably not. I'm not available now for a relationship, because of my breakup."

"No, of course, not now, but three, six, nine months down the road?"

"I care deeply for you, but that's not a relationship. Because I used to be your therapist, there are different layers to the way I feel about you, and the shifting of them would be hard. Plus, it's not ethical. And I just screwed up the relationship I was in."

"If you really meant 'definitely not' when you said 'probably not' but you were trying to be nice, you should tell me. I need to know what is reasonable to hope for."

"No, regarding the ethics of it, definitely not. But at least now you are aware of what can be possible for you."

So much more *was* possible for me now—it went way beyond sexuality. My soul had been restored. I could no longer live with oppressive energies, fear, and wrath.

I dropped off the kids with a friend, found a furnished three-month sublet, and moved us in that day. The landlord had stocked the kitchen "right down to the garlic press," and I appreciated it. I had landed, and it felt right, but I knew this was going to be a big transition for us all.

We were welcome to borrow my landlord-cum-new friend's two small dogs, Milk and Honey, whenever we wanted. I knew my children would need those little balls of fur, their loving, licking tongues and warm brown eyes, their wee nails clicking on the tile floor.

"You deserve a future that's not contaminated," said my *new* therapist, whom I did not have any disruptive feelings for.

And when I went home, I could lock my door and feel safe—on the inside.

25

The New Basics

MOVING OUT made my freedom from compulsory cooking real. It was one more bittersweet thing for me to both miss and revel in. I went to the supermarket and bought about twenty Weight Watchers frozen meals, a twelve-pack of Guinness stout, and then "mom on autopilot" food for the kids. Frozen macaroni and cheese, carrot sticks, chicken nuggets. Honorée never liked anything but the plainest food anyway, and Nathaniel was less picky, but just getting through each day was enough of a challenge for me. Cooking fell off my map.

Although I still had heaps of feelings for Céline, I knew that I needed to figure out if I indeed had just been walloped with transference—or if this lesbian thing had legs. I'd been in a marriage for seven years and had thought my romantic future was both known and dreary. She and I agreed that it was no longer appropriate for me to be her client. I missed her but also felt hopeful that another kind of relationship would begin.

This was my chance to find out the answer to the question that had been padding around the outskirts of my consciousness on kitten feet since my youth.

My quest to date women was also a way to distract myself from the way the divorce pain was smashing my soul like chicken under a brick. The terrible thing about divorce is that even if you don't love or desire or even respect your spouse anymore, you still mourn the death of the marriage, of your hopes and dreams, of the dearness of your long-ago naiveté as you took the leap. You mourn your family's disappointment, and sometimes you even find yourself comforting them. Witnessing your children's fractured world is excruciating: their anxiety, their pleas, their questions as you pick them up at school for your half of the week with them—"Why you not live with Daddy in our house? Why you not come home?"—and sometimes you can't even get out of the car to sign them in because you're crying so hard.

Some people gain weight when they're grieving. But once again, grief burned up my fat deposits and winnowed my appetite. It helped that I went religiously to Nia. Dance class—even if I ended up crying during the cooldown—was a lifesaver. And the more I did it, the better I got, which gave me *something* to feel good about. I'd spent my whole life feeling slow, awkward, uncoordinated, and also victimized, but suddenly I was spry, agile, and even graceful. It made me feel more confident as I posted my profile on Match.com.

Will posted his profile there, too, and within a week of my moving out, he had sex with a woman on their first date and told me about it. That hurt. But as he kept lashing out, I kept withdrawing from him. He zigzagged between acting out toward me and pleading that I come back to him, but he wasn't doing anything to optimize that very slim chance. He was so angry. He even threatened to call my father up and tell him that I was a lesbian, in very crude terms.

"Go ahead," I said. "I'll dial the phone for you," scrolling to his number and hitting "call." I wasn't ready to own that label, or even to share my situation with my father, of all people, but I refused to be threatened.

"No, no, no, Candace, forget it, just forget it!" He strode away from me, but my father's phone was ringing at this point, and then I heard his voice.

"Hi, Dad. Happy Easter," I said, oddly cheerful.

"Hah . . . hah." I heard his voice break. "Your brother told me . . . that you and Will . . ." He was crying.

"It's okay, Dad, it's okay. It's for the best." I wished that he didn't care—it was a touching surprise that he did. Of course, he'd always liked Will, and he was losing a son-in-law. "Why don't we talk later? It sounds like you have company."

He asked me to call him that night. When I did, he spent an hour giving me very valuable legal advice. I didn't expect him to be so pragmatic, and so loyal, because he was basically giving me hundreds of dollars' worth of advice on how to screw Will six ways to Sunday in terms of alimony and settlements. I had no desire to do so.

I could tell that my father was disappointed that I had so little fighting spirit. I could have pleased him by giving him a way to feel that he was helping me. But it felt wrong. I wanted to sever our marital bonds and receive equitable child support, but New Mexico had a worksheet for that based on the custody agreement and each parent's income, and there was really nothing you could do to come up with a different result.

My mother, when I told her the news, said, "I feel like you just stuck a knife into my heart." I was crying hysterically in a taxi in L.A., on an ill-timed business trip, so my patience was short.

"This isn't about you, Mom! This is *my* marriage that's ending." Of course, it was about her, too, because this was happening to her grandchildren and her son-in-law and her daughter, but I wasn't in the mood to hear about her stabbed heart when mine was so in need of comfort.

Will was a devoted dad, and joint custody gave him a more active parenting role. I spent my time alone recharging my batteries, meditating, going to therapy, and healing; I could also spend more time getting up to speed in my new position as features editor at *Mothering.* I had so much more to offer when the kids returned.

Céline had invited me to come to her meditation center after I told her about my Kundalini experience. And on my bachelorette Wednesdays, I put all of my newly underutilized culinary energy into cooking dinner for the entire group, although the true fire burning in my loins, that is, tongs, was the desire to woo Céline, to nurture and pleasure her, with mouthfuls of food.

But as it was for a vegetarian community, I was forced to work within those boundaries. No demi-glace, no chicken broth, no bacon fat. Since I worked at the office all day, I turned to the slow cooker to create food that seemed unhurried, attentively made.

Tuesday evenings had me shopping for ingredients, Wednesday mornings had me chopping and sautéing. I used the *Fresh from the Vegetarian Slow Cooker* cookbook and made French White Bean and Cabbage Soup (a.k.a. garbure), Moroccan-Style Lentil and Chickpea Soup, French Onion Soup, Three-Bean Chili with Chive-Flecked Cornmeal Dumplings. I also pulled from the urban, girlfriends-y *The New Basics,* which my friend Marijane swore by.

Céline gave me lots in return: With each bite, she closed her eyes and sighed or very faintly moaned with pleasure. She then opened her eyes, lowered her head, and smiled, looking at me through her lashes as if to say, *Oh, no you didn't.*

I think I brought forth the most attenuated moans from her heaving chest when I served an olive oil–lavender honey cake with fresh whipped cream. I saw her mouth spasm with pleasure and her shoulders curl inward.

And when I found a recipe for a lavender honey–yogurt refrigerator pie, I decided that would be my next dessert. Except the store was out of lavender honey. So I chose the chai honey and had the whole group practically on their knees. Chai honey–yogurt icebox pie—at a meditation center. Not a sliver was left.

It was one of the most satisfying cooking gigs of my life—I was cooking only once a week, for a deeply appreciative crowd, while high on *shakti,* and I was *also* cooking to seduce Céline, and I got to stick around to watch her flail with pleasure.

Others who cooked for the center introduced me to new dishes as well. Savory cereal was a community favorite—a mix of whole grains, shredded coconut, chopped onion and tomato, cumin and fenugreek, plus ginger root, a hot pepper, nutritional yeast, and fresh cilantro.

But after *satsang,* I went home to an empty house and knew I wouldn't see Céline until the following week, unless we bumped into each other (which we did so frequently that it began to be a little awkward. *She must like me,* I thought, *because it takes two to manifest the energy to run into each other almost daily*). So I went searching for gay women in a city without a single gay bar or bookstore.

My Match profile was attracting its fair share of winks, emails, and so on, which felt good—although women were usually reticent regarding my "separated" and "two kids" status. Who would ever want to take a chance on me?

Amber. My first date was with a ridiculously beautiful woman in her late twenties who also had a young child. She had hair down to her butt and a smokin' body, and if I had actually been attracted to femmes, she would have done it for me. But I realized, as we sat across from each other at a tapas restaurant, that I had a type. I liked older women. Not necessarily as old as Céline, who was a whopping twenty years my senior—but not younger than me. And more of a tomboy. I had always found the nape of a woman's neck very fetching, especially when the hair was cropped short, to reveal its winnowy places. Amber and I kissed chastely good night and didn't manage to ever have that second date.

More followed. I worked my way methodically through the list of potentials, feeling more and more discouraged as a love connection failed to materialize. But the great thing about dating women was that if the chemistry wasn't there, there was a really good chance that we could become friends.

I soon had a posse of about fifteen new women friends to show me the ropes of being sociable in Santa Fe's under-the-radar scene.

Gia and I went to our first dance together, burned up the dance floor, drank about four too many Cosmos each, and ended up being hit on separately by women who soon thereafter held our hair while we booted on different ends of the parking lot . . . and then still wanted to date us.

Nancy and I went out to dinner at a resort that had an outdoor swimming pool for the guests, which was closed for the night. "Want to sneak in and skinny-dip?" Nancy asked.

"No! Well . . . okay!" In we slid, giggling, our breasts bobbing in the warm water. And yes, we did get busted.

Céline and I did do a few "friendlike" things. But as much as I wanted to coast into a groovy post-therapy friendship with her, every moment I spent in her presence was overwhelmingly charged.

I invited her to the opera, and she agreed to go with me. I had half of the season tickets Will and I had bought the year before, and although it was tacky, I took her. The seats were killer—orchestra center, and I got to thrill as she whispered comments in my ear, her hair brushing my neck and cheek, her scent wafting into my nose from just centimeters away. Afterward, I drove her home, pulling into the driveway I used to park in when I was her client, but now it was close to midnight and we were both dressed up.

"Good night, sleep tight," I said nervously.

"Don't let the bedbugs bite," she said. "And if they do, come back!" She smiled in the semidarkness.

I couldn't believe she had actually said that. If she had actually said that, it would have been a come-on. But I couldn't believe she had actually meant it. If she had meant it, I should have taken her up on it. That was the quest I'd been on for a year—the seduction I'd been building with every bite of food, pair of stockings, flirty word, gaze and breath and smile.

I told every lesbian friend I had about it, and their reactions were unanimous. I had blown it, biffed it, choked. But although I knew that intellectually, I didn't feel regret. It was entirely possible that, per the silly laminated inspirational poster saying, I really *had* been in it for the journey, not the destination. The journey pulled me out of my marriage. It showed me the delight of loving her, a woman, dressing for a woman, cooking for a woman, tempting a woman, so I could notice how incomparably, lusciously right it felt. For me.

26

First Course

"COMING OUT is like going through a second adolescence," my friend Judith told me. It was! I felt puppylike, clodlike, sweaty, and insecure. I was faking it until I made it, from the moment I woke up to the moment I fell asleep. Sometimes I dressed like a boy, in hoodie sweatshirts, jeans, and Converse sneakers. Sometimes I dressed like a soccer mom. And sometimes I dressed like a wannabe slutty teenager, in slingback wedges, tight capri cargos, and cleavage-y tanks under skimpy cardigans. I even . . . dyed my hair a shade of blond. Running into Will's dad in that outfit was quite mortifying, especially when he looked at me dismissively as if I were a cheap tart. Of course he hated me now. I'd ruined his son's life. And I was fine with his having that take on it.

I remembered what he told me well into a wine-soaked family dinner, in his thick French accent. "When I first saw you, I wanted you for myself. But I told myself, *It is not my time. It is my son's time.*"

Great! Can you please pass the salt?

But what's more a rite of passage than the first girlfriend or boyfriend of adolescence? When I was fourteen, a boy named Bobby talked to me at a party, and the next thing I knew, he was calling me and asking me to the movies. He had the hairstyle of a first grader and snaggly teeth, but warm brown eyes and soft lips. And when he kissed me for the first time, in the darkness beside the back screen door, I melted. (And then my mom slapped me across the face on the other side of that door. But that's another story.)

It didn't really matter whether I would have picked Bobby out of a room full of boys (I wouldn't have). But he noticed me; he put me on the map. He was significant because he was first. Once I got that first bit of validation, I was on my way and could stop obsessing about whether or not a boy would ever like me.

It occurred to me that in this newfound adolescence, I was stepping out of that passive role. Coming out was about what I wanted. If I wanted to have a girlfriend, I had carte blanche to take on as active a role as my potential suitors (suitorettes?). And that was wild. I texted a woman I met at a dance to ask her out. She texted me back to say that she was very flattered, but she had a partner of fourteen years. *Whoa! Sorry!* I plunked down next to another woman and chatted her up, until she mentioned that she was in a relationship. "Oh, that's cool, no, I just wanted to meet you. You seem like a really interesting person." *Cringe.*

And there was interest coming my way—a Sam's Club assistant manager *(eeee),* a woman who emailed me and confessed that she kind of resembled Shrek (and she did!), another woman who sent me her photo and, unfortunately, even in the blurry snapshot, looked eerily like Will. I told her this, which completely enraged her, even though I tried to couch it in the most polite way imaginable. Then my friend Gia went out on a date with her. "Not only did she rant about it to me, not knowing we were friends, but you were totally right! She looks *exactly* like Will. It's so freaky."

And then there was the woman who disclosed, minutes before our meet-up, that she was missing a limb. "My dog bit off my finger —I was trying to separate her and another dog during a fight."

"Do you still have the dog?"

"Of course!"

Next.

It was really hard to hit on women, and it was really hard to turn them down. But if it led to finding The One out there, it was a small price to pay. But would I ever?

"How's Kelly?" Kimber asked me.

"Oh, honey. Kelly was three dates ago."

"Wow."

"I think they refer to it as a burn rate."

"You're scaring me, girl. You sound like such a player."

"I'm just trying to find the right woman."

I first met Maxine at my friend Judith's potluck—but didn't pay her much attention because Céline was there as well. I might have struck up a conversation if I hadn't been eating right out of the bowl of pasta Céline held in her hands while she threatened to go. Or was it a salad? I remember the loaded subtext way more than the dish. "I'll stay until you're done," she huskily intoned, thrilling me.

She was excited to find out what I had brought, but I hadn't expected her to be there, and as it turned out, I had brought two gummy cakes from Smith's supermarket. I was busy, and I assumed Judith's potluck bar would be set pretty low, resulting in the usual glum assortment of hummus, crudité, tabbouleh, crackers and cheese, and the ever-present, low-effort New Mexico canapé—tortillas spread with green chile and cream cheese, rolled tightly, and cut into pinwheels.

After most of the women left, including Céline, Judith invited us to come soak in her deluxe hot tub.

"I didn't bring my bathing suit," I said.

"Who needs a bathing suit?" said one of the women, and she slipped out of her clothes.

So did everyone else. So here I was, at a lesbian backyard party, and everyone was getting naked. *When in Rome* . . . I thought, and pulled off my dress, wishing Céline were there to join us. Now, *that* would have been a good story.

I next saw Maxine at a women's singles party. She wore cute striped trousers and a button-down shirt, and looked kind of dashing. Not only that, but she renovated houses, and I had plenty of questions for her. I was looking to buy a house cheaply and fix it up.

We talked for hours, and then we made a coffee date. Of course, she didn't drink coffee. And it ended up turning into lunch. "I've really been wanting to meet someone younger, who has kids," she said. "Because I want kids!"

Maxine was older than me, and tomboyish, with short hair and glasses. As in older-older. Céline's age. That gave me a subversive thrill. *Take that, Céline. Watch me date someone exactly as old as you—to show that I can do it.* When I saw her seeing me on a date with Maxine at a theater performance, I preened. Céline was also there with a date—a butch gal in a tux.

Maxine and I moved rather fast. We were an item within the week. I really liked having a girlfriend, after all of the dating and doubting. But it was also really intense to have one. Every time I went out in public, I had to steel myself for the distinct possibility that I'd run into friends or acquaintances who not only did not know that Will and I had split up, but also did not know that I had switched teams. It was a lot to communicate—or avoid communicating—and it made me feel panicky and sick.

And on top of that, it wasn't like I was dating your average cute lesbian. She was way older, she had odd taste in clothes, and she often had a dour, stern look on her face. It was hard enough to come out, but to come out as someone who was both gay and dating a much older, very dykey woman wearing a Hamid Karzai hat and a vest made out of a kilim rug? That was a rough way to get jumped in.

"I feel so shallow," I said to Sarah, one of my new friends-via-Match. "If I like her as a person, what she wears shouldn't bother me. But it *does!* It makes me feel absolutely wretched! And she doesn't take it very well when I suggest a wardrobe change."

"No," she said. "It *is* important. You should just tell her that you had the wrong idea of who she is, and that it's not a good fit." Sarah didn't play well with the dominant Santa Fe lesbian sect— the women named Wolf and Bear and Crow and Fox, who had feathered Flowbee haircuts and wore turtlenecks with jeans that came up to their boobs. She was fiercely pretty, and she hung out with beautiful women who could have been extras on *The L Word.*

"It's not supposed to be this hard," my friend Julie told me. "Especially not in the very beginning. It's supposed to be fun." And it definitely wasn't fun to have someone cross-referencing your food with the ayurveda guide *A Life in Balance*. Maxine was really into ayurveda, an ancient Indian form of medicine that categorizes people by their *dosha* (*vata:* airy, *pitta:* fiery, and *kapha:* earth) and then recommends and discourages the consumption of foods accordingly.

"You're a *kapha-pitta,*" she said, after giving me a quiz. From then on she was solicitous about my food choices. It was kind of sweet. One thing that was new about dating a woman was that the cooking duties didn't default to me. But wouldn't you know it, she was a terrible cook. She made greasy, soggy skin-on chicken surrounded by sweet potatoes, covered with water, and then baked until it was close to goo; buffalo stew (meat cubed but not browned—imagine!); and every morning, steamed acorn squash sprinkled with spirulina powder. One night, I pled a stomachache, left her at the table, and ran off to eat a burger and french fries with Nancy. We cackled like naughty children.

Maxine also didn't approve of drinking. "It's okay if you have one drink while we're at a party. But if you have two, I'd just rather drop you off and go on home."

"Why?"

"I like to be able to read people, and I can't do that very well when they've been drinking."

I couldn't imagine ending things, as much as I sometimes felt uncomfortable. I had finally made it inside, after hours in a snowstorm, of pressing my nose against the glass of a cozy firelit chalet. I was *in*. So what if the shag rug was too shaggy? So what if the incense was too pungent? So what if the art on the walls was tacky? So what if the stucco was too craggy? I couldn't eject myself back onto the tundra. Not yet.

And in the meantime, I had a trip to Prague to look forward to. Jack had been living there for years and had always wanted me to come visit. Now I could. I would leave on Christmas Day and come back right after the new year. "It's my divorce present to myself," I said. Any other person would have bought tickets to Cancún and lounged in the warm sand, drinking tropical cocktails. I had to go to a frigid-ass (albeit gorgeous) city to visit a man with whom I had a very tumultuous history. And not only that, but the one thing that could have made it more of a fun, carefree romp was off the table. Sex. Especially now that I had a girlfriend. I would not cheat on her.

Feeding Maxine was even harder than being fed by Maxine. She was gluten-free, wheat-free, sugar-free, alcohol-free, and caffeine-free, and ate only *pitta-vata*-friendly foods. And then there were the surprise problems.

"I've had gas for days!" she groused. "I think it was that damned garlic in your baked chicken." Or, after I made her the very thing she ate every single morning for breakfast (steamed acorn squash, sprouted almonds, two pieces of rice-bread toast, two organic turkey breakfast sausages), plus customized *pitta-vata* chai, the only thing she had to say was, "The chai wasn't hot by the time I sat down."

In the days before I left for Prague, Maxine and I ran around, buying a tree, decorating it, wrapping presents, taking the kids to events, going to parties. It was hectic, but hectic was good for me—it kept me from spending too much time dwelling on the fact that this was my first post-Will Christmas since I had hauled that tree home, strapped to my yellow bicycle.

I was running away from Christmas in many ways—getting on a plane early in the morning, lifting off into the air, and staying there until the day was over.

Apparently, my subconscious wanted a vacation from my vacation. The morning of my flight, I found that I had driven twenty miles past the airport without noticing. I should have kept going, because Juárez would have been more fun. I got a beastly flu on the way over, Prague was freezing, and Jack both criticized my body and engaged in a days-long campaign to get me to sleep with him. I wouldn't.

I'd slept with so many guys because it was easier to say yes, it was less scary to say yes, it was more polite to say yes, and I had terrible boundaries. But that was before I faced up to the abuse and before the kundalini awakening reset my meters. *I* didn't want to sleep with him, and I wouldn't be changing my mind.

Finally, after yet another night of fending off his advances, I proposed that I go stay in a hotel. I was ready, I had the money to pay for it, and I think I might have really preferred the high thread count, room service, and solitude. A hotel would certainly have had cleaner towels.

He had no bargaining chips, no pull. It was amazing how much fun we had after we got clear on that one. Things shifted. He became the older brother I never had. He even confessed that he did cheat on me—a lot. With the women I suspected.

"Why didn't you just tell me the truth, then? It made me feel crazy to sense it but have you deny it."

"I didn't want to make you upset."

"It made me more upset to doubt myself and have someone I loved lie to my face, but not be able to prove it."

"Good point."

He introduced me (on separate occasions) to the three twenty-something chicks whom he was currently driving batshit. Same pattern, different decade. I dropped the 411 on each of them whenever he went out of earshot. I was relatively ancient to them, ten years their senior, and a mother of two. My body was soft and stretchy where theirs were taut and untrammeled. But my oracle was one they were eager to consult. And I felt proud to ally myself with them, instead of being catty and cagey, like Danielle had been ten years before.

Jack also brought me out dancing with his Russian sometime girlfriend, who was bi, and her sometime girlfriend, also bi. They were Bond-girl gorgeous, and they sandwiched me on the dance floor. The one who looked like Helena Christensen kissed me quickly on the lips, and then smiled guilelessly. A threesome in Prague was there for the taking. But shit! I had a girlfriend. I danced away.

Jack and I tried to make osso buco with the terrible Mitteleuropa meat (some pig shank riddled with bone splinters). He thought it was a roaring success, but I knew what we were missing.

We did, however, go on a very memorable culinary tour of the best goulash and dumplings *(knedlicki)* joints in Prague. One was in the shadow of Prague Castle, and one was way out in an unfashionable neighborhood with a toothless waitress and kelly-green carpeting. Although it was a close call, I preferred the latter. He told me, over the lovely *knedlicki,* "Candace, you know, I would have married you if you hadn't run off with Will so quickly. You're the one person I could have done that with—right down to having kids."

Somehow I wasn't surprised. I had known it, back in my little cocaine-bender brain, that it was right there, waiting to be lived.

"But I wouldn't have been one of those dads who change diapers and feed them and all that nonsense. I'd have done things the old fashioned way." Or rather, *not* done things, the old-fashioned way. That's when I told him the dream of the ham sandwich. He chuckled. "You're probably right. I would have asked you to just make me a ham sandwich."

"That's why I didn't wait."

"And it all turned out for the best, didn't it? Except I still think this lesbian thing you're on about is rubbish." He smiled, taking the poison out of the bite. "You know, it wouldn't be half bad if you were dating a hottie. But this Maxine looks like my auntie back in Perth!"

I wondered if I should break up with Maxine. Or rather, I knew that I should, but the thought just seemed so unpleasant. I didn't have to worry about it for long, though—she beat me to it.

27

A Moveable Feast

MAXINE WATERED my plants while I was away, and I wondered if maybe she snooped and read my diary. That tearstained, crush-soaked journal was such a crazy-girl brain dump that if she did, it might explain her about-face.

"I feel like I've been on a spa vacation since you went away," she said. "Being with you has really exhausted me! Between the Christmas stuff and the kids . . . when I used to come over for dinner, while you cooked, it felt like you expected me to be a babysitter!"

"Oh, the way you used to read to them and play with puzzles while I whipped potatoes and basted the chicken? I thought it was cozy and sweet."

I remembered how she'd been so keen on the fact that I had kids. Unfortunately, that feeling hadn't survived a couple of half-hour stints on the living room floor with my nonhellions.

Even though there were so many things I didn't like about Maxine, I fell apart when she broke up with me. "I'm not breaking up with you," she said. "I just want to go back to the beginning, and go slowly. Let's just get to know each other without being physical."

"Okay. What kind of time frame do you have for this?"

"I don't know—six months, maybe more."

She had to be kidding. I hadn't spent my whole life waiting for this so that I could hang around cuddling with someone for the foreseeable future. Women were winking at me on Match, friends wanted to set me up, I was thirty-five years old, in my sexual prime, and Maxine wanted to literally *create* lesbian bed death. Right after I'd been so good in Prague. What a waste!

I was single again. And all the postdivorce pain that had been held in escrow by the pleasure of my Céline dreams and my feelings of triumph about being in my first relationship blew through me like a gale force hurricane.

Will caught me in tears and came over straightaway, a six-pack of sympathy beer in hand. He sat beside me on the couch, wrapped his arms around me, and held me tightly as I cried.

More than only crying about my breakup with Maxine or my divorce, I cried out my grief at my deepest fear: that I was inherently unlovable and flawed, incapable of being happy ever again; that I was like so many women of my mother's generation who divorced or had been widowed, and spent the rest of their lives monastically solo.

"You're a wonderful person," he said. "I married you! That's got to count for something. You and I split up, and it was the right thing to do, but there are lots of other people out there who will appreciate you and enjoy you for who you are. That woman was not right for you. You spent all this time settling for our relationship, which was not enough. That relationship was not enough either. I know you really wanted to be in a relationship with a woman after all this upheaval, but don't sell yourself short. She doesn't drink, she doesn't eat this, she doesn't eat that, she can't stay up past eight, she doesn't want to have sex. . . . Candace, when there are more don'ts than dos, *don't.*"

Will was a big enough person to be there for me as I mourned someone who was *not* him. And he was there for me, so much so that he let me soak his dress shirt with my tears. It didn't hurt that he was happily in a new relationship, with someone who was even geekier about classical music than he was. I wondered if now that we weren't married, we could have a better overall relationship. I hoped so.

After that, my friends began to collect around me. Susie arrived, all blustery indignation that someone could cut her best friend loose, comfort groceries in hand. Then Gia arrived, and we drank more and made lists of what I wanted in my next girlfriend and, just as important, what I didn't.

"Must get you and know that you are great," Gia said.

"Must be able to fall asleep where you are," Susie said.

"Yes to consciousness of what's reasonable," said Gia.

"She can't smell like soup," I said.

"She can't tell you how to parent," said Susie. "And she has to love your kids."

"Yes to a little bit of butch swagger," said Gia.

"Oh, yes," I said.

"And good nighttime skills," said Susie.

But I was no longer in any kind of rush. It was nearly March, which would make it a year since I had moved out. And since then, I'd been a dating machine, and how well had that really worked out for me? I hadn't waited, because I had something to prove, and I had more than proven it. I loved sex with women way more than sex with men. It wasn't a stretch, or stressful, or a chore, or a performance. It was doubtless what truly straight women loved about sex with men—it was the right fit.

That's not to say that I looked back and saw my sexual history with men as a disappointment. I pursued, wooed, loved, and savored men. I just didn't realize how much more there was to enjoy.

If you spend your whole life eating pork chops and applesauce with sauerkraut, you have no idea how much you prefer pork served with a mole of cacao nibs, six kinds of chilies, cinnamon, anise, cloves, coriander, ground almonds, pumpkin seeds, and garlic . . . until you try it.

I still found men attractive. But all I wanted from even the most compelling man I saw was a really good hug. The last man I had a crush on before I met Céline was Greek; he hailed from Lesbos. I was on a track, all right.

I decided to take a hiatus from dating, just to give myself a little downtime and space to grieve in case I needed to really fall apart. The year had been full. Chasing relationships down had not worked; it was time to put down my butterfly net.

On February 27, I got an email from Match.com with "Your

Matches." *Oh, pshaw,* I thought. Most of the time I didn't even open those. When I did, I'd see about fifteen women who were most certainly *not* my matches—instantly disqualified by bad mullet hairdos, joyful employment in the trucking industry, or monikers like "I_love_snoopy." Match had been good for making friends. That was it.

But, what the hell . . . I clicked on it.

Right in the top row, I saw a photo of the most adorable woman ever. She epitomized my type. She looked at once intellectual, boyishly pretty, smartly dressed, witty, intelligent, kind, and gentle. All that from a photo the size of a postage stamp.

Her profile text was probably going to show me that I was jumping to conclusions—but it did not. She was smart and witty, and joked that she loved home improvement so much that she fantasized about working at Home Depot. Coupled with her up-until-recent university professor status, it was a sexy combination. I shot her a flirty email, subject line: "wow."

Her reply, subject line: "and wow," was filled with tasty sentences. I couldn't believe it. No misspellings, no cringe-inducing admissions, no desperation, no hubris. Just charm, and an endearing transparency. And I learned her name: Laura.

"Your profile knocked me out. Really. Suddenly, I'm very nervous. I have a million questions for you and would love to hear more. I know email—especially this kind, can sometimes invite stilted language, so I won't pepper you with all of them. But I do want to hear about your work, your kids(!), your house project, your ideas on spirituality, your thoughts on dwr.com, etc. Oh, and your cooking. What I wouldn't give for polenta in marsala gorgonzola ANYWHERE, ANYTIME."

"Oh, and your cooking." Game on.

Our first phone call—I worried that it would break the spell, particularly for two admittedly phone-avoidant people. But the conversation (all three and a half hours of it) did not. After one long, sprawling, giggly, somber, sometimes on the daybed, sometimes en route to the kitchen conversation, we asked and answered questions, commiserated, told the next tale that spun out from the other's one before, dropped and recognized references, flexed every single verbal muscle we could to win the other. By the end of the call, I was on the living room couch, and I can still remember the feeling of the firm blue cushion supporting the back of my head as I took a deep breath and asked her, "Would you like to have dinner with me on Sunday night?"

"I would *love* to have dinner with you on Sunday night," she replied. She lived in Nob Hill—the Albuquerque neighborhood I used to feel so called to, the one I covered with my children in their double stroller. We agreed to eat at the Gruet Steakhouse, in an old firehouse on Central. I realized after we made the date that it was on my father's birthday.

I drove down to Albuquerque, nervous. My stomach felt like a piece of gum that was being chewed vigorously. I blasted the Strokes, howling along with the lyrics, allowing them to drown out my brain's nattering. Was the fear telling me to turn around and go home? It was so muscular. It was like being in line for a bungee jump (and I'm afraid of heights). Being buckled in. Watching the earth's surface retreat.

I learned that night that sometimes fear accompanies the best things that ever happen to me.

Laura's hair was precociously silver, her eyes cornflower blue with ice flecks. Her smile was girlish, and also a little bit rakish. Her vocabulary was killer, and her hands were sexy. She had a beautiful sense of style. Well-cut trousers, cute oxfords, a white button-down shirt with cuffs pierced with silver gear-shift cuff links, under a dark jacket. Her clothes were boyish, but her body was dizzyingly womanly. The contrast made my heartbeat quicken.

She talked and she listened. She laughed and made me laugh. *There's no way,* I thought. *If I like her this much, and she's this perfect, she does not like me back.* But she did.

After dinner, I asked her if she wanted a ride to her car, because it was snowing lightly and I wanted to be kissed. She said yes. We parked in front of Objects of Desire, the store in which I had so innocently bought Christmas ornaments a few years back. We sat. We fidgeted. She leaned, infinitesimally and definitely.

She told me later that I moved toward her in slow motion. I just remember that I felt like the air was suddenly more tensile around me, that I had to lean through it deliberately, to get to her mouth with my own. It was the slowest . . . it was so slow, this kiss. First our lips grazed against each other, then seemed to land like birds on a certain branch of a tree. We kissed, and kissed, and kissed, while intangible things that have no name entwined around and inside us.

When I felt her tongue, it was like a little bird wing fluttered up, and the vertebrae in my lower back liquefied into warmed amber honey. She placed her hand on my left cheek, and I was sure that nobody had ever done that. If they had, her hand replaced the memory seamlessly. I unsteadily raised my left hand to her shoulder and rested it there so gently, because I was deliciously weak. And we kissed. And paused to rest our foreheads together. I opened my eyes and saw her, the planes of her face my new way home.

That was four years ago. Laura, who wrote on her Match.com profile, next to "Do you drink?"—"Definitely." Laura, who can be relied upon to order cheeseburgers, or slutty piles of nachos, whenever we eat out. Laura, who is a sensualist. My onion chopper, my dinner appreciator, a reluctant cook who nonetheless does a singularly lissome spaghetti carbonara. She appreciates fine wine but quaffs the simple stuff with satisfaction. She is my culinary soul mate, although there are several things she just flat out won't eat. (Like soup.)

Through Laura, I discovered all that's good about the intersection of holidays and food traditions: our first Easter, for instance.

I had planned ahead. The ramekins were in the refrigerator, dolloped with mounds of creamy polenta, lined with thick slabs of pliable applewood-smoked bacon. I sprinked freshly grated Gruyère cheese on the polenta, then cracked an egg into each cup, topping it off with more cheese and chives. Then I placed the ramekins on a cookie sheet and slid them into the oven. The champagne chilled in the refrigerator, right next to the bottle of peach nectar for Bellinis.

Laura emerged from the bedroom, following her nose to the kitchen, where I was peering into the oven to gauge the egg whites' opacity. I needed to catch the eggs when they weren't too runny, yet far from rubbery-solid. To know how far I could push it before abandoning the next minute of cooking and its effects. I needed to sense, surrender, intuit.

Laura mixed the Bellinis as I fussed over the eggs. We sat down in my living room, in the house that I had cleaned from top to bottom—the way you only clean when fueled by love, lust, and benevolent anxiety. Diffuse light bathed us, as did the glow of our endorphins. The polenta mixed with the strands of melted Gruyère and the piquancy of the grassy chives. The yolk bathed everything in splendor, and the bacon added a crispy, savory backbone. We sat in the quiet of our dawning life together, stared into each other's eyes, and breathed "*mmmm*" with each bite. And then we went back to bed. Though not to sleep.

Weeks before our first Thanksgiving together, Laura and I pulled all of my November food magazines and favorite cookbooks into bed and paged through them, and assembled the most kick-ass menu to date. Pancetta-sage turkey and gravy; artichoke, sausage, and parmesan stuffing; chestnut dressing; mashed potatoes; sweet potato wedges; green beans with pecans and feta; spiced streusel apple pie; and more. We crammed my little house so full of people —Laura's parents, aunt and uncle, friends, Susie, coworkers—that we re-created the flushed exuberance of my grandparents Marie and Jimmy's Thanksgivings. And like them, I had fresh things to mourn and old things to forget. But those just made me appreciate my exquisite love for Laura, and hers for me, all the more, the way a pinch of something salty brings out the flavors of dark chocolate and caramel.

My parents weren't there, but they never travel on Thanksgiving. Over time, they each got their head around my gay self without too much agita. They love Laura. Even Will loves Laura. "I've known for years," my mother said. "When I visited you when you lived with that girl in college."

"Well, then, why didn't you say anything?"

"I was hoping you could work around it."

My dad cornered me on the phone one evening, after I told my stepmother in a series of emails, "in confidence." That was one time that I used her leaky confidence skills to my advantage. I was fine with her being the lead messenger. But he wanted to hear it from me.

"So, what are you dating, a woman, an Indian?" he asked.

"I have . . . a . . . woman . . . partner," I squeaked out, sweating profusely, my entire body scrunching into an involuntary flinch.

"Well, that's exciting," he said. "It's fun to explore. Just, you know, don't do anything that makes it into something that limits you in the future, that prevents you from . . . other options."

I couldn't promise that, especially since Laura had slipped an engagement ring on my finger just a few weeks before, six months after we met.

Before that, I didn't know if she would ever want to marry me. We were two women and we couldn't get married in New Mexico. She hadn't ever considered getting married to her previous partner, of twelve years. Why would she think of it with me?

My divorce had been finalized for five days when we found ourselves out on my patio, well into a bottle of chewy red wine, with stray pasta strands on plates that had moments before held caramelized squash, onions, and wilted greens from the farmers' market. We were staring at each other, grinning until our faces hurt.

"I could marry you," she said, with a smile both soulful and cheeky.

My body replied. It vaulted me into her lap, my chair flying across the porch sideways from the force of my launch. For what seemed like an hour, I just held her, hot tears streaking down my face, which was buried in her neck. I couldn't say anything. I just held her. And she held me.

"I'm so moved," I said. "And I do want to. I do."

"I know," she said. "I took that as a yes."

Ours was a movable feast. A trip to Yelapa, Mexico, and one to her family home in Ojai, California (I brought the fondue pot), and New York City (we ate at wd~50), and hundreds of trips up and down I-25, where we wore grooves in the road, poised to land in each other's arms. I cooked at her house, I cooked at my house, we ate and drank, feasting on our love, our capacity for enjoyment, our utter lack of food and wine restrictions. She bought me a milky aqua KitchenAid for our first Mother's Day together—honoring my mama self, my kitchen-centricity, and edging Bella into her next life, as my friend Nancy's new love.

Although Laura had never imagined having children, she did now. I fell in love with her even more as she read to Nathaniel and thought hard about what to get Honorée for her birthday.

We moved in together after two and a half years of courtship. For the first time, I didn't rush in. And I understood why I had been a fool to do so before. Our engagement rings remained on our fingers, unpaired with bands. California's same-sex marriage laws were mired in contention, and my loyal California girl didn't want to go get hitched in a random state. I sometimes got the marriage bug, but wanted it to be something we were both enthusiastic about. So I focused on what we did have: a beautiful home together where we curled up like spoons every night, a kitchen that would turn out untold numbers of meals, rooms for my children, beds for her dogs, boxes of mingled Christmas tree ornaments in the garage, and a sideboard filled with her parents' registry china.

Raw

I'D ALWAYS THOUGHT that this society's emphasis on weight loss and being skinny was screwed up. Watching my mother hate her body turned me off to dieting, and to looking at my body critically. Her never-ending conveyor belt of diets, the gastric bypass that caused two near-death experiences (her gall bladder failed, and a hernia caused internal bleeding), the hundreds of meals that laid her out, traumatized me. Watching her care so much, and to such a destructive degree, made me not want to care at all. I thought that was loving and accepting my body as it was, but really, I was in a state of dissociative self-neglect. I ate unconsciously, and when that meant I ate too much, I came back online long enough to empty my stomach.

But I couldn't continue to purge now. The first time I did it after a restaurant dinner with Laura, I kept it a secret. But I noticed immediately, and over the next few days, that I felt a new distance come between us. That ugly act isolated me from my love, and probably had been doing the same thing in other relationships for decades. It was a shameful thing that I didn't talk about, a way to have my cake, eat it too, and then not have it after all. To people-please, and self-please, and then do a twisted kind of take-back that hurt only myself. Cheaters never win.

So I came clean and apologized. "If I feel like doing it, I will tell you. And I swear that if I do it again, I will tell you. I want to be accountable."

She was sad for me and more than willing to help.

Without purging, I had no idea how to actually control my own weight in a healthy way. I dropped pounds when I was grieving or overly stressed out. But now I was happy, and after three years of nightly epicurean delight with Laura, I was shocked to discover I weighed over two hundred and five pounds. I had no idea—because I, like many women, eschewed the practice of weighing myself. It allowed me to totally kid myself. I wore "yoga pants" because I found my regular pants confining. My bras were causing me pain, and so I switched out underwire for big, stretchy, ACE bandage–looking things. I noticed that I was looking really bad in photos, though, so I decided to go on Weight Watchers. After months of being obsessively correct points-wise, I had lost about three and a half pounds. I felt betrayed by my body, like a failure.

I was lucky enough to attend a press event with Ashley Koff, dietician to the stars. Someone mentioned the study floating around about how women would rather go without sex for six months than gain ten pounds.

"That's so stupid!" she exclaimed. "First of all, if I gained ten pounds, I would *lose them,* and second of all, who designs these studies?"

Wow, I thought. She felt so empowered to lose unwanted weight. I asked her for advice, and she taught me about her eating philosophy. I followed it, and it worked better than Weight Watchers, but I still felt like one bad weekend of eating could undo all my hard work.

So I did what I do whenever I'm completely out of answers: I called my psychic. The conversation we had, along with three other factors, changed everything for me.

My psychic isn't some lady in a turban, in a room filled with other psychics who string you along with an eye on the clock or read from a script. Her name is Lisa, and she talks like the girl who sat next to you in biology class in high school—the really nice girl who was chatty and breezy and deeper than she appeared at first glance. She has a day job in retail, and recently got divorced, and sometimes posts on Facebook about partying too hard the night before. Ninety-five percent of the time, she's dead-on.

"I feel like I wake up wanting to move, wanting to walk or run. I see fit people, jogging along as I drive to work, and my desire to be in that place is as strong as the way I crave chocolate. I know it's good. I'm sitting there, waiting for it, but it's out of my reach. I feel like my depression is sitting on me, not letting me move. And I can't write," I told her.

"You're stuck," she said. "You need to break up that energy by moving your body. I know you don't feel like it, but don't decide it in your head. Decide it in your body. If you leave it to your mind, your mind will talk you out of it and then attack you for being lazy later. Your homework is to start doing yoga—or something that you enjoy, that has worked for you in the past."

"Okay," I said, not feeling like I could remotely go to yoga. "I also feel like I want to lose weight, but my body is hanging on to it so stubbornly. I'm trying so hard, doing everything right, and it's not happening."

"Most of the success or failure you'll have with weight loss has to do with energy. Here's another homework assignment I have for you. When you have some quiet time alone, put your hands on a place where you're carrying weight—your hips or your stomach or your thighs, and just ask your body, *What is this? What am I carrying here?* and see what comes up. And then journal about it."

"Okay," I said, doubting I would actually do so.

The next morning, when I awoke but wasn't ready to actually get up, I gently rested my hands on my stomach. "What's here?" I asked myself silently. I waited without mentally tapping my foot, just trying to drift like a bird coasting on its wings above the question.

The reply surfaced. It had to do with my motherhood. Thoughts and feelings came up—of being gravid, expectant, and so determined to do it right. Also of being a failure, not as good a mother as I had wanted to be, nowhere near perfect. I couldn't protect my kids from having divorced parents. I yelled when I didn't want to yell, was unfair and unreasonable, spaced out while they were telling me things, forgot to give them money on pizza day, and had to scramble through laundry baskets at the last minute to find two matching socks. I had no idea how to get them to eat the recommended daily allowance of vegetables, especially since they didn't like most of them, and I wasn't about to force-feed them.

I thought of my mother's belly—when I was a child, it was crisscrossed with angry, raised cesarean scars, and the flesh fell out of her otherwise trim torso when she unzipped her jeans, like a laundry bag stuffed in a closet. When she had her fourth cesarean, she ordered a tummy tuck and came home with a stretched, flat, shocked abdomen, adorned with a quite realistic man-made navel. Her scar was a low wide smile, a bikini cut, hidden. The navel once fused to the umbilical cord that notched into her mother's placenta was resting wherever they send medical waste.

When I had Honorée and Nathaniel, I learned what my mother never got the chance to know: Our hips weren't just abundantly shaped on the outside; on the inside, the birth canal was so roomy that my babies almost fell out. I was born to give birth. If only the rest of motherhood were that easy.

My stomach right then was the size it had been in my first trimesters of pregnancy—rounded and puffy. It was as if I were stuck in that place where I thought I could be the perfect mother, where I was still scornful not only of my mother, but of anyone who was clearly failing at perfect motherhood in public. And from that stance, I judged myself every day—even though Honorée had been on the other side of my stomach for almost a decade.

It's okay to be imperfect, I told myself. *Love yourself more to love your children better.*

I was ready to receive more insights, but then a sudden wave of nausea rolled through my abdomen, and I pulled my hands away from that place as if from a hot stove. It was time to step away.

The next day, I placed my hands on my thighs. They were rounded, full, as if I had another set of hips below the first. *What am I holding here?*

Again, I drifted. *On the left, this is the place where the front grille of a car hit me when I was thirteen, walking across the street, holding an ice cream cone.* I don't remember this incident; my mind decided to spare me.

I spent weeks in the hospital, in traction. One of the rings inside my pelvis had a hairline crack, that's all. But it was enough to keep me strung up for weeks, and enough to cause me to have to learn to walk again, with crutches. Without the crutches and the traction and the physical therapy, I would have had a pronounced limp.

Until I discovered Nia, I felt most attracted to being still. But the practice I loved so much during my divorce had fallen by the wayside, thanks to all the time I spent on I-25, and Susana's reduced schedule, and the complacency I felt about my body, now that it was so unconditionally adored by Laura.

My left thigh has a small lump of scar tissue at the point of impact. Probing it makes me slightly panicky. So does the rusty wail of sirens. Nobody has ever said they could see the difference, but I do. My other thigh, over time, filled out to match closely enough. Did I will it so? I sensed that my thighs thought they needed to be like bumpers, needed to be ready to absorb blows.

No. They don't, I thought to myself. *I'll be very careful crossing the street. I don't need you to protect me this way anymore.*

I'd always tried to give my father the benefit of the doubt. I counseled my siblings to accept him the way he was. "He's not going to change, so do you want to have a relationship with him or not?" I would always mourn not having a Michael Landon/Pa Ingalls dad, but I had a strong, unexamined desire to have *a* dad, even if our relationship was close to nonexistent. I thought it was the healthiest option.

But then that changed.

I emailed my dad and stepmother to let them know that Laura and I planned to get married if California relegalized marriage, the following spring. No reply. I resent it two weeks later. No reply. Then he stopped responding to any emails or phone messages.

"Life is too short to be estranged from people you love, don't you think?" I emailed.

The email I got back was so vicious that my hands shook as I scrolled down the vitriolic lines. Tears squirted out of my eyes. He told me that I was such an angry person that whenever he was in the same room with me, he always kept an eye on the closest exit. He said that I was anti–senior citizen, antiheterosexual, and seven other crazy things. Then he accused me of being an alcoholic. "You know, they have gay AA meetings!" he urged.

Laura read it and became apoplectic with anger. I talked to my sister on the phone about it. Although his assertions were random and some were outright comical, I still felt weepy for days.

He would never see me. No matter how good I tried to be, how much I accepted him, if I had a relationship with him, it would be a tacit acceptance of his terrible version of me. All the things that he hated about me, that he tried to beat, force, ignore, starve, and coerce into or out of me. As long as he was my father, I was the little girl cleaning my plate of an unwanted second helping to earn love.

I wrote him an email telling him that we no longer had a relationship and bounced his reply. I was sad about losing my dad, but that sadness was dwarfed by the huge weight that lifted off my spirit.

Laura got me a juicer for my birthday, and it was a brilliant present. I was completely surprised, but it was the kind of thing I didn't realize I wanted until I opened it. One of my PR contacts at *Mothering* had met me at a conference and then sent me a book on juicing. I could tell that she was trying to help me lose weight, without my even bringing it up.

I went hunting for a juicing weight-loss book on Amazon and found *The Juice Lady's Turbo Diet,* which had a slightly cheesy title, but amazing customer reviews. As soon as it arrived, I began the plan: 100 percent raw foods and vegetable juices for a week, then mostly raw meals and juice two times per day. I lost thirty pounds in six weeks. It didn't hurt that I joined a Nia studio and danced almost every day. I felt restored and beautiful. Being forty pounds heavier wasn't my truth. I shed the pounds in connection with shedding the last toxic relationships left in my life. What remained: a stronger, tauter, more glowing me.

"These are your kids?" people asked. "You're so young-looking! You must have had your kids early on."

"I wasn't a teen mom," I said. "I'm thirty-eight years old!"

Dancing flirted with my injuries, physical and emotional. It teased them into movement. I swiveled, pumped my pelvis in all directions, kicked forward, back, to the side, and across. I dropped my tailbone and my head, and then rolled them back up, engaging my thighs, channeling their oomph. My teacher ordered us to rumble and shake and shiver through our hips and legs, which rattled my crystallized trauma so that it, too, broke away, coursed with my blood through my liver, and out.

While eating raw, I noticed cravings come up for other foods. When I told myself no, I actually had to deal with the feelings behind the cravings. And they weren't pretty. I had spent my life literally throwing food on top of my feelings like you'd throw a blanket on top of a fire. And then a couple of drinks on top of that, for good measure. I eliminated more: sugar, caffeine, alcohol because I wanted to reset my system.

Eating raw was surprisingly fun and delicious—a new culinary playground to explore. I made zucchinis into a trompe l'oeil of linguini with a spiral slicer. I made pâtés out of ground-up nuts, aromatics, and vegetables. No sugar, hardly any grains, loads of vegetables, and a little bit of fruit. My new protein and fat sources became avocados and nuts. I craved bread, and then I didn't think much about bread, and then it seemed beside the point.

Instead of bread or pitas or tortillas, I wrapped my sandwich fillings in big, emerald chard leaves with ruby veins that mirrored the tree of life design that graced my placentas.

The depression and low energy that had dogged me my entire life went away, and I digested like a champ.

I'd spent my whole life evolving through the process of cooking, eating, and studying different chefs, food magazines, and cookbook authors. This latest rung in my self-evolution was food-related, too. But just as I used to cook and bake to woo, please, and nurture others, I had now discovered how to cook to truly nurture myself. Not by throwing food down my hatch to blanket unwanted feelings. Not by cleaning my plate to get approval. Not by making performance-y, one-upping meals that were too rich for my system. I could make myself satisfying meals that gave me energy without making me feel burdened or backed up.

And the best part of all was that after I lost the weight I wanted to lose, I was able to add things back—in a conscious way that kept my body humming like a finely tuned machine. It just so happens that *my* body loses and gains weight in a specific way—and I was lucky enough to stumble across the right formula.

29

Carryover Cooking

AFTER LAURA asked me to marry her, we swung into planning mode, unlocking our limbs from the proposal chair and heading toward the kitchen.

"I've always wanted to get married at the Wayfarers Chapel in Palos Verdes, California," she said. "It's made of glass and was designed by Frank Lloyd Wright's son. They have same-sex ceremonies."

We peered at the website's photographs, which looked enticing. And at the time, California, Laura's home state, was performing same-sex marriages.

Let's have a cake tasting!" I exclaimed. "The only thing that's open is the grocery store, but we can buy lots of different slices and celebrate with champagne."

We drove the few blocks to a big, fluorescent-lit supermarket, which had that middle-of-the-night zombie-occupied feeling. Not that we noticed. Usually shy about PDA, we held hands as we picked out a bottle of Gruet sparkling wine (which we had on our first date), a piece of red velvet cake, a piece of German chocolate cake, and a piece of carrot cake, each in its own small plastic clamshell. I knew we wouldn't buy our wedding cake at Smith's, but it was a fun gesture and the humble squares tasted better than my first wedding cake by a mile.

And then, a few months later, California did the do-si-do that reversed same-sex marriage, and reinstated it, and clamped down on it, and brought us both to a place of impotent frustration. There was a chance that California would make it legal again, enough of a chance that it kept us from tying the knot in, say, Iowa. (Bless those Iowans, mind you, but I didn't have warm fuzzies for Iowa or any of the other gay-marrying states.) At the same time, it was demoralizing to wait on California like orphans asking plaintively for more porridge.

I'd had a wedding dress hanging in my closet for just shy of three years when New York began to seem like a strong maybe.

I immediately started flogging my Facebook wall with every kind of call to action I could find. I emailed and called Mark Grisanti—who was not only an undecided swing voter, but the state senator of my off-campus neighborhood in Buffalo—and asked my college classmates to do the same. I called the un-undecided senators on Long Island, which felt pointless but necessary. I hoped, I prayed, I dreamed, I signed petitions, I held space and visualized and did every woo-woo thing you can imagine. It was like being on a turbulent airplane. I got very spiritual very quickly.

I didn't know if it would make a difference, but I did know that if I didn't give it my all, I would feel deep regret.

Laura swung from guardedly optimistic to resignedly pessimistic. Our hearts lurched every time the vote was seemingly delayed or passed over for discussion by the New York Senate.

We watched the vote on the eve of Santa Fe's Gay Pride weekend. And same-sex marriage beautifully, circuitously passed, as we once again cried happy tears in each other's arms.

I slid on the brown suede lace-up minidress I used to rock back in my German *Vogue* days, and Laura and I ran out to the party at Rouge Cat, Santa Fe's gay bar, and danced our soon-to-be-wedded booties off.

So I'd be a two-time New York bride, but my weddings would take place on two entirely different planets. Unlike with my first wedding, my family did not rush forward to hustle us through the preparations, planning, and execution, throwing money our way at every turn.

Some relatives were fantastic, mind you, but others didn't respond, or bowed out because they "wouldn't feel comfortable." That made it much easier to have an affordable, intimate guest list. Only people who were absolutely jubilant for us received a beautiful, creamy, thick invitation envelope.

Laura's best friend from high school, Peter, volunteered his gorgeous, historic home just outside Hudson, New York, and we found an all-candlelit space called the Tin Ballroom. We rented a townhouse on the main street of Hudson for the week, for lots of practical reasons. But to be sure, the most important factor for me was its stocked kitchen and Viking range.

I did not take on serving forty people dinner (full disclosure: I thought about it!). That, we outsourced to Mary DiStefano and Dana Wegener, who ran MOD Hudson, a snug, lovely restaurant that turned out comfort food. We decided on a Thanksgiving theme for the dinner: turkey, mashed potatoes, gravy, cranberry sauce, and pies. My grandpa Jimmy would not be there—and I had no idea if he would have been able to get his head around having a gay granddaughter—but his stuffing was on the buffet. My diner-owner grandfather Charlie's gravy would gild the turkey and mashed potatoes.

My mother *would* be there. "I wouldn't miss it for the world," she said, after a quiet receipt of the news.

She was bringing Lenny, her new boyfriend. Unlike her other fellas, Lenny was kind and low-key and thought my mother walked on water.

"Shush," she told him. "That's blasphemy."

He was the Jewish boyfriend she'd wanted her whole life. She'd wanted it for me, she'd wanted it for Lisa. She'd wanted it so badly that she'd made up stories about Constantin from Crete being Jewish. But Lenny didn't need her to be Jewish. He just needed her to be Linda.

Best of all, my mom had found a way, post–gastric bypass, to eat enough calories. She was comfortingly curvy and filled out once more—and she really liked herself that way.

❦ ❦ ❦

This time, I was making my wedding cake. It only took me eleven years, and a world of changes, to be back in that position, and I was primed to make the most of it.

My chocolate hound Laura requested that for one tier, but it took me weeks to figure out what flavor "my" tier would be. Would I go linzer torte with almond cake and raspberry jam between the layers? Or coconut? Or *natilla*-inspired, cinnamon-vanilla custard? I trawled Martha Stewart's wedding website and others, but then turned to *The Cake Bible*. As I turned the pages, I saw a banana cake. What about . . . Chunky Monkey–inspired banana cake studded with chocolate slabs and walnuts? It was offbeat and yet familiar, and paired well with the chocolate. It had a history with me, not free of a dark side, but I was reclaiming it and changing the medium—not to ignore the past, but to reclaim it in a healthier context.

I chose Beranbaum's white chocolate–cream cheese buttercream, the same stuff that adorned the cupcakes I had brought to Honorée's childbirth preparation class. If there had to be a bible on our wedding day, let it be one that gives the recipe for the one true buttercream—not the one "right" way to love and live.

Honorée chose the accent color: a beautiful dark teal, and our flowers were rusty, autumnal, like our favorite season. Nathaniel and Laura wore matching pale gray suits, Laura's bespoke so that it nestled against her shape as intimately as I like to. Like the first draft of our wedding plans, my initial dress went by the wayside. I chose a backless, fitted trumpet mermaid dress—far more body-conscious than my blousy first wedding dress, during a season when Will and I had eaten many a stress-driven dinner at Panna in Little India. In the weeks before this wedding, I'd slipped back into religiously raw, juicing mode and climbed the small mountain down the road before Nia, and I was keen to show off my figure.

Our guests seemed to bear witness to our former selves in their gazes. When I looked at them, I was reminded of the me's they used to see: the child, the teen, the clueless twentysomething; the burgeoning mother. And so those versions of myself attended my wedding too, and that added to my contentment.

Our guests included Emily, my best friend from junior high; Rachel, who brought me Madeira for my first osso buco; my cousin Kristieanne, Gustav's granddaughter; Laura's high school friends; our close family; and Julie, my favorite July mama, who'd received the post–gestational diabetes brownies.

My father wasn't there, since I'd ended our relationship. I did feel like he should have the chance to see his grandkids if he wanted to, so I gave him the opportunity to spend the afternoon with them on Thursday. Under the best of circumstances, it would have gone smoothly, but I was being overly optimistic. He was four hours late, which screwed up our wedding-prep plans. It reminded me of how my siblings and I used to wait for him to come get us on Saturday mornings. It was dinnertime by the time he pulled up. I brought the kids out from our townhouse to his car in the midst of a sudden rain.

"Hop in," he said.

"Oh, I need to stay here," I said.

"Why, you don't want to get dinner?"

For a second, I was ready to comply. I noticed that the agreement was in my cells, not my mind. *Father wants to take me to dinner. Must go.* But then I realized: *I can't!*

"You know what? I wish I could, but I can't. I have to make my wedding cake."

"What, they don't have bakeries up here?" He seemed confused.

"No, I *want* to make my wedding cake. And I have to do it tonight; it's my only window."

"Oh, okay."

A few hours later, he called to say he was outside. I fetched the kids, who had about ten pounds of plastic toys in bags. "I took them to the dollar store and told them to pick out whatever they wanted."

He got out of the car to help the kids gather everything. There he was, my dad, in front of me. In spite of my nonrelationship with him, in spite of our horrid history, he was standing there with the smile I recalled from earliest memory. I hugged him.

"Good luck to you both," he said, and I know he meant it.

Julie arrived that night after I'd baked the Chunky Monkey cake successfully. The chocolate layers, however, were proving problematic. They were the large cake layers, and although I'd stared at Beranbaum's helpful chart on how to adjust the recipe for larger layers, my brain refused to grok the formula. As a result they came out flat.

"It's fine!" Laura's mom said. "Nobody is going to care."

Julie and I looked at each other. "I need to make another layer, don't I?"

She knew me. She knew I wouldn't want a cake that looked like a top hat, that it would gall me until the end of time. Even though I was tired.

"Let's make another layer," she said. "We have the ingredients, right?"

Julie and I had made a cake together the first time we met: the coconut cake that my friend Casey had at her Little Rock wedding. I'd fallen in love with it and begged the caterer for the recipe. Little did I know that nine years later, she'd be helping me make my wedding cake—and that I'd be getting married to a woman, in New York.

But here she was, saving the day, washing out bowls, patting me on the back, running interference. And the cake looked (not just tasted) perfect. Not Martha Stewart perfect, nor even Rose Levy Beranbaum perfect, bless them. But it was proportional, and covered in white chocolate–cream cheese buttercream frosting, nonneurotically applied with the frosting spatula I'd bought at New York Cake Supply so many years ago.

Laura and I also made our vows from scratch, in the canopy bed of the Hudson townhouse, the day before we walked down the aisle. And unlike the cake, which we didn't freeze for our first anniversary, we read these vows to each other whenever we get the yen for their mouthfeel, sweetness, texture, layers, and loft.

I choose you as my One, and I vow to be the most encompassing
   One to you
to champion your boldest and most desired quests
to applaud your triumphs and to soothe you when you stumble
to shield you from life's nuisances and blows, great and small
to constantly remind you of your beauty and my love
to reflect all the best in you so that you walk in your greatness
to cherish all the worst in you so that you may be fully present
to honor your soul's path, knowing when to assist and when
   to refrain
to bring the power of the first blush of our love into every day
   we share
to thrill at the sight of you
to never forget the incompleteness I felt before encountering you
to be humbly thankful that we chanced to meet
to stand by your side and sleep in your arms as long as we both
   shall live.

Our wedding, like our first encounter, almost didn't happen. New York's legalization hinged on Senators Grisanti and Saland. Had they swung the other way, we would still be waiting on California. Instead, passages from their speeches made it into our ceremony.

The judge, whom we'd scheduled months before to marry us at the city hall ceremony that would precede the one at Peter's house, didn't show up. He plain forgot. But the sergeant on duty, Randy Clarke, who cut a jocular, cop-like, Irish profile that struck me as far from promising in terms of him being an eleventh-hour champion of out-of-state lesbians left at the altar, made it his single-handed mission to find another judge. He called every one in a 200-mile radius and finally connected with (Republican, mind you) Mark Portin, who abandoned his Saturday of muddy home chores to drive two hours to come marry us. Not only was Portin gallant, he was so handsome that every woman there—from Ana, my photographer, to Julie, to Laura's mother, and Laura (and me, it should be admitted)—got a little silly and flustered.

"Do you have vows?" he asked.

"The other judge said we couldn't do our own vows, we had to stick with the legal verbiage," I said.

"You can't do your own vows?" he snorted. "What in the world. It's your wedding!"

And so our no-show judge was part of the greater plan to deliver us the best wedding possible. We got to say our vows twice, at the courthouse and just barely an hour later, in front of our guests.

Which was not the worst way to begin to remember.

Recipes

HANDS-ON *SPANAKOPITA*

This recipe from Chapter 1 was brought over from Crete by my great-grandmother Maria. In tracking down the recipe, I reconnected with my cousin Stacie, who gave it to me. I then passed it on to another cousin, who thought the recipe went to the grave with Maria's daughter Christina.

Yield: 12 servings

2 cups curly-leaf, a.k.a. savoy, spinach (not baby or flat-leaf spinach)

1 pound cream cheese

½ pound farmer cheese, or chèvre in a pinch

½ pound of large-curd pot cheese or cottage cheese

Salt and pepper

⅛ cup of freshly chopped peppermint, or a tiny droplet of peppermint extract ("Don't overdo it, or it tastes like mouthwash," according to my cousin Stacie). I also sub in oregano if I don't have peppermint.

1 pound of phyllo dough

3 eggs

3 tablespoons melted butter

Preheat oven to 375°F.

Wash the spinach, remove stems, dry the leaves, and then chop them. Add salt, pepper, and peppermint and toss.

continued ▶

Put the cheeses in a large mixing bowl and break them up with your hands. Mix them together. Whisk eggs separately, then add to cheese and stir briskly to incorporate.

Start adding the spinach mixture into the wet mixture. You need to squish the spinach with your hands. Keep adding spinach and squishing it until it's all added into the main bowl and has an even consistency. I think my great-grandmother squished it until it was completely broken down, but I stop before that because I like the texture.

Make a phyllo base, in your rectangular oven-safe pan, by buttering and stacking a couple of layers. (When I'm working with a smaller pan, I take about 6 phyllo layers from the package and lay them flat in the pan. There's a lot of extra length, so I pack the spinach mixture in and then wrap the phyllo ends over the filling, like flaps.)

Pack the spinach mixture on top of the phyllo. Top with more phyllo, then brush top with butter. Before baking, cut rows through phyllo, because it's way messier to cut it after it is cooked. Bake until phyllo is brown, for about 40 minutes.

LUNDY'S BISCUITS

This recipe from Chapter 2 was handed to my grandfather Charlie Vourakis by Irving Lundy in the 1950s.

Yield: 18–20 biscuits

2 cups flour	¼ shortening
3 teaspoons baking powder	¾ cup milk
½ teaspoon salt	

Preheat oven to 450° F.

Sift flour, baking powder, and salt together. Massage shortening in with fingertips. Add milk slowly and mix until it becomes a soft dough. Knead lightly 20–25 times on a floured board. Roll out dough on a floured surface to ½-inch thickness.
Cut with a 2-inch biscuit cutter or glass. Bake on ungreased sheet 10–15 minutes.

KOULOURAKIA (GREEK BUTTER COOKIES)

These cookies from Chapter 4 have been enjoyed by five generations of my family in this country. I can only imagine how far back
they stretch into the daily life of previous generations in Crete.

Yield: 6–8 dozen cookies

2 cups unsalted butter,
softened

2 cups sugar

2 teaspoons vanilla extract

6 eggs

8–9 cups flour

3 tablespoons baking powder

¼ cup sesame seeds

Preheat oven to 375°F.

Cream butter and gradually beat in sugar. In a separate bowl,
whisk eggs until fluffy. Add eggs and vanilla to butter and sugar
mixture and beat until uniform. In a separate bowl, sift flour and
baking powder. Add flour mixture to wet ingredients, in batches,
until a soft dough forms. Lightly flour your hands and pick up a
handful of dough. Roll it into a snake shape, and then roll it into
a tightly wound C with curled-in edges or a tightly wound S with
curled-in edges, or bend it in half and twist the lengths over and
over each other.

Place on a greased and floured (or nonstick) cookie sheet, brush
with egg, and sprinkle with sesame seeds. Bake for 20 minutes or
until golden brown.

YIA YIA'S PIECRUST

This recipe from Chapter 4 was passed down from my great-grandmother Maria to my mother, Linda, and forms pies that are both toothsome and shapely.

Yield: 2 single-crust pies or 1 double-crust pie

4 cups flour, unsifted

2 cups organic vegetable shortening or unsalted butter

2 teaspoons salt

1 egg

1 teaspoon sugar

1 teaspoon vinegar

¾ cup very cold water

Combine flour and salt, and cut in shortening. Whisk egg in separate bowl, and add water, sugar, and vinegar to egg mixture. Combine wet and dry ingredients and knead briefly. Wrap dough in plastic wrap or place in container and refrigerate for 1 hour.

Divide dough in half and roll out thinly between 2 pieces of wax paper. Remove 1 layer of wax paper, transfer dough to pie plate, then peel off top piece of wax paper. Add pie filling, and if you are making a double crust pie, top pie with second layer of dough. Repeat previous dough steps. Form excess dough into a ruffled edge.

Bake as directed by pie recipe.

APPLE PIE FILLING

This recipe from Chapter 4, along with the crust, is a mandatory dessert at every Thanksgiving in my family.

Yield: enough filling for 1 pie

⅓–⅔ cup sugar

¼ cup flour

½ teaspoon cinnamon

½ teaspoon ground nutmeg

Dash salt

8 cups sliced tart apples

2 tablespoons butter

Preheat oven to 425°F.

Prepare pastry.

Mix sugar, flour, cinnamon, nutmeg, and salt in a large bowl. Stir in the apples, turn out into pastry-lined pie plate, dot with butter, cover with top layer of pastry, and cover outer 1 inch of crust with a strip of tinfoil, leaving 3 inches foil all around. Bake for 40–50 minutes or until crust is brown and juices bubble through slits in crust; remove foil during the last 15 minutes of baking. Cool on a rack.

MUTE duROI's FRIKADELLEN

I enjoyed these meat patties, referenced in Chapter 5, both in Germany and in my German grandmother, Marie's kitchen.

Yield: 6 servings

Just over ½ pound ground beef   1 onion, minced

Just over ½ pound ground pork   Salt and pepper to taste

1 crusty roll   1 teaspoon dry mustard

1 egg

Tear the roll to bits and soak in hot water or milk. Then squeeze out excess liquid, put in a food processor, and tear or chop finely with a knife. In a medium-size bowl, mix bread bits together with the meats, egg, onion, salt, pepper, and dry mustard. Form into uniformly sized, palm-flattened patties and sauté in a lightly oiled skillet, on a medium-high burner, about 7–10 minutes per side.

Best served with potato salad and vegetables.

SCHNEEWITTCHEN KUCHEN

This recipe, from my German host family's mother, appears in Chapter 5.

Yield: 12–16 servings

3 cups flour	2 teaspoons baking powder
2 sticks plus 1 tablespoon butter, softened	2 cups frozen dark sweet cherries, thawed
5 eggs	

Preheat oven to 355°F.

Blend together first 4 ingredients with electric mixer.

Pour into 11 x 7-inch rectangular baking dish. Drop in cherries, individually, at regular intervals.

Bake for 30–45 minutes, until middle springs back lightly when tapped.

Let cool on counter or in refrigerator.

BUTTERCREAM

2 sticks plus 1 tablespoon butter, softened	1 egg yolk
⅔ cup powdered sugar	2 packets chocolate glaze a.k.a Schokoguß (available in German markets)

Beat together the butter, sugar, and egg yolk and spread evenly on the cake. Spread chocolate glaze lightly over the top with a rubber or silicone spatula. Chill in the refrigerator to set, and then cut into squares and enjoy.

GRANDMOTHER MARIE'S CHICKEN FRICASSEE

This recipe, which appears in Chapter 7, is a beloved family classic. During my research for this book, I was asked for the recipe and happily passed it on to my Aunt Carole, Marie's daughter. Sometimes, recipes skip a generation!

Yield: 8 servings

1 whole chicken,
skin mostly removed

2 stalks celery,
cut into 1-inch lengths

2–3 carrots,
cut into 1-inch lengths

1 onion, quartered

3–4 tablespoons flour

Salt and pepper to taste

4 cups chicken broth or stock

Place the chicken and vegetables in a tall pot and add stock and water to cover it. Bring water to a boil, then simmer for an hour or two. Rotate chicken periodically. Cook until the meat is falling off the bones. Keep adding water as needed, to just cover the chicken.

Place a colander in another large bowl or pot and strain the pot's contents. Reserve the broth. Transfer broth back onto stove and cook it at a low boil to reduce and concentrate the liquid.

Separate chicken from carcass and place in a separate bowl. You can add the vegetables to the chicken mixture, or compost/discard them along with the chicken bones. Once that step is complete, bring broth on stove to a rolling boil.

In a medium-size bowl or large glass liquid measure, add 1 cup of water and whisk 2 tablespoons of flour into it—hard—so that no lumps remain. It should look like milk, rather than water with flour bits in it. Slowly pour this into the broth and whisk briskly

continued ▶

together. Lower the heat; stir it some more. Repeat the steps above 1 or 2 more times until the liquid reaches the desired gravy consistency, coating the back of the spoon.

Add the chicken to the gravy, stir for another few minutes, and serve over rice.

PEA SOUP

This recipe from Chapter 8 was a thrifty favorite in my college apartment.

Yield: 8–12 servings

1 bag dried green peas

1 large onion, chopped

Salt and pepper to taste

Fill large pot halfway with water. Add bag of dried peas (you're supposed to rinse the peas and make sure no pebbles tagged along, but we never did). Toss in onion. Bring to a boil, then simmer for hours, stirring occasionally (as the kitchen windows steam up against the bitterly cold Buffalo winter air that whistles through the cracks), until the peas liquefy. Season with salt and pepper to taste.

HASTY HUMMUS

I've been enjoying this Chapter 12 recipe since my mid-twenties, and now my children love it as well.

Yield: about 2 cups

1 (15.5-ounce) can organic garbanzo beans, drained and rinsed

2 tablespoons tahini

1½ tablespoons extra virgin olive oil, plus more for serving

3 tablespoons water or nut milk

Lemon juice to taste (about 1–2 teaspoons)

Salt and pepper to taste

Add garbanzo beans to food processor or blender with tahini, olive oil, and water or nut milk. Puree until smooth. Scoop into a bowl, drizzle olive oil over it, add salt and pepper, and enjoy as a spread or dip for fresh vegetables and toasted pita points.

DAPHNE'S FLAN

I could never forget Daphne Mascarello's flan (Chapter 19) or her beautiful smile. Luckily, she and I reconnected via Facebook and she very graciously provided the recipe.

Yield: 12–16 servings

CARAMEL

2 cups sugar   3 cups water

CUSTARD

4 ounces cream cheese

1 can evaporated milk

1 can sweetened, condensed milk

3 eggs

2 tablespoons sugar

½ teaspoon vanilla extract

1 pinch salt

Preheat oven to 325°F.

Begin by making the caramel. In a saucepan, heat sugar and water over medium heat. Do not shake or swirl; otherwise it will crystallize. The sugar will dissolve on its own and begin to brown. Lift the pan 4–6 inches above the heat source and continue to brown the sugar until it becomes a dark golden brown.

Pour caramelized sugar into a round 8-inch cake pan and swirl to coat the bottom and sides of the pan evenly.

Bring a pot of water to boil (this will serve as a hot bath for the cake pan).

continued ▶

On to the custard. In a blender, combine cream cheese, sweet-ened condensed milk, evaporated milk, eggs, sugar, vanilla extract, and salt. Blend on high for 1 minute. Pour over the caramelized sugar. Place the filled cake pan into a larger pan and carefully add hot water to larger pan until it is 1 inch deep. Bake in preheated oven for 50–60 minutes or until set.

Daphne shares: "The secret is to make it 2 to 3 days before you will be serving it and to bake it at a low temperature. What makes it special is its creaminess. The reason I love it, and enjoy making it for people I care about, is because my grandmother and my aunt used to make it for me and my cousins. It is a family tradi-tion. In fact, when at times they had no gas (which happened often on a third-world Caribbean island), she would make the flan on a makeshift outdoor grill—a pile of sweet-smelling wood. Instead of a regular cake pan, she'd use recycled metal cans. The flan tasted of smoky creaminess, heaven in your mouth!"

PAPPARDELLE BOLOGNESE

(Recipe courtesy of *Bon Appétit*)

Although this recipe from Chapter 20 led to an argument with my first spouse, my second spouse loves it.

Yield: 4–6 servings

¼ cup olive oil

2 slices thick-cut bacon, diced

1 cup chopped onion

½ cup chopped celery

½ cup chopped carrot

4 garlic cloves, minced

1 tablespoon chopped fresh thyme

1 pound ground veal

1 pound ground pork

1 cup dry red wine

2 bay leaves

2 14-ounce cans beef broth

1½ cups canned tomato puree

1 pound pappardelle or mafaldine pasta

Freshly grated parmesan cheese

Heat oil in heavy large pot over medium-high heat. Add bacon; sauté until beginning to brown, about 6 minutes. Add onion, celery, carrot, garlic, and thyme; sauté 5 minutes. Add veal and pork; sauté until brown and cooked through, breaking up meat with back of fork, about 10 minutes. Add wine and bay leaves. Simmer until liquid is slightly reduced, about 10 minutes. Add broth and tomato puree.

Reduce heat to medium-low; simmer until sauce thickens, stirring often, about 1 hour, 15 minutes. Season with salt and pepper. (Can be made 1 day ahead. Cool slightly. Refrigerate uncovered until cold, then cover and keep chilled. Bring to a simmer before using.)

continued ▶

Boil pasta in large pot of boiling salted water until just tender but still firm to bite, stirring often. Drain. Transfer to pot with sauce; toss. Serve with parmesan.

PARMESAN-SCALLION MASHED POTATOES

This Chapter 21 recipe goes very well with a roasted chicken.

Yield: 8–12 servings

3 pounds russet potatoes	¼ cup parmesan cheese
½ bunch scallions	½ cup chicken or vegetable broth
1 tablespoon olive oil or butter	Salt and pepper to taste

Bring a large pot of water to a boil. While that's heating up, wash and peel potatoes (or leave the skins on), and cut into uniform slices (about 1 inch thick). Add potatoes to water at rolling boil.

Wash scallions, cut off and discard the root and top ends, and then thinly slice the trimmed stalks crosswise, all the way up. In a skillet, sauté in butter or olive oil and a dash of broth.

When potato pieces are cooked through, drain and add to mixing bowl. Use a mixer on medium speed to mash the potatoes. Then, once they have come to a uniform consistency (lumps are fine), add the parmesan cheese, sautéed scallions, and broth. Blend everything together; add salt and freshly ground pepper to taste.

KIMBER'S VINAIGRETTE AND SALAD

Before I met Kimber, I felt like eating salad was a chore. She showed me that sometimes salad (such as this one from Chapter 23) can be better than dessert.

Yield: 6–8 servings

SALAD

About 6 cups mixed greens

1 avocado, sliced

1 ruby red grapefruit, halved, pieces segmented out from the membranes (do this step over the bowl of greens so that the juices drip in)

VINAIGRETTE DRESSING

1 cup extra virgin olive oil

⅔ cup balsamic vinegar

1–2 tablespoons tamari

1 tablespoon grainy or Dijon mustard

1 clove minced garlic

Add all ingredients to 1-quart mason jar or other sealable container. Shake, taste, add more vinegar if desired. (I add a squirt of honey and salt and pepper, too.) Kimber got this recipe from her first husband's dad, her son's grandpa Will.

Bacon-Wrapped Eggs with Polenta

As Easter approaches every year, Laura and I look forward to making these delicious baked eggs, mentioned in Chapter 27. Polenta, cheese, bacon . . . what's not to love? Make sure to pair them with fizzing, peachy Bellinis (champagne peach nectar cocktails) in tall champagne flutes . . . though we've been known to enjoy them in Bonne Maman jelly jar glasses.

Make the polenta a couple of days ahead, then assemble each serving an hour or so before guests arrive.

Polenta

2 tablespoons (¼ stick) butter	1 cup polenta (coarse cornmeal)
¼ cup minced green onions	½ cup (packed) grated Parmesan cheese
3 cups water	1 tablespoon minced fresh thyme
1 teaspoon salt	

Melt butter in heavy medium saucepan over medium heat. Add green onions and stir until wilted, about 1 minute. Add 3 cups water and salt; bring to boil. Gradually whisk in polenta. Bring to boil. Reduce heat to low and simmer until thick and creamy, stirring occasionally, about 13 minutes. Stir in cheese and thyme. Season with salt and pepper. Cool to lukewarm. (Can be prepared 2 days ahead. Cover and refrigerate; polenta will become firm.)

continued ▶

BAKED EGGS

20 thick slices applewood-smoked bacon

6 ounces extra-sharp white cheddar cheese, grated

6 ounces Gruyère cheese, grated

8 large eggs

¼ cup thinly sliced green onions

1 teaspoon minced fresh thyme

Heat large skillet over medium heat. Add bacon; fry until beginning to brown but still pliable, about 4 minutes. Transfer bacon to paper towels to drain. Cool slightly. Reserve 2 tablespoons bacon drippings for Spring Greens with Sherry Vinaigrette.

Line sides of eight 1 ¼-cup custard cups with 2 slices bacon each, forming collar. Place ½ slice bacon on bottom of each cup. Divide polenta among cups, about generous ⅓ cup each. Press polenta over bottom and up sides of bacon. Mix cheeses in bowl. Sprinkle ¼ cup cheese mixture over polenta in each cup. (Can be prepared 2 hours ahead. Let stand at room temperature.)

Preheat oven to 400°F. Crack 1 egg into center of each cup. Sprinkle eggs with remaining cheese, green onions, thyme, and black pepper. Transfer cups to rimmed baking sheet. Bake until egg whites are almost set, about 20 minutes. Let eggs stand at room temperature 5 minutes (eggs will continue to cook).

Run small sharp knife around edge of cups; tilt cups and slide bacon, polenta, and egg onto plates and serve.

LAURA'S SPAGHETTI CARBONARA

Laura first encountered this Chapter 27 recipe while traveling in Siena, Italy, as a student. Carbonara is often served in American restaurants as a kind of alfredo plus bacon. This version has crispy, caramelized qualities instead.

Yield: 6–8 servings

1 pound dry spaghetti	Salt and fresh pepper
8 ounces thick-cut bacon	½–1 cup grated or shredded Parmesan cheese
1 medium onion, chopped	
3–4 cloves garlic, minced	2 eggs, slightly beaten

Bring 4 quarts of water to a rolling boil in a large pot. While the water is heating, cook the bacon until it's crispy in a 3- to 4-inch-deep, straight-sided skillet. Drain bacon on paper towels, but reserve the drippings in the pan.

Sauté the onions in the bacon drippings until they soften and become transparent, then add the garlic. Continue to cook the onions and garlic over medium to medium-high heat, making sure not to let the garlic scorch. After the garlic softens, turn heat to low.

Add about 1 teaspoon salt to the boiling pasta water and stir to dissolve, then add the pasta and stir. Cook the pasta for about 10 minutes or until al dente (slightly chewy).

While the pasta is cooking, chop or crumble the cooked bacon into ¼-inch pieces and add to the onion-and-garlic mixture. Stir until evenly mixed.

Right before you drain the pasta, turn the heat up on the skillet to medium-high to prepare it for the pasta addition.

continued ▶

Drain the pasta (do not rinse) and add it to the skillet, stirring well to mix the ingredients and heat up the pasta. The pasta should be sizzling hot.

Sprinkle Parmesan cheese on the mixture and toss the pasta to distribute the cheese. (Laura uses two wooden spoons to toss the pasta.)

When everything is well heated, drizzle the eggs over the pasta and quickly toss the mixture so that the eggs coat the pasta and do not fall to the bottom of the pan (otherwise you'll get scrambled eggs!). The eggs will cook on the hot pasta almost instantaneously. Grind fresh pepper over the top to taste. Remove from heat and serve immediately.

My Perfect Morning Juice

The Juice Lady's Turbo Diet, which I talk about in Chapter 28, contains a wealth of vegetable-based juices. I Frankensteined this concoction from a few of my favorites.

Yield: 2 servings

1 cucumber, cut in half crosswise

3 stalks celery, cut into 1-inch lengths

2 carrots

¼ beet

1 nub ginger

1 nub turmeric root

½ burdock stalk

½ lemon

½ Granny Smith apple

1 small handful greens (kale, spinach, or even parsley or cilantro)

Run through the juicer and then enjoy. (It's great any time of day.)

RAW SESAME NOODLES

Although most people think that a raw diet involves feelings of deprivation, it's impossible to eat this Chapter 28 recipe without feeling ecstatically satisfied.

Yield: 4–6 servings

3 zucchini

1 carrot

½ red bell pepper (if you have it)

3 scallions, thinly sliced

3 tablespoons toasted sesame oil

3 tablespoons tamari

1 tablespoon apple cider vinegar (or rice wine vinegar)

1 tablespoon honey

Juice from ½ lemon

1½ teaspoons grated ginger

1 teaspoon minced garlic

⅛ teaspoon cayenne powder

1 teaspoon sesame seeds

1 tablespoon peanut butter (or more to taste)

¼ cup peanuts, chopped coarsely in food processor

Cut the zucchini, carrot, and pepper in long noodle shapes (use a Spirooli or a mandoline, or even a grater). Mix together the 3 different varieties of "noodles" and scallions in a large bowl. In a small bowl, combine the rest of the ingredients and mix well. Toss the noodles in the sauce. (So good right away, and even better the next day.)

Acknowledgments

I WANT TO THANK my editor, Krista Lyons, for her patience, faith, and enthusiasm, and my agent, Emmanuelle Morgen, for her scope expansion, precision, and vision.

Endless gratitude to my wife, Laura André, who literally made this happen through her tireless rereadings, fortnights of solo parenting, and bottom-of-the-ninth, one-woman pep rallies. And thank you to my sweet, supportive children, who had to put up with this verbose paper sibling siphoning off so much of their mother's free time. Let's play!

To family members who handed me gems of remembrance: my mother, Linda Karlson Shaw; my uncles Gustav Albert Karlson and Rickey Vourakis; my aunt Carole Sullivan; my sister, Lisa Walsh; my cousins Stacie Vourakis Junghans, Suzanne Hollingsworth, Kristieanne Karlson, Tara Moylan, and Marie Sullivan. More family who threw this Nancy Drew clues: Alex and Paul Calogerakis, Eileen Duggan.

I want to thank people who believed in me before, during, and after this project: Peggy Gaugy, Melissa Chianta, Michelle Michalski, Shelley Thompson, Tara Baxagocsy, Frank Gitro, Jeannette Curtis, James Michael Nolan, Susan Martin, Nancy Judd, Karen Bassett Stevenson, Rusty Gaston, Kyky Knowles, Rose Ademulegun, Nick Pietrocarlo, Jason Fundalinski, Jennifer Esperanza, Shawn Bluejacket-Roccamo, Maureen Rooney, Tricia Desimone, Leslie Goldman Alter, and Nancy McManus Miller.

My writer and foodie friends who kept my head out of the oven

and my hands on the keyboard, with a special thanks to those
who read the manuscript: Theo Pauline Nestor, Julie Geen, Barbara
Straus, Louise Smith, Jennifer Margulis, Gretchen Rubin, Hope Edel-
man, Jennifer Singer, Meredith Maran, Corbyn Hanson Hightower,
Rachel Aydt, Ashley Young, Muffy Bolding, Toddy Eardly, Audrey
Bilger, Michele Kort, Melissa Lavrinc Smith, Deena Chafetz, Ariel
Gore, Tonia Caselman, Maggie Odell, Peter Spears, Gabriella West,
Ana June, Emily Withnall, Lauren Piscopo, Kelly Smith, Jake Mar-
cus, Jodi Rodgers, Canon Wing, Kathleen Beardsell, Elaine Soloway,
Meadow Braun, Susan Martin, Elizabeth Nall-Grogg, Amelia Sau-
ter, Rob deWalt, Candelora Versace, Brooke Elise Axtell, Melissa
Chianta, Gabriella West, Jodi Rodgers, and Valley Haggard.

My freelance editors, who gave me free, fruitful rein to talk
about food: Sara Wilson at the *Huffington Post,* Trish Bendix of
AfterEllen.com, Audrey Bilger and Michelle Kort of the *Here Come
the Brides* anthology, Julia Goldberg and Alexa Schirtzinger at the
Santa Fe Reporter, Cynthia Baughman at *El Palacio,* and Carlos Lopez
at the *Santa Fe New Mexican.* And my extraordinarily wonderful
colleagues, Dave Herndon, Jodi Vevoda, and Cheryl Alters Jamison
and Bill Jamison.

My teachers: high school composition: Audre Allison; memoir:
Tanya Taylor Rubinstein; intuitive: Lisa Toal; juice lady: Cherie
Calbom; raw-food celebrator: Cassidy André Barbeau; Nia: Holly
Nastasi; therapist: Lauren Zarozny; dietician: Ashley Koff; pitcha-
paloozer: David Henry Sterry.

My Nia tribe: Jamie Berry Klein, Jan Pitlak, Kelle Rae Oien,
Loretta Milo, Sarah Mitchell, Kate Latimer, Corina Logghe, Barbara
Miller, Randy Miller, Susana Guillaume, Dani Reddick, Janet and
Jim Elder, Lily O'Leary, Mark Frossard, Margaret Connerly, Diane
Kennedy, Andrea Cassutt, and Wendy Higgins.

The final chapter of the book wouldn't be half as rich without
those who made our wedding weekend perfect: Peter Spears and
Brian Swardstrom, George and Lenene André, Mary DiStefano and
Dana Wegener, and Malcolm and Janet Travelstead.

I want to thank writers who inspired me with their own heart-stopping bravery and candor bathed in grace: Nora Ephron, Gabrielle Hamilton, Ruth Reichl, Kim Severson, Dani Shapiro, Caroline Leavitt, Jeffrey Eugenides, Jill Soloway, Faith Soloway, and André Dubus III.

And, of course, Full of Beans Coffee House, Flying Star Café, and Real Food Nation, three joints that were more than hospitable as I sat at their two-tops day after day, churning out chapters.

About the Author

CANDACE WALSH edited the Seal Press anthologies *Dear John, I Love Jane: Women Write About Leaving Men for Women* (a Lambda Literary Award finalist) and *Ask Me About My Divorce: Women Open Up About Moving On.* She was the features editor at *Mothering* magazine for six years, was cofounder of *Mamalicious* magazine, and is currently the managing editor of *New Mexico Magazine.* She lives in Santa Fe with her wife Laura André, their two children, and two dogs. Find more *Licking the Spoon* stories and recipes at http://lickingthe spoonbook.com.

Selected Titles from Seal Press

For more than thirty years, Seal Press has published groundbreaking books. By women. For women.

Bento Box In the Heartland: My Japanese Girlhood in Whitebread America, by Linda Furiya. $15.95, 978-1-58005-191-0. A uniquely American story about girlhood, identity, assimilation—and the love of homemade food.

She-Smoke: A Backyard Barbecue Book, by Julie Reinhardt. $16.95, 978-1-58005-284-9. The owner of Smokin' Pete's BBQ in Seattle lays down all the delicious facts for women who aspire to be BBQ queens.

The Quarter-Acre Farm: How I Kept the Patio, Lost the Lawn, and Fed My Family for a Year, by Spring Warren. $16.95, 978-1-58005-340-2. Spring Warren's warm, witty, beautifully-illustrated account of deciding—despite all resistance—to get her hands dirty, create a garden in her suburban yard, and grow 75 percent of all the food her family consumed for one year.

Something Spectacular: The True Story of One Rockette's Battle with Bulimia, by Greta Gleissner. $17.00, 978-1-58005-415-7. A piercing, powerful account of one woman's struggle with bulimia, self-image, and sexuality, set against the backdrop of professional dancing.

Sex and Bacon: Why I Love Things That Are Very, Very Bad for Me, by Sarah Katherine Lewis. $14.95, 978-1-58005-228-3. A sensual—and sometimes raunchy—book celebrating the intersection of sex and food.

Find Seal Press Online
www.SealPress.com
www.Facebook.com/SealPress
Twitter: @SealPress